Praise for *Devils of Democracy*

"With a deep dive into American history, literature, and popular culture extending back into the eighteenth century, Michael E. Heyes finds that Americans' abiding fixation with demons, especially when mixed with apocalypticism and seasoned by misogyny, created a witches' brew that has fed conspiracy movements from QAnon to the Dominionism that animates the New Apostolic Reformation—and even helps to explain the domestic terrorist attack of January 6, 2021. Thoroughly researched and carefully argued, *Devils of Democracy* deserves serious attention."

—**Randall Balmer**, John Phillips Professor in Religion, Dartmouth College, and author of *Bad Faith: Race and the Rise of the Religious Right*

"This fascinating book lays out in great detail and digestible narrative the intertwined political and religious history of demons, spirits, and the like in America. From the papal and royal antichrists in the Revolutionary Era, to demons who offered all types of freedom to females in the 1800s, to the origins of the vibes of the Ouija board, to the call for Christian dominion in the twenty-first century, this book is a tour de force of forces from another world. I was skeptical that I would learn anything new from this book: Demons seem a well-covered subject. But I was converted when page after page of letters, sermons, editorials, and a dash of scholarly citations seemed to take over my mind. Entranced, I read it almost in one sitting. In that second reading, I discovered the most important part of the book: how all these spirits matter today. As Heyes makes clear, all this history currently impacts our nation because we just can't seem to shake the demons from democracy."

—**Matthew Boedy**, author of *The Seven Mountains Mandate: Exposing the Dangerous Plan to Christianize America and Destroy Democracy*

"Michael E. Heyes has written the definitive guide to a dark and often misunderstood corner of the American psyche. As one of the foremost experts on demonology in the United States, Heyes demonstrates that demons have always been more than just monsters in stories; they are mirrors of our deepest cultural fears. By tracing this obsession from its biblical origins in Genesis to the modern political stage, Heyes reveals how supernatural beliefs now provide the framework for social warfare. This is an urgent and necessary look at how labeling an opponent 'demonic' changes the rules of engagement and makes democratic compromise nearly impossible. *Devils of Democracy* is a must-read for all who wish to understand the religious logic driving today's headlines."

—**André Gagné**, full professor at Concordia University in Montreal, Canada, and author of *American Evangelicals for Trump: Dominion, Spiritual Warfare, and the End Times*

"*Devils of Democracy* is frighteningly relevant for our current political moment. Heyes offers haunting insight into America's centuries-long project of demonizing religious, racial, and sexual outsiders—showing the real monsters among us are (and always have been) those most determined to undermine the nation's commitment to individual liberty and religious freedom."

—**Dr. Megan Goodwin**, senior editor at *Religion Dispatches*, nerd-in-chief of Feral Nerd Consulting, cohost of the *Keeping It 101* podcast, and coauthor of *Religion Is Not Done with You*

"In this bracing and historically grounded book, Heyes traces the long history of Christian demonology, revealing how an ancient theology has come to shape today's volatile political climate. By grounding today's spiritual warfare in its deep theological past, he asks a vital question: If demons are not going away, what does their resurgence mean for American democracy?"

—**Elle Hardy**, author of *Beyond Belief: How Pentecostal Christianity Is Taking Over the World*

"*Devils of Democracy* reveals how, for millions of voters, the ballot box has become a front line for 'strategic-level spiritual warfare,' transforming political opponents into cosmic enemies whose defeat is imagined as reclaiming dominion over the earth. Michael E. Heyes traces the democratization of spiritual warfare that first empowered individual believers to battle personal demons, then expanded their moral anxieties into a global political theology in which 'territorial spirits' govern nations and shape world events. As a sociological autopsy of the American electorate, he shows how demonology operates as a form of social control by recasting progressive movements as supernatural threats and framing political compromise as a kind of sin. The result is a modern demonology that erodes democratic empathy, encourages citizens to view neighbors as monsters rather than partners in a shared civic life, and furnishes a powerful rationale for political violence. In the end, the devil takes shape not in distant fantasies of hell, but in the everyday suspicions that turn fellow Americans into evildoers who must be destroyed."

—**Gerardo Martí**, William R. Kenan Jr. Professor of Sociology at Davidson College and author of *American Blindspot: Race, Class, Religion, and the Trump Presidency*

"Michael E. Heyes's *Devils of Democracy* exposes a simultaneously fascinating and sobering history of the rhetorical use of demons and demonization in American political discourse and action. Appeals to the end times and to demon possession in periods of crisis as part of an effort to vilify the political other and to dial the stakes up to eleven are not unique to the United States, but good grief, do we seem to have a particular penchant for it. Heyes shows that from the witch trials to the Satanic Panic to the Seven Mountains Mandate, and down to today, the gravitational pull of the demonic has a way with the tide of American history. Most sobering of all, Heyes demonstrates that thoughtful folks concerned for the nation's future ought to start taking far more seriously the influence of conspiratorial demonology."

—**Dan McClellan**, author of the *New York Times* bestselling book *The Bible Says So: What We Get Right (and Wrong) About Scripture's Most Controversial Issues*

"When Michael E. Heyes writes, 'We are cosmic warriors fighting on the side of God himself; we've been chosen by the Almighty to combat the demonic threat,' he captures the theology of 'demonic warfare' that defined my childhood. As the son of world-famous American evangelical leaders Francis and Edith Schaeffer, I was taught that we were God's chosen people on Earth, charged with fighting Satan, his demons, and their human servants—namely, anyone who did not share our beliefs. To take part in this eternal cosmic struggle, we had to believe that our true enemies were demonic forces. Consequently, those who disagreed with our political or cultural views were not merely wrong—they were evil. Our opponents were deemed undeserving of empathy, kindness, or even fact-based understanding, no more than the demons they were said to serve.

"As the Religious Right—an entity my family helped to shape in the 1970s and '80s—rose to power in the Trump era, it unleashed the merciless certainties that now define the Christian nationalist movement. Heyes exposes this history, revealing how the extremist delusion of 'spiritual warfare' has become a profound threat to American civility, tolerance, and neighborliness. Anyone who seeks to understand the current state of the United States—and to rescue it from delusion and conspiracy-fed lies—must urgently read *Devils of Democracy*."

—**Frank Schaeffer**, author of *The Gospel of Zip* and *Crazy for God*

"This is the ideal book for anyone puzzled by the sudden surge in talk about angels, demons, and spiritual warfare in our politics. Heyes ably demonstrates that the American religious imagination has always tended toward the lurid and apocalyptic. While openly agnostic about the existence of actual demons, *Devils of Democracy* offers a valuable (and alarming) history of the role of demonizing in American rhetoric and politics."

—**Matthew D. Taylor**, author of *The Violent Take It by Force* and *Defying Tyrants*

DEVILS
OF
DEMOCRACY

DEVILS OF DEMOCRACY

AMERICA'S LOVE AFFAIR WITH POLITICAL DEMONS FROM THE REVOLUTION TO TODAY

MICHAEL E. HEYES

BROADLEAF BOOKS
Minneapolis

DEVILS OF DEMOCRACY

America's Love Affair with Political Demons from the Revolution to Today

32 31 30 29 28 27 26 1 2 3 4 5 6 7 8 9

All biblical quotations are from the New King James Version, unless otherwise noted.

Library of Congress Control Number: 2026932361 (print)

Cover image: Leviathan Ouroboros by Danny Gonzalez M.

Cover design: Broadleaf Books / Carlos Esparza

Print ISBN: 979-8-3419-0093-6
eBook ISBN: 979-8-3419-0094-3

Printed in India

CONTENTS

Introduction

THE PEOPLE OF the United States have a demon problem.

Before I explain, let me set the stage with the following example.

On May 12, 2023, a two-day event in the far-right political and religious ReAwaken America Tour movement launched at the Trump National Doral resort in Miami. The tour program featured a combination of COVID-19 denial messages, speeches against "globalist" agendas (often an extremist antisemitic code term for Jewish people), and speaker engagement with a host of other conspiracy theories. The event was seemingly blessed by Donald Trump, then actively campaigning for reelection, who called in at one point to wish the event's co-organizer Michael Flynn well, as Flynn held up his phone to the audience.

A host of strange statements were made at the conference. However, arguably the most peculiar claim made at the main sessions came from Amanda Grace, Trump supporter and self-styled prophetess of Ark of Grace Ministries, a group Grace founded "to preach the Gospel to all creation."[1] Grace proclaimed to the crowd: "There's wickedness attempting to completely cover this nation in perversion and seductive, seducing spirits. I have never seen more images of more mermaids and water people in my life. That's a division in the Kingdom of Darkness and they're highly technologically advanced."[2]

That declaration was too outlandish for some observers not to share on social media, and many personalities weighed in with their own takes. My favorite remark came from David Corn, a journalist in Washington, DC, for *Mother Jones*, who commented, "When the mermaids attack, it might be foot-to-fin combat. That's to our advantage . . . on land."[3]

But Grace's wild, confusing vision itself is not the problem. The problem has to do with the very next thing that she said, a statement that, following her previous astonishing proclamation, many people missed:

> We have to understand the rules of engagement in spiritual warfare. . . . We are meant to bring our cries before the throne of God to bring judgment on the rulers of darkness of this world and of this nation, because the rulers have set up a throne in this nation. They've set it up. Darkness has completely covered and eclipsed the White House of this nation![4]

What Grace was talking about was the idea of demons. More precisely, she was asserting what everyday American men and women can do to prevent demons from exerting political control over the nation. That demons already can, and do, exert such control is an idea that many people today already believe.

This concept is nothing new. Many Christians, past and present, consider "spiritual warfare" (a modern term for the process of banishing or defeating demons) an important religious practice. In the views of those who believe in spiritual warfare, such actions as offering up numerous prayers, struggling personally with sins of desire, and even opposing certain social movements all can counteract the work of demons, which are thought to be constantly swarming around the believer, poisoning everything that they do.

Spiritual Warfare and the Rise of Trump

In the early twenty-first century, Donald Trump's presidential campaigns have served as a significant intersection between politics and these beliefs. One of the key works that galvanized and turned out evangelical voters for Trump in the 2016 election was author Lance Wallnau's *God's Chaos Candidate: Donald J. Trump and the American Unraveling*. In it, Wallnau claimed "Satan considers taking this nation down to be his number one priority. . . . We are up against a malevolent and demonic agenda aimed to destroy the global force for kingdom expansion that is America."[5]

After Trump's election that year, Paula White, founder of Paula White Ministries and the president's personal spiritual advisor, landed in the news for commanding "all Satanic pregnancies to miscarry" in an explosive sermon she gave in Apopka, Florida. *The New York Times* described her words as having been aimed at fighting "witchcraft . . . and demonic manipulation."[6] In the previous year, White even evoked specific demons by name—Leviathan, Jezebel, Abaddon, Belial—during her prayer that she gave in a conference call from Washington, DC, launching a Christian nationalist initiative called the One Voice Prayer Movement.[7]

After COVID-19 was declared a global pandemic in 2020, Trump retweeted a post made on Twitter (now X) by Stella Immanuel, a medical doctor who advocated hydroxychloroquine as a treatment for COVID-19. Journalists looking into Immanuel's background quickly found that she had also made the claim that sex with demons can cause reproductive issues like cysts and endometriosis.[8] Once more, as in the days following Grace's mention of battle-ready mermaids, the mouths of Democratic Party supporters hung open while millions of others quietly nodded their heads, a stunning figure that journalist Emily Brumfeld-Hessen cites in the title of her piece published in *Foreign Policy*: "Millions of Americans Believe Trump Is Fighting Literal Demons."[9]

Spiritual Warfare and Trump's 2020 Loss

Paula White, Trump's aforementioned spiritual advisor, officially launched his 2020 reelection campaign at a 2019 rally in Orlando, Florida, where she encouraged the audience to hold hands and pray with her. In the midst of this opening prayer, she commanded, "let every evil veil of deception of the Enemy be removed from people's eyes in the name which is above every name, the name of Jesus Christ." White went on to invoke the demons cited in Ephesians 6:12 when she told the crowd "I'm gonna deal with some principalities now" and commanded the "demonic networks" (that is, collections of demons) fighting against Trump to be broken.[10]

As I point out to my students in a course I teach entitled Angels and Demons, this essentially means that Trump's second presidential campaign started with an exorcism. By that, I mean that White engaged in a practice that was meant to expel demonic influence from a person, place, or thing. White herself might instead think of what she did as "deliverance ministry," but this is largely a term adopted by Protestants to distinguish what they do from Roman Catholic practices. The intended outcomes are the same.

After Trump's loss in November 2020, other exorcisms equally as political as White's began to occur. After some Trump supporters began to speculate that the election had been somehow rigged against him, a Catholic priest in Wisconsin followed up one Latin mass with an exorcism in which he commanded the demons who were supposedly attempting to influence vote recounters to depart.[11] The month prior, when protests against racial injustice occurred in Portland, Oregon, the Archbishop there conducted a public exorcism at a park, with the intention of banishing the evil influences that were causing unrest.[12] That same day, the archbishop of San Francisco performed an exorcism over the remains of a statue of Father Junipero Serra—a controversial figure due to his brutal treatment of Native Americans in his conversion process—following its toppling by protestors advocating for the rights of Black and Indigenous Americans, before the statue was replaced.[13] All of these exorcisms suggest that, to varying degrees, demons are becoming bound up in political matters.

From Trump's Second Election to Today

The 2024 election cycle continued this pattern. Speaking at his opening rally in Waco, Texas, Trump claimed that "the stakes of this election could not be clearer. Either we surrender to the demonic forces, abolishing and demolishing—and happily doing so—our country, or we defeat them in a landslide on November 5th, 2024."[14] During this campaign season, Trump-supporting far-right commentators and religious leaders often leveled accusations at his opposition, Kamala Harris, claiming that she was receiving aid from, or "had," something called a Jezebel Spirit: a kind of demon of seduction and division.[15]

Whether the use of such language was a deciding factor or not, Trump won the 2024 election. And whatever one thinks about such spiritual-political rhetoric, it's hard not to wonder what its ongoing use means. Exactly why are demons and politics suddenly being combined in the first half of our century? Why are religion and politics becoming so intertwined? What is it about our present political moment that has produced such strange bedfellows? These and similar questions seem to be circulating actively in both liberal *and* conservative circles, yet the answer is often a dismissive hand wave. To many, this spiritual-political shift signals not a long-term problem, but rather a unique aspect of Trump's presidency, a demon-styled version of the so-called Trump Effect, "the idea that Trump's bombastic rhetoric has made significant changes in many areas of American life."[16]

Or as a colleague of mine once put it: "Once Trump goes away, the crazy will too."

Let me offer you another way of viewing this pattern. Because although it may feel to us as though what's going on today is very different than anything that has happened in the United States before, what our country is experiencing is nothing new. And that fact can both inform and comfort us in this moment.

Over the chapters of this book, I will introduce you to numerous intersections of politics and demons in America. From the Revolutionary War to today, America has been steeped in the demonic, the diabolical, and the devilish. It is a part of our culture and communities, our history and heritage, our religion and recreation, the personal and the political. Demons populate the spaces of our daily life in ways we would never be inclined to imagine—even in ways that we might be inclined to dismiss. I encourage you not to do so. Instead, in these pages, I will help you to confront them head-on, revealing that we live in a nation that would not exist in its present form without the demonic beliefs that built it.

I also argue that failing to understand the political demonic could spell the downfall of our democracy.

Cards on the Table

I understand that you may be skeptical. Perhaps, you're thinking that there can't be enough public interest in demons or material about them to warrant yet another book on the topic. And indeed, there are already many excellent books on the subject, many of which are dense scholarly tomes such as Brian P. Levack's *The Devil Within: Possession & Exorcism in the Christian West* (346 pages),[17] Stuart Clark's *Thinking with Demons* (827 pages!),[18] or Jeffrey Burton Russell's four volume series on the history of the Devil.[19]

My own research and scholarship have added modestly to the groundwork that these stellar scholars and others have laid. In this way, I too have made a name for myself as something of an expert on the topic of demons. I say this not to toot my own horn or to raise my professional profile but simply to establish myself as a credible authority on the topic with which you are about to engage. To that end, I will note that I received my PhD from Rice University, with my dissertation focusing on the demonic elements of a medieval work called the *Life of St. Margaret*. This work became the foundation of my first book, *Margaret's Monsters* (2020). Through my teaching in 2019, I became interested in the ways that ancient and medieval ideas are, and are not, reflected in the modern United States. This led me to begin studying the intersection of demons and politics that resulted in my second book, *Demons in the USA* (2024), which covered some of the historical frames and problems that we'll be looking at here.

One might observe that literally *thousands* of books about demons have been written over the course of history, including some that defend belief in them, some that deny their existence, and those that study demons apart from the question of belief or disbelief. The purpose of this book, which falls in the third category, is to give you a readable understanding of what has turned out to be an important social issue in our time.

Perhaps, you're worrying that I am going to try to secretly convert you, either to a belief in demons you don't have or away from a belief in them that you've accepted. This is not my intention. If you are a firm believer in demons, I think that's okay, and I can understand why you would believe the way that you do (though I would argue that there are "bad"—i.e., socially irresponsible—ways to believe in demons, as we shall see). If you adamantly reject the idea that demons exist, I think that's okay as well, and I can understand why you would believe in the way you do. In fact, you might be surprised to find out that I don't believe *or* disbelieve in demons myself.

That's all right too, though my failure to come down on one side or the other surprises a lot of people. Often, we assume believing or not believing in something is required; that we have to have an opinion on everything. This way of thinking essentially turns the world into a vast series of light switches that are all either on or off. The truth is that things are often a lot more complicated, and as a scholar of religion, I often have to navigate these murky waters, a variety of different views, and a host of loud voices that all claim they know "the TRUTH."

Let me offer a different perspective on belief. Instead of light switches, let's think in terms of money. In this case, your money is your time, energy, and credibility, rather than actual dollars and cents. If someone came to you with an opportunity to "invest" (that is, to believe or disbelieve), would you throw your money around without first understanding what they were offering? Personally, I'd want to make sure I was "getting the most bang for my buck," as my dad used to say; I'd want to know I was making a wise "investment." To do that, I'd need to know quite a bit about the possible investment, what it would mean for me to invest in it, and what I might expect in return.

To put it back into the terms of belief, I might ask myself the following questions: What do I get from aligning myself with a particular conviction? Do I get a connection to a community I enjoy being a part of? Do I gain greater aptitude to explain my environment (as, for instance, believing in the scientific method gives me)? Do I become better able to relieve stress or anxiety that I feel? Do I get a new way to view the world that fills me with hope or excitement? Expressing belief (or disbelief) can do all these things, but I need to be wise with my investments: I only have so much "money."

For me, belief or disbelief in demons doesn't "get me" anything that I feel I need, so I don't invest. Truth be told, I'm a rather frugal investor to begin with: I value my time and credibility too much to just sink it anywhere. That being said, belief is not the same thing as knowledge, and it is my experience that, belief aside, knowing something concrete about demons is both interesting and useful to me when it comes to understanding how others see the world. I am "agnostic" with respect to demons—that is, I don't receive anything from my "investment" of believing or disbelieving so I choose to adopt neither position. However, I do believe without question that people's *beliefs* in demons have in the past and will in the future alter the world.

Ahh, there it is, you might be saying. *He's just "demon crazy."* Now, there you're right. There's something about how we as people believe in things that transcend our senses, from principalities like angels and demons to particles like quarks and neutrinos, that I find endlessly fascinating and that stirs my curiosity.

And I think the beliefs you'll read about here—beliefs that cover the entire stretch of American history—will do the same for you.

The Road to Conspiracy

While there are thousands of interesting facts about demons, one of the most unusual and odd is the focus of this book. Americans, as it turns out, love political demons. Perhaps this can be traced back to the religiously extreme positions held by some people who composed early America, or maybe a love of demons has always been at the heart of democracy beating in the breast of the United States. Whatever the cause of that love, when we look at American history, crisis always seems to engender the political demonic.

If you are to understand how uniquely people in the US view this phenomenon, we first need to get you caught up to speed. Before we get to the political demonic in the United States, we need to give you some idea about how demons and the Devil were understood in the history of Christianity before our country was born. Not only is this history interesting as its own independent topic, but it will also really make the differences between the dynamic in other nations and our own "pop." To give you this needed background, the first part of the book will cover issues from the presence (or absence) of the Devil in various works of the Bible to how Christians thought about demonic "bodies." We'll cover almost two millennia worth of demonology in what has been designed to be an easily digestible form.

From there, we'll move straight to the topic of the Apocalypse, the focus of part 2. Specifically, the one that was believed to be coming before the Revolutionary War. In this section, we'll see that in the years leading up to the war and the ones in which it unfolded, many Americans felt that King George III was the foretold Antichrist of the Apocalypse, his tax collectors were demonic accomplices, and the Revolutionary War was the last battle that would herald the End of Days.[20] Afterward, many of these same people came to believe that the defeat of the British instead heralded a new advent, one in which America became the millennial "Land of the Saints" that would welcome the return of Christ, the "New Jerusalem" hailed in Revelation. Forever after, countless Americans would think of the Apocalypse as an event that would occur in America or one in which America would be a significant actor.

As we'll see in part 3, it took less than a century before demons roared back into the American consciousness. In 1849, as Spiritualism began to rise in the US, two siblings from New York known as the Fox sisters demonstrated their supposed power to communicate with the dead, and in under a year some writers and critics had reframed this purported communication with the dead as communication with demons. As more and more Americans became entranced by séances and Ouija boards, these authors—whom I've collectively termed anti-Spiritualists—wove a grim picture of demons deceiving people, filling their heads with political lies that led them to advocate for the abolition of slavery and women's suffrage. In this period, the idea of a new, previously unimagined threat developed: a kind of secret possession, a sneaky backdoor into people's brains by which the Devil and his minions could exploit a person without the victim ever knowing they were there.

Eventually, this rhetoric was woven into the threads of the Civil War, and both sides eagerly invoked the Devil as the leader of their enemies. For Union soldiers, the idea that "the first secessionist was Satan" predominated,[21] casting the Confederates as on par with the Fallen One himself. Confederates also made use of Satan in images in pamphlets,[22] to claim that members of the Union had been deluded by demons posing as the dead to get them to turn from what they framed as "just" practices (i.e., slavery). During this time period, Americans imagined their first demonic political conspiracy, one in which untold numbers of Americans, consciously or unconsciously, marched to the Devil's drum and in which Lincoln made demonic pacts.

At the end of the Civil War crisis, most of America turned its gaze away from political demons again. More and more, demons came to be regarded as intellectually backward and medieval by the general populace. It wasn't until after the Second World War that belief in demons would come into vogue once more. We'll pick up the thread here in part 4. While there are many authors and speakers who contributed to this resurgent popularity, I argue that four personalities—Merrill Unger, Michael Harper, Billy Graham, and the Hammonds—had an outsized influence upon this development. This growing movement was further aided by Hollywood's production of demonically oriented films (like *Rosemary's Baby*, *The Exorcist*, and *The Omen*) and authors of tell-all memoirs who claimed to be ex-Satanists, witches, and other nefarious personages. Eventually, this movement informed the so-called Satanic Panic, the widespread fearful idea in the 1980s and 1990s that an underground conspiracy of Satanists was actively predating upon children and teens.

In part 5, we'll see that as the second millennium dawned, these fears lived on. Although investigations found no evidence for the over twelve thousand accusations of "Satanic Ritual Abuse" documented by psychiatrists and police around the country, the idea of Americans being the victims of demons endured. These beliefs fed new movements like the far-right conspiracy theory movement QAnon, which began in 2017 and the New Apostolic Reformation (NAR), a charismatic evangelical Christian movement with a theological obsession with demons that emerged in the late twentieth century, and that turned the tide for presidential candidate Trump in 2016 and 2024 and supported the false narrative that the election was stolen from him in 2020. Both movements saw the Democratic Party as a source of demonic evil and used language that slowly recast their human political opponents. QAnon imagined their opponents as child-eating monstrosities whose hearts beat with demonic malice, while the NAR saw them as the dupes of devils who were running the country to ruin at the behest of their unseen overlords. These are the conditions in which we find ourselves today.

After the book's second, third, and fourth parts, I've included what I call a Modern Takeaway: a sort of epilogue for that part of history that points to its relevance to today. (More recent history to the present is covered in part 5.) Even though those earlier historical moments have passed, the effects of our collective belief in demons from that moment remain. As we'll see, these moments stack together like a tower of blocks, collectively creating a larger structure than any one alone ever could.

Unfortunately, the structure that those blocks have created is what I will refer to as a "conspiratorial demonology," a term that refers to the "bad" or "socially irresponsible" way to believe in demons I noted earlier. This way of believing not only threatens people on an individual level—for instance, by exacerbating differences to such a degree that friends and families become divided—but it threatens us on a national level as well. Like many other kinds of conspiracies, conspiratorial demonologies erode public trust, increase both individual and collective anxiety, and in many cases eventually lead to harm (or even deaths) that could be avoided.

For instance, as Matthew D. Taylor points out in his 2024 book *The Violent Take It by Force: The Christian Movement That Is Threatening Our Democracy*, members of the NAR played an outsized role in the insurrection attempt on the capital on January 6, 2021. Conspiratorial demonology encourages Americans not to see the present moment as business as usual, the playing out of political differences between well-intentioned fellow citizens, but instead as a conspiracy of demon-worshipping, child-devouring political actors with legions of unknowingly demonized people at their beck and call who are trying to usher in the End of the World.

"Come and See"

And here is where we come to the importance of this material. Given our history, it is unlikely that America will soon quit a trend it has maintained since its inception. Demons will continue to crop up around political crisis points. We can't do anything to stop that. However, we can arm ourselves with the balance of history to prevent us from giving in to the seductive pull of conspiratorial thinking.

If we forget about this simple pattern, then every crisis will seem like the End of Days instead of the End of Just Another Day. But if we remember, we have the information we need to peacefully counteract a set of dangerous beliefs that are held not only by a disturbing number of our friends and family but an increasing number of those in power. We can develop strategies for how we can inoculate ourselves against the viral conspiracy theories we face every day. Doing so can ensure we can coexist with our demons while still maintaining a healthy and thriving democracy.

So, as one of the four beasts of the Apocalypse rumbles, "Come and see" (Revelation 6:1), within these pages, we will find demons undermining the Republic and whispering to Americans searching for messages from the Beyond; allegations of witchcraft and child sacrifice to the Devil in the American heartland; and the demons of film, whom some claim refuse to stay put on the screen.

Come and see. We'll have a hell of a time.

Part I

Thousands of Years of Demons

A History

CHAPTER ONE

In the Beginning . . .

In September of 2024, while seeking to learn more about what was happening at the meeting point of spiritual warfare in politics, I found myself waiting in line at an event on what was being called "The Courage Tour." The Courage Tour is a religious and political rally that launched that year, put on by leaders in the NAR, a Christian movement that is significantly invested in the idea of demons. The Tour's intention was to encourage attendees to vote for Trump and to evangelize others to do the same.

This was the second day of the event. The previous night, we attendees had been told by organizer and headlining speaker Lance Wallnau that we were going to get to enjoy a surprise guest: then–vice presidential candidate JD Vance would be joining us for the Saturday meeting. (Luckily, the hearing loss I suffered following the deafening roar that greeted this announcement would prove to be only temporary.)

"Get there early." This had been the organizers' prevailing message. The reason for the warning was clear: There were only two metal detectors that could be set up to check guests as they came through the doors. That left me standing in an asphalt parking lot in the morning sun with the rest of the attendees as we awaited our turn to enter.

I was keenly aware that as a scholar rather than one of the faithful, I didn't exactly belong in that crowd. But I knew that the group was obsessed with demons, so I stuck it out. The previous night's message had covered a bit of the "Seven Mountain Mandate," a prophecy in the NAR movement that held that the Antichrist or Satan lorded over seven metaphorical "mountains" of influence through its demonic minions.

The seeds of this belief had been planted years before by Campus Crusade for Christ leader Bill Bright and Youth With a Mission leader Loren Cunningham, who both claimed that God had called them to transform society in seven areas: religion, family, education, government, media, arts and entertainment, and business. Lance Wallnau, one of the Courage Tour's founders, had since adopted the seeds of these beliefs and was now clearly associated with the idea. I had found

Wallnau's book on the Seven Mountain Mandate interesting and was hoping to hear more. Now, standing in line, I figured I might be able to find more demonological pearls if I trained my ears on the things people in the crowd were saying.

Eventually, listening in on these conversations paid off: Someone near me started to talk about demons, and others joined in. Time has since passed, and I no longer recall the substance of the discussion, but I do remember how the conversation about demons ended. One of the members of the group remarked, "I don't think most Americans are ready for 'the D-word.'"

A fascinating observation: one that suggests a need by true believers to be secretive about the true motivations of their influential group, as well as a conviction that America will be ready in time to accept demons but might, if not properly prepared first, reject this vision of the world. All the more reason for you and me to engage with this subject now, rather than waiting for intellectual tides to turn in favor of such a politically motivated group.

So, let's talk about the "D-word." What are demons? You probably have a lot of ideas about what they might be (or might not be), and we need some common ground before we start moving into the history of demons in the United States. America, after all, isn't known for doing things halfway, so it makes sense that the history of the demonic in the United States is pretty different from that of the rest of the world.

In order to make the topic of demons more manageable, we're going to focus on some specific areas. In this chapter, we'll cover demonic origins. Specifically, we'll discuss where the Devil *isn't* in the Hebrew Bible and introduce the important concept of allegory.[1] Finally, we'll see where the demons—and their head honcho, the Devil—got their start.

The next chapter will focus on New Testament and medieval ideas about the demonic and the Apocalypse. We'll learn about possession, what demons are able to know and why, what their bodies are made from, and when the events of Revelation will happen (or, as I'll argue, *have* happened).

Adam, Eve, and the Devil That Wasn't

Our story starts with the Bible. Now, you might be thinking, "Well, sure, it all starts with the Devil! If he hadn't offered the apple to Eve, we'd all be sitting pretty."

Not really. It might seem strange to those of us who grew up equating the serpent in Genesis 3 with Satan, but historically speaking, the snake in the garden is just a snake. It might further surprise you to know that there really isn't a devil in the Hebrew Bible, nor do any demons (at least, not as we think of them) appear in the text.

In order to get to the root of this misunderstanding, we should start with the text itself. Bible passage incoming! Genesis 3 starts out in the following way:

> Now the serpent was more crafty than any of the wild animals the Lord God had made. He said to the woman, "Did God really say, 'You must not eat from any tree in the garden'?" The woman said to the serpent, "We may eat fruit from the trees in the garden, but God did say, 'You must not eat fruit from the tree that is in the middle of the garden, and you must not touch it, or you will die.'" "You will not certainly die," the serpent said to the woman. "For God knows that when you eat from it your eyes will be opened, and you will be like God, knowing good and evil." (3:1–5 NIV)

Look at the language that we use to describe the serpent here: he's not described as a demon, a devil, or anything of that sort. He's just a "wild animal." Is it odd that he talks? Sure, but there are plenty of myths, stories, and historical narratives from cultures around the world that feature talking animals. The snake isn't even the only talking animal in the Bible: You've also got a talking donkey in Numbers 22:22–40[2] and a talking eagle in Revelation 8:13.[3] And to date, no one has accused them of being the Devil in disguise!

Next in the text, Adam and Eve have their ill-advised snack. When they're done, God returns to the garden, and he is pissed. He's so angry, in fact, that he curses everyone involved. Here is the curse he pronounces on the snake:

> *"Because you have done this,*
> *cursed are you above all livestock*
> *and all wild animals!*
> *You will crawl on your belly*
> *and you will eat dust*
> *all the days of your life.*

And I will put enmity
between you and the woman,
and between your offspring and hers;
he will crush your head,
and you will strike his heel." (Genesis 3:14–15)

Let's take a moment to observe that the text—this time, reporting God's voice—identifies the serpent, *yet again*, as a "wild animal." Then, God curses him to do all the snaky things that snakes do: crawl on their bellies and bite stuff. As scholar and theologian Bill T. Arnold writes in his Bible commentary *Genesis*, this passage is simply defining the relationship between humans and snakes: natural enmity.[4]

God's identification of the snake as a wild animal throws a serious wrench into the idea that the snake was also the Devil. That's because, if we want to read the snake as the Devil, we then have to make a problematic assumption: God didn't *know* that the snake was really the Devil in disguise. Considering that this creates a host of theological problems concerning a God who is widely understood in Christianity to be all-knowing, it's easier to make the obvious conclusion: In the story of Genesis 3, the snake is just a snake.

Desperately Seeking Satan

The Concept of Allegory

The obvious question here is this: How did Christians come to associate the snake with the Devil such that this becomes a kind of standard reading of Genesis? The association certainly didn't happen overnight. Instead, many generations of readers interpreted the character in different ways, each one building on the interpretations of readers who came before.

Recognizing this brings us to an important concept that we'll return to again and again in this book: allegory. An allegory is a literary device in which social, political, or cultural meaning is conveyed through a narrative that uses symbolic representation. For example, in Aesop's fables the animals represent human traits, and their actions teach lessons about how humans are meant to behave in the world. Thus, when a person says that something is "allegorical" or should be read "allegorically," what they're saying is that there is a greater or more important message behind the story than one might first think.

Creators of allegorical stories, then, are encouraging their audience to see the events of the story as pregnant with meaning, and to thereby interpret those events as metaphors or symbols for bigger ideas. This process layers the text with additional meaning that continues to grow, reading after reading. Because we can't unlearn meanings about a text that others taught us, and since a story's or text's meaning is constantly changing over time, every generation moves farther and farther away from an author's original meanings and contexts.

In the case of the serpent in Genesis 3, many Jewish and Christian authors—starting around the first century BCE—allegorically read the snake as another serpent from the Hebrew Bible: Leviathan.[5] Leviathan is *the* sea serpent that is depicted in the Hebrew Bible. It's a kind of primordial chaos beast that represents God's power and control, and it gets referenced in Psalms, Isaiah, and, perhaps most famously, in Job. Leviathan is the "Big Bad" of the Hebrew Bible, yes, but it is a chaos beast that is firmly under God's control.

A snake is, of course, not the same thing as a sea serpent. So how did Leviathan ever come to be associated with the Devil? The answer begins with the fact that Leviathan is referenced in the Bible by titles, such as "the fleeing serpent" (Job 26:13) or "the twisting serpent . . . the dragon that is in the sea" (Isaiah 27:1 NRSVUE). In Revelation, we see these titles of Leviathan associated with the character of the Devil: as in "the great dragon was cast out, that serpent of old, called the Devil and Satan" (Revelation 12:9) and "the dragon, that serpent of old, who is *the* Devil and Satan" (Revelation 20:2). By the time of the Church Father Irenaeus's *Against Heresies* (~180 CE), it appears to be a standard reading that the "serpent . . . who is the Devil" had also come to be associated with the serpent in the garden. This allows Irenaeus to read the curse upon the serpent as prefiguring Christ's defeat of Satan, an interpretation referred to as the "Protoevangelium" (or "first Gospel").

All of the Bible's other references to Satan or the Devil received a similar treatment from early Christians. By the late antique period, it was common to read the Devil allegorically into several juicy characters in the Hebrew Bible. For an example, let's return to Job, which starts off with the character Satan approaching God at a kind of "divine mixer" with all the angels in attendance. "One day the angels came to present themselves before the Lord, and Satan also came with them" (Job 1:6 NIV).

It seems like a pretty clear reference: Satan is Satan, right?

Well, sort of. The term here isn't actually a name, it's a title: "the Satan" (ha-Satan), which can be translated as "the Accuser." In a legal context, this figure is something like the prosecution (the accuser) in a court case, but in this story, it is a kind of spiritual court case in which the Accuser tries to point out the flaws in humankind.[6]

As the story unfolds, this is exactly what "the Satan" does. When God suggests that Job is the most righteous man alive, the Satan zeroes in on a flaw in the argument, claiming you'd be righteous too if you got everything you ever wanted. At this point, God apparently accepts that this is a reasonable argument, and he sends the Satan to destroy Job's family and property in whatever way it chooses to test this theory. Just like Leviathan, the Satan in this passage is still firmly God's minion, a legal opponent and *not* a cosmic opponent.

Once again, a passage that Christians today widely believe is populated by the Devil is in fact devil-free. The truth is that the Hebrew Bible doesn't really need a devil to explain the presence of evil. Isaiah 25:7 says, "I [God] form the light, and create darkness: I make peace, and create evil: I the Lord do all these things." The Israelites didn't need a devil to pin negative things on, because God did *all things*, the good and the bad. They considered God good not because he's capital g-o-o-d *GOOD*, but because he's the God of their tribe, Israel.

But this line of thinking doesn't work in the New Testament. That's because the New Testament stars a different kind of God, a God who represents absolute Good, one who is just and not just the God of the Israelites. For God to work, we need an opponent, an Enemy who's bad to the bone, as well as a population of minions to do this enemy's dirty work.

The Weird Stuff

The Birth of the Devil and His Demons

This Enemy and his army can be found in the gradual Israelite adaptation of one of the weirdest sections of the Hebrew Bible: Genesis 5–6. Genesis 5 is a genealogy—a list of dads and their sons, in this case—from Adam to Noah. If you've ever skipped over it, don't worry: everyone does. It's just a whole lot of "So and so was born, lived a while, had a kid, lived some more, and then died" over and over and over again.

But there's also a weird nugget in there; blink and you'll miss it. In Genesis 5:21–24, we read:

> Enoch lived sixty-five years, and begot Methuselah. After he begot Methuselah, Enoch walked with God three hundred years, and had sons and daughters. So all the days of Enoch were three hundred and sixty-five years. And Enoch walked with God; and he *was* not, for God took him.

As one of my students once asked incredulously, "What?! What actually happened to Enoch? What does it mean he 'walked with God' or that 'God took him?' Everyone else dies, but Enoch just 'was not'!"

It's a good point: What happened to Enoch isn't at all clear. Then, as if this confusion wasn't enough, in the very next chapter we find out about the Nephilim. In Genesis 6: 1–4 (NRSVUE), we read:

> When people began to multiply on the face of the ground, and daughters were born to them, the sons of God saw that they were fair, and they took wives for themselves of all that they chose. . . . The Nephilim were on the earth in those days—and also afterward—when the sons of God went in to the daughters of humans, who bore children to them. These were the heroes that were of old, warriors of renown.

Here's the thing: You can't just give people two very strange ideas (here, Enoch's disappearance and the existence of the Nephilim) with no explanation and expect them to take it in stride. So it makes sense that the Israelites started to think about how these two strange things could be connected. As they thought, they wrote, as did subsequent generations, and by the third or fourth century BCE, these writings started to form into a work called "the Book of Enoch." If you've never heard of it, again, don't worry; it's not in the Bibles of most Christian denominations and is not considered canonical by a lot of religious groups. However, it is one of the most influential extrabiblical Jewish works of the antique period, and we can see its long shadow quite clearly in the development of modern ideas about the Devil and demons.

In 1 Enoch,[7] we find a group of angels that watch over humankind. Disobeying God, they mate with human women, producing the Nephilim as their children (1 Enoch 6–7). As a result of this disobedience, these angels are expelled from heaven and are bound in "the bonds of the earth" until the Final Judgment (1 Enoch 14). Their children, the Nephilim, are fated to die by violence. God summons Enoch to him in order to record the verdict and eventual punishment of these disobedient angels.

There's just one catch: The Nephilim can't actually die because they are partially immortal in their parentage. As a result, "the giants, who are produced from the spirits and flesh, shall be called evil spirits upon the earth" (1 Enoch 15:8–9). First Enoch then proclaims that these evil spirits go on to bedevil humankind at every juncture, sowing discord and suffering wherever they invisibly travel (1 Enoch 15:10–12).

Progress in our search for the Devil and demons! We've got an angelic fall, and we've got "evil spirits" that roam the earth and hate humanity. We're just missing one crucial thing: a leader. Sure, we get a couple of figures that bear some responsibility,[8] but no one really distinguishes themselves as the worst among the bad.

That won't really happen until the second century BCE with the writing of Jubilees.[9] Jubilees combines material from Genesis and 1 Enoch and expands on both. In the book, Noah prays to God to remove the "dead" Nephilim from the earth because they are accosting the survivors of the Flood. However, in chapter 10, verse 8, just as God is about to consign these evil spirits to the "place of condemnation," one spirit, Mastema, pleads with God:

> Lord, Creator, let some of them remain before me, and let them harken to my voice, and do all that I shall say unto them; for if some of them are not left to me, I shall not be able to execute the power of my will on the sons of men; for these are for corruption and leading astray before my judgment, for great is the wickedness of the sons of men.

According to Jubilees, God agrees, placing the majority of the Nephilim spirits in the "place of condemnation" and a tenth under the control of Mastema (Jubilees 10:8–9), a leader whose name literally means "hatred." As this horrific being claimed he would do in his speech above, he goes on to lead the contingent of demons under him to harass and assault humanity at every turn, punishing them for their "wickedness."

Et voilà! There's our Devil, before he's called the Devil.

Enter the Devil

Great, we now have a Devil. Unfortunately, not many of the sources these ideas came from actually give us an idea of what the Devil and his demonic minions are capable of *doing*. The "dead" Nephilim are clearly capable of "corrupting" and "leading astray" (Jubilees 10:8), but what else is within their power? Could they strike a human being dead if they were so inclined? Under what conditions would Mastema allow a human being to be assaulted by these evil spirits, and if that happened, how might a person turn aside their attacks?

If the idea of demons is going to be useful—really useful—to us as an explanatory device for human misery and woe, then we need rules: We need to be able to say how demons are able to act in the world and what they're (not) able to do. We need to lay down guidelines for people to understand their interactions with the world of demons.

Luckily, there's a little addendum you might have heard of that starts to set down these rules a bit, written after the writings of the ones we just covered.

It's called the New Testament.

CHAPTER TWO

Dealing with Demons

THERE EXISTS A biblical account of exorcism so lurid and strange that it has virtually seared itself into the collective Western mind. In a passage that we find, in slightly different forms, in Luke (8:26–39) and Mark (5:1–20),[1] Jesus and his disciples come to the region of the Gerasenes. As soon as they step onto the shore of the region, a nude, gibbering man approaches them from the nearby tombs.

This man, we learn, is possessed by demons, and every day is bound in chains (presumably, by his fellow Gerasenes) only to break out of them again. When we see the man, he falls at Jesus's feet and the demons inside of him beg not to be expelled from their host. When Jesus asks what the name of the demons is, they claim that it is "Legion" (a Roman military term that designates a unit of three to six thousand soldiers) since there were so many demons inside the man. Jesus swiftly casts out the demons, sending them into a herd of pigs who throw themselves down the embankment and into the sea.

Although the scene is somewhat confusing to us today, this and other depictions of the demonic in the New Testament actually serve as points of clarity because they begin to establish for us what demons are and are not capable of. From tales of possession to oblique references to aerial demons, these details served up by New Testament authors help develop the world of demons and organize their interactions with human beings—interactions that are later used to establish sets of rules and principles for dealing with demons. Some of these principles are quite long-lived and are still used by contemporary Americans to this day.

The "Good News" About Demons

Possession

Of all the miracles that Jesus performs, none are more numerous in the Gospels than his exorcisms. All told, there are seven major accounts of exorcism by him (such as the exorcism of the man just discussed, often referred to as the "Gerasene Demoniac"), plus a range of minor mentions and oblique references to many more (like Jesus casting seven demons out of Mary Magdalene).

The exorcisms performed by Jesus in the Gospels function as a kind of "baseline" for how we can understand the phenomenon of demonic possession. Possession is a state in which a demon comes to influence the behavior of a human being. We can think of the demon as effectively being "inside" of the person, though interpreters of Scripture sometimes disagree on exactly what this means. An abundance of films has come out in the United States over the past five decades that feature possession as a part of the plot, but a lot of these depictions are rather sensationalized and horrific (like spinning heads, prodigious vomit, and crawling backward up walls). The rules for possession laid down in the Gospels are a bit more even keel.

The first rule is that possession occurs when a person is in bad health. Many of the miraculous cures that Jesus performs, such as healing the mute and the blind,[2] are for illnesses that were caused by demons. In fact, the authors of the Gospels often refer to curing disease and casting out demons in the same breath, making it difficult to determine when Jesus is "curing" people and when he is "exorcising" them.[3]

This is a problem that has been observed from antiquity to the present day, as summed up by the question: How does one tell demon from disease? As Sir Thomas Browne notes in his spiritual and philosophical memoir *The Religion of a Doctor* (*Religio medici*, 1643), "the devil doth really possess some men; the spirit of melancholy others; the spirit of delusion others." By that claim, he means that some people really *are* possessed by the Devil or demons, but it is difficult to distinguish these people from those with mental illness or who have been merely deluded to believe that they are possessed.

(Un)Truths

Demonic Knowledge and Lies

Not being able to tell when someone is possessed is a problem. Consider this for a moment in terms of a medical paradigm: How can one suggest treatment if they are unable to first diagnose? This is basically the same question that plagued specialists treating spiritual conditions. The answer was simple: In order to resolve this problem, we need demons to be able to do things that human beings are not capable of.

This need brings us to what appears to be another rule of possession: The possessed person can sometimes speak with the voice of the demon. For example, when Jesus asks the Gerasene demoniac, "What is your name?" the demoniac doesn't answer "Chuck," or whatever the man's name was. Instead, he says "Legion." (In Mark 5:9, the text explains the name's meaning—"for we are many"—in a way that clearly indicates that it is the name of the possessing demon rather than the man being possessed.)

While a change of name isn't significant evidence of possession, someone talking like a demon *could* be, and dramatically so. In particular, if the person knew things that they otherwise were incapable of knowing, people could take this as concrete evidence of the person being inhabited by one or more demons.

Because from what Scripture shows us, demons are knowledgeable. For example, time and time again, when Jesus's disciples and close associates fail to understand Jesus's true nature, it is the demons that he casts out who *do* understand. In Mark 1:24, a demon inside a human host shouts, "Let us alone! What have we to do with You, Jesus of Nazareth? Did You come to destroy us? I know who You are—the Holy One of God!"

This idea of demonic knowledge went on to extend far beyond the pages of the Gospels. As American medievalist and religious historian Richard Kieckhefer notes, exorcism and conjuration, the practices of calling up demons, were nearly identical practices in the Middle Ages.[4] In the conjuration work that Kieckhefer analyzes, "Fully seventeen experiments are divinatory techniques for gaining knowledge of future, past, distant or hidden things."[5] During that time, magicians sought to use demonic knowledge for purposes such as discovering a thief or uncovering hidden treasure.

The promise of such hidden knowledge likely forms the backdrop of an injunction found in the *Rituale Romanum*—a Roman Catholic liturgical book that contains the rite of exorcism. In the *Rituale*, the exorcist is told not to ask "superfluous or prying questions, particularly concerning the future or hidden things not pertinent to his office."[6] Put another way, the text is instructing the exorcist not to engage in the types of conjurations discussed by Kieckhefer: Demons should only be asked questions as required to expel them and not for informational purposes.

Demonic truth, however, was not a guarantee. The Bible tells us that despite being knowledgeable, demons are also very capable liars. John 8:44 refers to the Devil as "the father of lies," and Ephesians 6:11 uses the word "methodeia" (μεθοδεία)—meaning deceit, trickery, craftiness—to describe his assaults upon Christians. Likewise, Acts describes individuals related to the Devil as being infused with deceit and villainy.[7] These characteristics of "the boss" were often also grafted onto his minions. For example, "early modern demonologists . . . warned against interrogating the demon [in a possession case] on the grounds that the Father of Lies was unreliable."[8] As the emissaries of the Enemy, demons shared in the Devil's deceitful nature.

Aerial Beings

Demonic Bodies

In 2 Corinthians 11:14, the apostle Paul warns people of this deceptive power in another way, saying: "And no wonder! For Satan himself transforms himself into an angel of light."

Paul's proclamation brings us to our next demonological issue, because it suggests that demons are not always invisible. If that is the case, we may ask, then what sort of bodies did they have? What were they made from?

Outside the Gospels, Paul refers to the threat of the Devil in Ephesians 6:12:[9] "For we do *not* wrestle against flesh and blood, but against principalities, against powers, against the rulers of the darkness of this age, *against spiritual hosts of wickedness in the heavenly places*" (emphasis mine). This line seems confusing at first, but it points to the idea that demons (the aforementioned "principalities," "powers," and "rulers") are not flesh and blood beings with bodies, like people.

So, then what were demonic bodies made from? One suggestion of the composition of demonic bodies can be found earlier in Ephesians, when the author writes that before coming to Christ the reader, "walked according to the course of this world, according to the prince of the power [ἐξουσίας] of the air, the spirit who now works in the sons of disobedience" (Ephesians 2:2). The term "power" here is not an incorrect translation of the Greek, but rather a term that might obscure a bit of meaning for us. Generally, the term ἐξουσία (exousia) refers to one's authority or right, a purview over which one has power. Thus, we might say that the Devil is being depicted here as something like the Ruler over the Domain of the Air.

If the Devil rules over the Domain of the Air, then it stands to reason that the subjects of his kingdom inhabit that air and are composed from it in the same way that humans inhabit terrestrial kingdoms and have terrestrial bodies. In *The City of God* (Book 8:14–15), Augustine of Hippo—one of the most influential Church Fathers—claims the same, arguing that demons inhabit the aerial realm and have bodies that are composed of air. However, Augustine assures his reader, "though they are aerial, [demons] are not better than we who are terrestrial because the air is higher than the earth, but, on the contrary, men are to be put before demons because their despair is not to be compared to the hope of pious men" (8:15).[10] Centuries later, physicians practicing medieval medicine took this to mean that possession occurred by the aerial bodies of demons entering a human body through one of the various entrances in the body through which air could travel.[11]

In this understanding, demons couldn't enter a person by "magic;" they needed a doorway to access the open spaces inside the human body where they could make mischief. While this image is terrifying, it also suggests that demons lacked bodies that could in any way act upon human bodies, that they were nothing more than puffs of smoke or gusts of wind. Here we get into one of the great debates of demonology: How solid are demonic bodies?

Arguably, it was the body of writing known as monastic literature that brought Christians their first cohesive suggestions that demonic bodies could interact with human ones. *The Life of St. Anthony* is our oldest example of a Saint's Life—a type of writing that gives a virtuous account of a saint's career—that focused on a monk. In this work, Anthony describes scenes in which he struggles with the "spirit of fornication;" fights off hordes of demons that appear to him as wolves, serpents, and leopards; and even meets the Devil himself.

These demons in Anthony's account accost him at every turn, titillating his senses and tearing at his body with their teeth and claws. In Michelangelo's *The Torment (or Temptation) of Saint Anthony* (1487), which depicts these struggles, a flock of weirdly formed beings lifts Anthony bodily above the lands of Egypt, clubbing and scratching him in flight. From this point in history forward, some people would understand demons as being able to touch and tease, beat and bruise the human body as they desire.

The "spirit of fornication" that sexually accosted Anthony was not the only demon perceived by Christians to have done so. In early Christianity, many influential voices argued that Christians should live the *vita angelica* (the angelic life). This meant that demons came to be associated with one thing angels didn't do: sex.

It's perhaps unsurprising, then, that many demons depicted in writing in the Middle Ages were shockingly sexual in their behavior. Modeled on St. Anthony's *Life*, saints throughout the period were described by hagiographers—the writers of Saints' Lives—as having been bedeviled by satanic stripteases and sexualized spirits who assaulted them in their dreaming and waking lives. This was perceived to be a big enough problem that John Cassian, a fifth century monastic author, suggested an entire chapter's worth of counter measures to his brothers in *The Institutes*, including draping a plate of lead across one's genitals.[12]

Eventually this problem of sex with demons found its way into non-monastic communities as well. For instance, when you and I think of historical depictions of witches, we might imagine a person wearing a pointy hat, riding on a broom, and casting curses upon unsuspecting townsfolk. On the contrary, the European Witch Trials tended to define witches by one simple question: Had the woman knowingly had sex with a demon or not?[13]

There were even specific demons who were assigned to this exact job. The most famous treatise on witchcraft during the European witch hunts, the *Malleus Maleficarum* (*The Hammer against Witches*),[14] called these demons the incubus and succubus. For Kramer, the terms actually refer to the same demon acting in two different positions:[15] the succubus—from *subcubo*, "I lie beneath"—has sexual relations with a man in the night. After stealing his sperm, it becomes the incubus—from *incubo*, "I lie above"—and inseminates an unsuspecting woman in her sleep.

These beliefs continue right into the present day, where you can find hundreds of videos on YouTube testifying to encounters with these demons or offering a means of warding them away. It is perhaps not surprising that these demons are undergoing a renaissance in the American mind: After all, most of the groups we'll read about in our contemporary material are deeply uncomfortable with the Sexual Revolution of the '60s and '70s. Given that, if one is inclined to resurrect an otherworldly enemy, what better demon to bring back than an entity that has sex with you in your sleep?

Demons as Opponents

The Other

Speaking of witches, you may have heard the argument that women who historically were persecuted as witches were simply women who had been displaced from the community, either because they refused to marry, appeared to be too wealthy, or were simply too outspoken or unpleasant. While I would say the issue is a bit more complicated than this (at least, in the case of the European Witch Trials, which were far greater in scope and deeply connected to conflicts between Protestants and Catholics), this claim points to one topic to which the idea of demons is deeply relevant, and that is the social construct of the Other.

The idea of the Other has been the subject of hundreds of books, but it is a fairly easy notion to summarize. First, think about one of the communities to which you belong: this might be a town, a nation, a special interest group, or anything else that collects groups of people based upon shared traits. These shared traits are a means of identifying the community—for example, citizenship is what technically makes someone an American, but people might also say that Americans love freedom, equality, individualism, or some other qualities—and those within the community have specific roles to play. When someone within the community is playing their specific role, they are operating as "the Self." Those outside of the community or those who reject their role become "the Other."

Now let's think about this in terms of Christianity and the demonic. Those individuals who identify as Christian in various ways (i.e., Roman Catholic, Methodist, Mormon, Jehovah's Witness, etc.) adopt certain traits and behave in certain ways so that they can be part of different types of communities we might refer to as "churches." Those outside of the community, for instance, Muslims or Buddhists, are generally considered, consciously or unconsciously, by those in the community to be "the Other." But so too could be someone who isn't playing their role properly, such as a medieval woman who creates social friction.

Historically, all three of these groups have been identified with the demonic at one point in time or another: During the Crusades,

Christian authors and Crusaders often accused Muslims of worshipping the demon "Mahomet" or "Mammon"; some contemporary Christian groups have accused Buddhists (especially, Tibetan Buddhists) of practicing rituals of demonic possession; and some women in the United States and Europe were definitely accused of being witches with no more substance to the accusation than that they aggravated someone (or multiple someones) in the community that accused them.

Similarly, many citizens of the US today have often associated political, social, or religious opponents with demons, or imagine that people who are different from themselves are somehow demonic in nature. This has led to everything from Jewish communities to yoga practitioners to the Democratic National Convention being branded a source of demonic activity.

The idea that these "Othered" groups worship demons, are possessed by demons, or even bear demonic traits is a persistent theme in the history of Christianity. Consider for example two images from the Middle Ages. The first is a fifteenth century fresco by the artist Giovanni de Modena that is at the Basilica di San Petronio in Bologna, Italy. Titled *The Inferno*, the work features an image of Satan in Hell, gnawing on the bodies of sinners. A woodcut by the painter Jörg Breu from Augsburg, made a century later, depicts a scene of Hindu worship as described by Christians who had visited Calicut (the modern city of Kozhikode in India). Put side by side, the two images are strikingly alike, illustrating how similar the Christian image of Satan is to Christians imagining Hindu worship![16]

The idea of the Other is insidious. As a tribal species, we are constantly seeking similarities and differences that can be used to unite and divide. Demons are often an important component of Christian communities thinking through the rationale for choices that divide.

Demons and the End

Apocalypse

Now, we come to the End. While to this point devils and demons in the Bible have factored into the Christian story in a relatively limited way, they loom large in the final reckoning of the world itself. A common term for this end in the Modern West is *the Apocalypse*, which is named after the Greek title of the book of Revelation ("The Apocalypse of John," or the *apokalupsis*/ἀποκάλυψις—a revealing, an unveiling of John).

If I had to describe Revelation in one single word, it would be "dramatic." In Revelation, demons spill from the mouths of false prophets and are worshipped by people as gods, through idols. Monstrous demonic figures rise from pits, the sea, and the land; great beasts emerge to accost believers; and fiery angels and a sword-mouthed Christ ride out to wage battle against the forces of darkness.

Yet, if I could have two words to describe the book, I would choose "frequently misinterpreted." You see, there's significant historical and archaeological evidence to suggest that the occurrences of Revelation had *already happened by the time of the book's writing.*

In the popular imagination today, the events of Revelation have yet to occur. However, when biblical scholars use their knowledge of the ancient world, both historical and linguistic, it appears highly likely that some of the events being described are actually things that happened long ago, slightly before or after the writing of Revelation.

Entire books have been written on this topic, which is more expansive than we have time to investigate in detail here. So let's just consider one of the most popular characters from Revelation, one almost everyone has heard of: the Beast, whose number is "666" (Revelation 13:18). One popular pastime of people who like to predict the Apocalypse is to assign this number to someone whom they don't agree with who is currently alive.[17] Viewing the text through this lens, they can then read the events of Revelation as if they are currently happening, with the Beast becoming an apocalyptic presence looming right on the horizon.

However, when we get to the biblical description of this Beast and his number, we read "Let him who has understanding calculate the number of the beast, for it is the number of a man: His number *is* 666" (13:18). The author is sending a clear signal to his ancient Christian readership: Hebrew, Latin, and Greek texts all could be read via systems of *gematria*—a way of assigning numbers to letters to convert names and titles into larger numbers. For instance, if we assigned numbers to all the letters of the alphabet starting with A-1, my name (Heyes) would have a value of 62 (H-8, E-5, Y-25, E-5, S-19). The author is inviting the reader to use one of these systems to identify one man, a particular individual whose name can be calculated to match the particular number 666.

Perhaps surprisingly, given a modern insistence on looking to the future to find the events of Revelation, finding a man who'd recently lived when Revelation was written, and whose name matched the number, is quite easy. At the time of Revelation's writing, estimated to be around the end of the first century, one of the most notorious persecutors of Christians in the Roman Empire had been the late Emperor Nero. The Roman historian Tacitus noted in his *Annals*, written in the early second century, that Nero had shifted the blame for the Great Fire of Rome to Christians. Worse, his tortures of Christians included having them torn apart by dogs, nailed to crosses, and burnt alive.[18] By the time of Revelation's writing, Nero had been dead for several decades. However, a popular myth surrounding the emperor suggested he would return to life and rule again.

It's notable that when one writes "Caesar Nero" in Hebrew, NRON QSRN as it was transliterated from Greek, the numbers for these letters add up to 666 in Hebrew *gematria*. Is this correlation a fluke? Maybe. But if we decide to believe that, then we also need to explain why some manuscripts of Revelation give the number as 616 instead of 666. Because if we accept that Nero is the man in question, then we already have our answer.

The explanation is simple: If you start from Latin instead of Greek and then move the name to Hebrew letters, you will likely come up with NRO QSR without the last *n*. Since the *n* is worth 50 in Hebrew *gematria*, this results in the following calculation: 666 – 50 = 616. The chances of being able to do the same thing with another name, and coming up with the same mathematical result, isn't impossible, but it is rather slim. This fact strongly suggests that 666 is a reference to the Roman Emperor Nero, and not to some future person who has yet to be born. Ergo, at the time when the book was written, the events of Revelation had already happened.

In the introduction, I promised not to try to convince you to believe in demons if you don't, or to not believe in them if you do. The same thing holds here about the interpretation of what's meant by the Beast in Revelation. My goal here isn't to identify precisely which interpretation of these verses is "correct." Rather, it is to draw attention to the fact that Christians today and throughout history have not shared a common understanding of what these passages mean. And that lack of consensus has contributed to how Christians see the world, spiritually and politically.

Even if you're not willing to buy the notion that the events of Revelation have come and gone, you and I likely can both say definitively that many people throughout history have thought the Apocalypse was happening in their lifetime and those lifetimes are now past. Pope Innocent III, for example, thought that the end of the world would happen 666 years after the rise of Islam in 618 (1284). Spoiler: It did not. Martin Luther, for his part, made multiple predictions about the Apocalypse and its actors, and he and his collaborator in reform, the theologian Philip Melanchthon, saw the end times as rapidly approaching—likely before the year 1600 CE.

False predictions about the end times of course are not limited to medieval theologians speculating about Christ's return a thousand years after the crucifixion. The Christian historian Sulpicius Severus, in his book *Life of Saint Martin*, recounted a prophecy by the Christian bishop, monk, and Saint, Martin of Tours, who claimed that the Antichrist had already been born and was soon coming to an age when he would achieve power and bring about the end of the world. This prophecy was delivered in the fourth century, and the world is still here.

In fact, the Apocalypse has been predicted perhaps thousands of times, every time in a very authoritative manner. And still, the earth continues to spin.

Challenges of Allegory

Let's return to the notion of allegory once more, particularly the notion of how we insert elements over time that are not there originally. The prophecy of Martin of Tours, for example, claimed that the Antichrist had already been born, which he said meant that the Apocalypse was almost upon the world. In this framing of the biblical text, the Antichrist is a necessary character within the "future events" that are laid out in Revelation.

Fascinating. Given that interpretation, how many times do you think the name "Antichrist" appears in Revelation? Ten? Fifty? One hundred? Guess again.

As it turns out, there isn't one use of the word *Antichrist* in the whole book. The term only appears in the letters of John (1 John and 2 John), where it is used in both the singular *and* the plural form: antichrist and antichrists.[19] Martin of Tours (not to mention, folks like you and me) arrived at the idea of the singular Antichrist—a kind of twisted reflection of Christ who ushers in the End of Days—through hundreds of years of people allegorically reading biblical books in conjunction with one another and then imagining their connections and similarities. It is through this layered reading process that this singular Antichrist came to be associated with various characters in Revelation. While allegorical reading allows readers to derive greater meaning from a text, it should be plain by this point that it can also mislead and create a gap between a text's original meaning and the way a reader understands it.

Much like us today, and like other Christians throughout history, early Americans were quite fond of reading elements of Revelation into present-day events and people. And that brings us, at last, to the pairing of politics and spiritual battles in America, which dates back even to before our country was born. In fact, as we'll see in the next chapter, the colonists of the eighteenth century would begin America's trend of the political demonic by allegorically reading onto the French and Indian War an apocalyptic figure that was foretold by Martin Luther: the Papal Beast.

Part II

The First American Apocalypse

The Seventeenth and Eighteenth Centuries

CHAPTER THREE

The Papal Beast and the French and Indian War

BEFORE GETTING TO the idea of the Papal Beast, let's take a step back to the conditions that led to its creation. We'll start at October 31, 1517, a date that looms large in the minds of many Protestants. While in modern, Western minds, October 31 might spark thoughts of Halloween, according to popular Protestant accounts of the time, this is the day that the monk Martin Luther nailed his *Ninety-Five Theses* to the church door in Wittenberg, where he was also a professor of theology at the university. While it is likely that the story of him nailing the *Theses* to the church door is a myth, the document itself was real and contained a series of condemnations of the Church's behavior that would trigger a chain reaction that fractured the Western Christian body and would go on to start various "Wars of Religion" over the next two centuries.

Luther himself hoped that the pope would see the need to reform the Church. However, the Papacy looked none too favorably on Luther's critique of its policies. Luther was duly condemned and offered the chance to recant.

At an imperial council known as the Diet of Worms—named for the city in which it was held, in what is now modern Germany—Luther issued his famous "Here I Stand" speech that marked his refusal to be silenced or to compromise his views. After the speech, Luther was condemned by the Holy Roman Emperor, a move that placed him in considerable danger and cemented his antagonism to the Church. Eventually, this course of actions led to the Protestant Reformation and contributed to the birth of the modern world.

Protestantism and the Papal Beast

Referring to "the modern world" here might lead you to believe we're about to discuss a time period in which people felt less concern about ancient creatures like demons and the devil. But assuming that, would be a mistake. In fact, our idea of Luther as a "modern" figure is the very thing that could prevent us from recognizing how deeply he believed in the Devil, whom he also believed appeared multiple times to him.

Some of Luther's reported personal encounters with the Devil are relatively well-known to contemporary Protestant audiences. One such encounter involves Luther being accosted by Satan as he was translating the New Testament into German. Depending on which version of the story one hears, either Luther throws an inkwell at the Devil to get rid of him, or the Devil throws one at Luther when the translator refuses to cease his efforts.[1] Luther claimed that such occurrences happened to him often. In another story, the Devil throws nuts to distract Luther, and in yet another, Satan appears to him in the form of a dog.[2] *Table Talk*, a collection of Luther's purported sayings, includes a pithy claim that he supposedly made about these encounters: "I resist the Devil, and often it is with a fart that I chase him away."[3]

Such stories are humorous or lighthearted, and so risk being easily dismissed as not reflective of Luther's "true" belief. As such, they are "allowed" by a modern Protestant audience to become a part of our conscious understanding of Luther as both a source of humor and a means to blunt the sting of some of his more aggressive apocalyptic comments that we'll discuss in a moment. However, for Luther, the Devil was no joke. As the Dutch historian and theologian Heiko Oberman notes in *Luther: Man Between God and the Devil*, Luther was consumed by the notion that humankind was caught within a cosmic battle that was being fought between God and the Devil. For Luther and many later Protestant reformers, it was impossible to do away with the Devil without doing away with God.

Luther was in fact constantly concerned with the Devil in both daily life and theology, and many of Luther's contemporaries and successors were equally obsessed. Although many US citizens today may think of Roman Catholicism as being more focused on the Devil in the modern world due to films like *The Exorcist*, it was actually Protestants in this period who were most concerned with the Devil, a concern that was significantly influenced by Luther's persecution by the church institution that, in a nod to its allegiance to the pope, became known after the birth of Protestantism as the Roman Catholic Church. (Prior to that, it was simply called the Church, or the catholic, i.e., "universal," Church.)

In particular, Luther saw his former boss—the pope—as an apocalyptic figure. When Luther condemned the condemnations of his ideas by the pope in the 1521 work "Defense and Explanation of All the Articles," he wrote: "But God's friend at Rome, the pope, would like to destroy this faith. . . . God keep all Christian hearts against this Antichrist and apostle of Satan!"[4]

The rest of the Reformers followed Luther's lead in casting the pope in an apocalyptic light. For example, Luther is well-known as one of the first vernacular translators of the Bible (in this case, into German, a process that happened gradually from 1522 to 1534), a project he undertook so that those not versed in ancient languages would have access to both the Hebrew Bible and New Testament. When carving the woodcuts for images that would be included in Luther's translation of the Bible, Renaissance painter and printmaker Lucas Cranach the Elder sprinkled papal imagery across the various depictions of monstrous beasts, especially from the New Testament book of Revelation.

In his *Treatise on the Power and the Primacy of the Pope*, Luther's aforementioned partner in reform Philip Melanchthon stated that the Papacy shared characteristics the Bible ascribed to the Antichrist, writing: "Now, it is manifest that the Roman pontiffs, with their adherents, defend [and practice] godless doctrines and godless services. And the marks [all the vices] of Antichrist plainly agree with the kingdom of the Pope and his adherents."[5] In other words, according to Melanchthon, in its present configuration, the entirety of the Roman Catholic Church is the Antichrist of the Apocalypse.

This work defined the Lutheran position on the papacy prior to the Council of Trent, an ecumenical council designed to clarify Roman Catholic doctrine in the face of Protestant critiques. The position Melanchthon expressed was important enough to warrant its inclusion in the *Book of Concord* (1580), the first textual collection of the Reformation compiled by Reformation theologians to end doctrinal disputes in the wake of Luther's death in 1546. It became a doctrinal standard for the emergent Lutheran Church, one which continues to see use as a work with varying authority in Lutheran denominations today.

While the idea that the pope might be the Antichrist was not a new phenomenon,[6] by the seventeenth century, Protestants around Europe had a well-developed notion that they were locked in an apocalyptic struggle with the Roman Catholic Church. Both religious and political authors were now significantly invested in the idea that disputes between Protestants and Catholics were necessarily rumblings of this cosmic conflict.

And this obsession did not stop at the borders of Europe. When people from England made their way to the shores of America, so too did echoes of the late Martin Luther's gripes. As the conflicts of the Old World bled into the New, British Americans inherited the well-developed idea of the Papal Beast, a spiritual concept that they eagerly turned to, to explain the conflicts in which they would soon become embroiled.

Both Religion and Politics

Before we move on, a few words of warning. Although from our historical distance, it might be tempting to think that all of the settlers shared virtually identical beliefs, in fact, colonial North America contained significant religious,[7] ethnic, and racial diversity.[8] We should keep in mind that not everyone was lockstep in their beliefs about the Apocalypse.

Still, the Apocalypse made up a significant strain of belief in the New World, starting with the "planting" of the colonies in the early 1600s. The English settlers, who represented the majority population, had been invested with anti-Catholic ideas, acquired both from their Protestant history and from an idea that many shared that the Anglican Church, which had persecuted many of them, was not sufficiently reformed from Catholicism (and thus, also was "Catholic"). Think back to our introduction, and to the metaphor of money and belief. A range of colonists would have "invested" differently in beliefs about the Apocalypse that were popular at that time. Still, all would have been aware and influenced by those ideas.

For instance, this "investment" in the Apocalypse was particularly pronounced among those involved in the First Great Awakening. Lasting from the 1730s through the 1740s, the movement swept through many Protestant denominations in the colonies, emphasizing the depravity of man and the hopelessness of redemption without God's grace.[9] Introspection and a proactive attempt to grow in God's grace were the only means of escaping damnation. Increased overt religious devotion led to a split in Protestant churches—the "New

Lights" who were proponents of the stoked fires of revivalism; the "Old Lights" their more traditional opponents. Many of the New Lights, buoyed by a sense that a new wave of faith was upon them, also felt that the signs of the end of time and the millennial reign of the saints were at hand.

Second, it may be tempting to interpret the concept of the Papal Beast as *either* theological or political, religious or secular. Certainly, this trend existed in scholarly works written about colonial America for many years. However, modern historians are increasingly turning to a view of this period that recognizes that in those years, the forces of religion and politics were bound together.

Early British American writers were in fact situated within a world in which politics and religion were closely entwined. Consider the following. The French Wars of Religion and the Thirty Years' War (both European conflicts supported by Britain), the instability of the Stuart Era in Britain, and the Puritan's and Pilgrim's quest for religious freedom (denied them by the British political body) all were key factors that brought British settlers to North America, and all of these conflicts were equally influenced by religion and politics.

Thus, the Papal Beast that was born in Europe was both a political threat and a religious one. Protestants in both Europe and the colonies perceived Catholic nations as members of the body of the Papal Beast, as hooved feet ready to trample or clawed hands ready to swipe. Likewise in Protestant eyes, priests, Jesuits, and even simple lay Catholics represented political and religious threats and were considered "marked" by the Beast.

In his book of sermons based on Revelation 16, *The Pouring Out of the Seven Vials* (1645), John Cotton—one of the most prominent Puritan theologians of the Massachusetts Bay Colony—called his readers' attention to this dual religious and political threat, condemning the "grosse blasphemy" of "Popish Priests and Jesuits" and enumerating the various ways in which they should be understood as apocalyptic heralds of the End of Days.[10] At the same time, he adds a political layer, claiming that both are engaged in "conspiracie and treason against the State."[11] According to Cotton, the "Beast of Rome" is not a simple religious body, but rather the head of the "Roman Antichristian State." The pope himself is to be condemned for he "claims to himself Supreme power, not only in Ecclesiasticall causes, but Civill too."[12]

In those days in colonial North America, organizations such as the Society of Jesus, commonly known as the Jesuits, and even simple priests were seen as clandestine actors, not dissimilar from how some Americans in the modern world perceive the activities of the CIA. In 1672, the Massachusetts Colony even went so far as to write into law that "no *Jesuite* or *Spiritual* or *Ecclesiastical* person (as they are termed) Ordained by the Authority of the *Pope* or *See of Room* [The Holy See, the Papal Throne]" should be admitted to the Colony.[13] The reason for banning what appears to have been a potential religious threat? Because they were viewed a political one as well: the law cites the "secret underminings" with which it was believed such figures would politically poison the colony and turn it toward division and war.

Even words that might seem to us in the modern day to have little to do with religion were, in this period, perceived as religiously charged. The leading Protestant voices of British America often understood liberty and tyranny to be not only political ideals but religious ones as well. For example, Ruth Bloch, an emerita professor in colonial and American history at UCLA, noted that Jonathan Edwards—one of the premiere theologians of the Great Awakening, the revival that swept the colonies in the 1730s and 1740s—condemned the "Papal Antichrist for robbing the people of both their civil and ecclesiastical liberties."[14] That is, Edwards allegorically read the "Papal Antichrist" as violating both civil and religious liberty. In her book *Visionary Republic*, Bloch suggests that many colonists understood the term "liberty" to mean both religious and political liberty without the need to specify.[15]

The Apocalypse, the Papal Beast, and the French and Indian War

As the 1750s progressed, prophecy seemed to those living in North America and Europe to be close at hand. Natural phenomena have always been a subject of religious interpretation, and the middle of the eighteenth century brought a series of particularly devastating earthquakes that wracked the world, stirring the apocalyptic imagination. Of particular note to the British were a series of several earthquakes that struck the area around London in 1750. Afterward, there was an exodus from the capital caused by predictions that London proper would be destroyed by just such a quake: divine justice for a populace who, some said, had engaged in the excesses of a Sodom or Capernaum.[16]

Closer to home, for the colonists, an earthquake in 1727 and its aftershocks had similarly struck New Englanders with the fear of God. In the wake of that quake, terrified colonists had prayed, fasted, and searched for explanations of the phenomenon. James Allin, a Congregational minister preaching in Brookline, Massachusetts, described the earthquake as follows:

> THE Surprise and Terror of it were very great: some thought their Houses were all on Fire about them, and made all possible haste to escape the Burning; others who were free from this Fear, were seized with the Terrors of the Last Day, and could think of nothing but the dissolving World, the sound of the last Trumpet, and the sudden Appearance of CHRIST their Judge; others expected to die by the falling of their Houses, or that the Earth under them would open, and they should go down alive into the Pit.[17]

Allin had little comfort to offer those who'd been affected by the quake. Quite the contrary, he noted that "THE *Design* of GOD in Earthquakes is not always the same; and from hence it follows that the *Effects* of them are different; sometimes they come in *Mercy*; but for the most part in *Judgment*; sometimes they are sent to *admonish* a sinful People, and often to destroy."[18]

This disaster was still fresh in the memory of many when a second series of earthquakes rattled the colonies and made them once again fear the end. On November 18, 1755, the Cape Ann Earthquake—to date, still the largest earthquake ever to strike Massachusetts—struck an area to the northeast of Boston, causing structural damage to that city. Modern estimates place its magnitude at between 6.0 and 6.2 on the Richter scale, and it was felt from Nova Scotia to South Carolina. Outside of the colonies in the 1750s, Portugal, Peru, Morocco, and Egypt were all struck by similarly large quakes with far more tragic results: tens of thousands of deaths, as were locations in the Middle East, South America, and the Caribbean. Christians throughout North American and Europe perceived the world to be teetering on the brink of destruction brought about by divine wrath.

The same people tracking earthquakes as signs of the approaching Apocalypse were likewise carefully monitoring a different kind of fault-line: political unrest between Roman Catholic nations and Protestant ones. Tensions between France (Roman Catholic) and Great Britain (Anglican, a branch of Protestantism) rose during this time, and eventually led to the French and Indian War, a near decade-long conflict between the two colonialist powers with North America as its theater. At the heart of the conflict were the territorial claims of each nation: the extent of the thirteen colonies rested on the eastern side of the Appalachian Mountain range, while New France began to its west.

While this geographical boundary in some ways served as a convenient barrier to keep the two claimed areas apart, disputes between the two powers sprung up along their edges. The Ohio River Valley was particularly ripe for such a dispute: Nearly a thousand miles long, the Ohio River runs from western Pennsylvania down to the southern tip of what is now Illinois and flows into the Mississippi River. This waterway made transportation by watercraft of people and goods easy along the vast and sparsely populated French territory, which stretched from what is now Northeastern Canada down to Louisiana. The British Americans, however, wanted to colonize the area, and British colonial governments issued land grants to private land companies in an effort to do so.

Tensions came to a head as the French began building forts to strengthen their claim along the Valley. In 1753, a young George Washington carried a message from the governor of Virginia to the French forces: An armed conflict would ensue if the French did not cease the construction of Fort LeBoeuf and vacate portions of the Ohio River Valley. Subsequent refusal by the French to do so led to a near decade long conflict between the French, British, and their respective Native American allies (who largely sided with the French).

This is the history many of us are offered in middle and high school, but it is one that conveniently sidesteps the apocalyptic fervor with which many British Americans approached the conflict, a zeal that often found grounding in the apparent evidence of the earthquakes. In 1755, a religious pamphlet by a Presbyterian minister in Scotland titled "A Letter from the Reverend Dr. David Imrie" promised the destruction of the "Romish Antichrist." The tract, which eventually drew substantial attention in Britain and the British colonies, stated that this destruction—as well as other prophetic acts like the conversion of the Jewish people and the beginning of the millennium of the saints—was all to occur in forty years or less,[19] a date that Imrie, as a "master of ancient chronology,"[20] had supposedly divined. An American editor added to the republished letter in 1756 the detail that Imrie later noted that the earthquakes of 1750 and 51 were "*only Preludes of more Prodigious ones*" and that "the *present Commotions* between *Us* and the *French* are a *Beginning* of the *Judgments* spoke of in his printed Letter."[21]

A few years later, a published pamphlet titled *The Strange and Wonderful Predictions of Mr. Christopher Love* proposed a timeline that shortened this time frame considerably. *Predictions* was believed to be an account of visionary experiences of the future that had been, a century before, experienced by Christopher Love, a famous Presbyterian minister who was executed in 1651. Love was widely believed to have issued numerous spiritual prophecies prior to his death, and the publication of his work in the colonies in 1759 claims to be an account of these prophecies.

The prophecies would have been eerily reminiscent of what the colonists had recently been experiencing. The prophetic occurrences that Love promised included worldwide earthquakes and great wars in Germany and America. Eventually, according to Love's "original" predictions, these events would lead to a worldwide reformation and to God being "known by all" in the year 1763, a development that would be heralded by a worldwide earthquake and an end to all war.

Of course, none of these things happened by 1763, a failure that necessitated the publication of multiple further editions of the work to push back the apocalyptic timeline. After all, it wouldn't do to have the dates for the Apocalypse printed in the pamphlet already be in the past![22]

The war was depicted in apocalyptic terms not just in published works, but from the pulpit as well. In 1756, the Protestant revivalist ministers Gilbert Tennent and Jonathan Parsons both published sermons in the colonies in which they interpreted the ongoing "war and the earthquakes as signs of 'some extraordinary event' or 'some extraordinary Revolution.'"[23] That same year, Aaron Burr (Sr., not the one who killed Alexander Hamilton), preached a sermon before the Synod of New York, in which he scathingly claimed that the "Kingdom of the Beast"—that is, the Papacy—had received a great wound from the

Reformation, but that the "persecuting Power of the Beast" nevertheless would continue for some time. He anticipated that the slaying of the Witnesses, a violent and symbolic event described in Revelation 11, was still to come; this meant that further bloodshed still lay ahead before the Beast would be defeated.[24]

A year later, the Presbyterian minister and revivalist preacher Samuel Finley took only a slightly less grim "carrot and stick" approach in a sermon he delivered in Nottingham, Pennsylvania, titled "The Curse of Meroz." The sermon's title evoked the name of a city whose inhabitants, the book of Judges says, were cursed by God for refusing to come to his aid (as described in chapter 5, verse 23). The sermon's subtitle, "The Danger of Neutrality, in the Cause of God, and Our Country," clearly states its intended message: Finley promises that God will curse those who fail to take up a sword in the present war but multiply blessings upon those who would be "the Instruments of his Vengeance on spiritual *Babylon, the Mother of Harlots, and Abominations of the Earth*."[25] In other words, take up arms against the Papal Beast or be cursed by God for all time.

Rise of a New Beast

The 1750s was a booming period for apocalyptic literature. While the "Great Awakening" of the 1730s and 1740s certainly sparked the apocalyptic imagination of many colonists, historian Ruth Bloch writes that "the French and Indian War was clearly the event most responsible for the numerous millennial works published in the 1750s. It was viewed as a great turning point in world history, one that might well lead to the establishment of the latter-day kingdom on earth."[26]

This vision of a "latter-day kingdom" was, much like the apocalyptic exhortations to war offered by preachers like Finley, both politically and religiously charged. While those who dreamed of it predicted it would be a glorious end of the cessation of suffering and strife, it was also expected to be a kingdom blessed with "liberty" that had expelled "tyranny" from its boundaries. This was not just the worldly tyranny of unjust rulers but the spiritual tyranny of the Papal Beast. In this vision, the demonic and the political were so deeply entwined as to be inseparable.

Of course, the French and Indian War would prove not to be the End. As the American Presbyterian minister and evangelist Samuel

Davies, a figure in the Great Awakening, put it in his 1757 political and religious sermon titled, perhaps somewhat prophetically, given the war of independence that lay ahead, "The Crisis": "the present War is the Commencement of this grand decisive Conflict between the Lamb and the Beast, i.e. between the *Protestant* and *Popish* Powers . . . But . . . however bloody and desolating this last Conflict may be, it will bring about the most glorious and happy Revolution, that ever was in the World."[27]

Davies could not have known that the Colonies were about to become embroiled in the Revolutionary War. But that is not the only outcome that would have perhaps surprised him. Because neither could he likely have anticipated that in less than a decade, France would transform in British American eyes from opponent to partner while a new Papal Beast would rise to take their place: King George III, the ruler of the British Empire.

CHAPTER FOUR

A Revolutionary Apocalypse

IN 1763, A TRIUMPHANT Britain stood victorious over all its opponents. Not only had it come out on top in the French and Indian War, gaining all French territory east of the Mississippi River, but Britain and Prussia had also emerged the clear victor in the larger Seven Years War that had been waged across the globe by the great powers of the century, in which the French and Indian was but a skirmish. Although the soon-to-be popular phrase "the sun never sets on the British Empire" was still decades away from being coined, there was no time in which an empire had spanned more territory than the British Empire did at that moment.

The cost of staging a war on such a global scale, however, had been substantial. The historian Steven Sarson summarizes the numbers in these terms:

> The war had required 100,000 soldiers and 75,000 sailors, and had cost £83 million to prosecute (including £8 million in North America). The national debt in 1763 stood at £133 million, with land taxes at 25 per cent of income, and taxes on cider and beer that provoked riots in the West Country and London. It would cost another £250,000 annually to station 10,000 troops in North America in the first year and 7,500 troops thereafter.[1]

Given these enormous expenses, the British Empire would need to recoup its losses and fast. And the crown knew just where to do so. With a seemingly limitless font of natural resources, North America was the treasure chest of the Empire and amid sentiment from British officials that the colonists had failed to sacrifice as much as they should have for the war effort, George III decided to plunder this treasury.

Parliamentary taxes were subsequently levied, one of which was the infamous Stamp Act of 1765. This tax required that an inked stamp be placed on all legal documents, from newspapers and contracts to marriage licenses and playing cards. From the perspective of British lawmakers, the tax was a fair one: British citizens had been paying a similar tax since 1694 (a practice that continues in the United Kingdom in a more limited scope to this day). Colonists rejected this interpretation: the idea that they should be directly taxed without having governmental representation appeared absurd to them, even tyrannical.

Demons and the Stamp Act

And tyranny, as we have seen, was understood to be a mark of the Papal Beast. As soon as the Stamp Act was enacted, the colonists rejected it, and some of its most vocal critics depicted the tax as apocalyptic and demonic.

In fact, even before the Stamp Act went into effect on November 1, in August 1765, a series of violent demonstrations later known as the Stamp Act Riots occurred across the colonies, conducted by the "Sons of Liberty," colonists who organized in response to the Act. In a letter to his brother on August 15 of that year, Cyrus Baldwin describes one such riot that occurred the previous day in which an effigy of the "Stamp Master of Massachusetts Bay swung from a noose by a tree on the main street. . . . Behind him was a Boot hung up with the Devil Crawling out, with a pitchfork in his hand."[2] This "Boot" with the Devil was a reference to Britain's Bute Ministry, led by the third Earl of Bute, which had proposed the Stamp Act.

In "A View of the Year 1765," a political cartoon printed by Boston craftsman and engraver (and eventual Revolutionary War figure) Paul Revere captures this mixture of demons and tax collectors. On the right of the image, an effigy swings from a tree labeled "Liberty Tree August 14, 1765," a clear reference to the riot described by Baldwin. To its left, a menacing dragon, a common apocalyptic figure, clutches the Magna Carta—which was the first document to suggest limits to the King's power under law—possibly in an effort to tear it in two, while a personified Boston attempts to claim the document for itself. Above, two demonic figures stand in opposition to the other personifications of the colonies, one of the figures is pouring out something from a syringe or large vial, a possible reference to the "vials of wrath" that God pours out upon the earth in Revelation.

Revere was clearly captivated with such devilish depictions. In 1768, he created another image for a broadside publication that condemned members of the Massachusetts House of Representatives who'd voted to, upon demand by the British government, rescind a letter that had been written to multiple colonial assemblies by political leaders in Massachusetts who were critical of Parliament and its taxes (the Townshend Acts). The piece, entitled "A Warm Place—Hell," features the seventeen Massachusetts House members who voted against the letter being forced into a hellmouth by two demons.[3] Another image engraved by Revere—the cover of Boston printer Nathaniel Gleason's "The Massachusetts Calendar; Or an Almanack for the Year of Our Lord Christ 1774"—captures Thomas Hutchison, the loyalist Governor of Massachusetts, "at the Hour of DEATH," attended by a draconic figure upon which stands a skeleton (Death) with a spear. A demon, possibly Satan himself, stands beside Hutchison with a large tablet marked "A List of Crimes."[4]

The trend of seeing Britain's Stamp Act agents, known as the "Stampmen," and those who created them as demonic quickly spread throughout the colonies. Connecticut's Stampman, Jared Ingersoll, was referred to by a New London, Connecticut speaker as "the Beast that Lord Bute set up in this Colony to be worshipped."[5] John Adams, then a lawyer who was emerging as a critical voice speaking out against British policy in the colonies, published a series of articles in the *Boston Gazette* that depicted the "rule of kings and aristocrats as a tool of the Antichrist."[6] In Adams's eyes, the Stamp Act was not a means to generate wealth for the Empire but rather a design against the colonists meant "to strip us in a great measure of the means of knowledge, by loading the press, the colleges, and even an almanac and a newspaper, with restraints and duties; and to introduce the inequalities and dependencies of the feudal system, by taking from the poorer sort of people all their little subsistence, and conferring it on a set of stamp officers, distributors, and their deputies."[7] Years later, in his *Origin and Progress of the American Revolution: A Tory View* (1781), Peter Oliver, a Massachusetts judge and British loyalist, reflected that fear of the demonic nature of the Stampmen had so impressed itself upon the population that to some people, these enforcers had become something of colonial bogeymen!

> Thus the common People had had that Act, & all the Acts of Parliament since, dressed up by their seditious Leaders, either

> with raw Head & bloody Bones, or with Horns, Tails, & cloven Feet, which were sufficient to affright their weak Followers.[8]

In the eyes of the many colonists, the Stampmen had been thoroughly transformed into demons, ones who were hell-bent on destroying the liberties that the people enjoyed.

George III, Secret Papist

The British Empire was forced to listen. In the end, the Stamp Act led to so many protests and boycotts across the colonies that it damaged British trade, causing more financial losses than gains. From widespread boycotts of British goods to physical threats to Stampmen and their property, the financial and political unrest caused by the Act was not worth its continued existence. As a result, the British Parliament repealed it on March 18, 1766, a scant four and a half months after it went into effect.

Still, unrest continued to grow in the colonies. The Declaratory Act, which was passed at the same time as the repeal of the Stamp Act, reasserted Parliament's authority over the colonies, claiming that it had the same jurisdiction over them as it did European Britain. In other words, *we'll do what we like, and you can't stop us*. As Massachusetts politician James Otis is said to have declared in those years of unrest, "taxation without representation is tyranny" (and we know by now how the colonists viewed tyranny). Additional taxation measures were variously leveled against the colonies by the British Parliament, including the Tea Act of 1773 that famously led to the Boston Tea Party and Parliament's response: the infamous "Coercive Acts," or as they were labeled by the colonists, the "Intolerable Acts," a set of punitive laws, that followed.

That four of these five acts would be termed "intolerable" by the colonists makes sense to our historical understanding as Americans. Let's look at them one by one. The Boston Port Act closed the same port until such time as the colonists paid for the lost tea. The Massachusetts Government Act stripped the colony of its charter. By stripping the colony of its charter, the British government denied Massachusetts the right to elect its own officials and restricted town meetings, thereby bringing it directly under the control of Britain. The Quartering Act required colonists to provide housing for British troops. In the event such housing was not provided, the troops were given leave to use unoccupied buildings. The Administration of Justice Act allowed royal officials to be tried elsewhere, that is, in Britain, for crimes that had been committed in Massachusetts, if it was deemed they could not receive a fair trial there. Taken together, these laws seemed to indicate that Massachusetts was being forced to pay for the fallout of a just protest, deprived of their right to self-govern, and required to provide housing for troops that could be sent to put down future protests. And if all this wasn't bad enough, representatives of the Crown who committed crimes could slip the noose (possibly, literally) by being whisked off to England for trial.

Colonists would later lump a fifth law, the Quebec Act, in among the Intolerable Acts. Yet, although it would be grouped in separately, some colonists would at the time perceive this as the most intolerable of the five. The reason requires a bit more explanation. Quebec had been claimed by the British as part of their spoils from France in the Seven Years War. On paper, the Quebec Act extended the province of Quebec and set its boundaries as the area around the Great Lakes. The Act also changed the wording of the oath of office taken by public officials in Quebec, eliminating language that had declared Protestant supremacy to that which simply acknowledged George III as sovereign. Finally, the Act allowed the practice of Roman Catholicism in Quebec and granted the Roman Catholic church the ability to once more collect tithes from its Quebecer members. These acts allowed the British Crown to assure the loyalty of the French-Catholics inhabitants as well as to better regulate the Ohio River Valley.

Some colonists saw this political move as evidence that the Beast was once more rearing its many heads. After all, not only did the new boundaries of Quebec overlap in part with the area claimed by the Ohio Company (seemingly reversing the success of the French and Indian War), but it also allowed Catholics, marked by the Beast, to amass on the northern and western borders of the colonies, a potentially apocalyptic army waiting to descend on the heads of New England. What's more, even before this descent, the coffers of the Beast (the Papacy) would be filled with the tithes of French-Catholics living in Quebec and individuals marked by the Beast could now hold office in territories owned by the British Crown. Intolerable, indeed!

The colonists' formal response to the Intolerable Acts—a document called "Address to the People of Great Britain" (1774)—references this anxiety. The appeal was created by the newly formed First Continental Congress, a governmental body created by colonial legislatures and made up of delegates from the American colonies. They wrote to the people of Britain that Parliament had tyrannically asserted rights over the colonies "which we consider as heresies in English politics."[9] The Congress asserted that Parliament was no more able to do so than "the Pope can divest Kings of scepters which the laws of the land and the voice of the people have placed in their hands,"[10] thereby drawing a direct connection between the Beastly power of the Pope and Parliament. The Quebec Act, the colonists argued, played a part in this tyrannical plot such that Canada "swelling with Catholic emigrants from Europe" would "become formidable to us, and on occasion, be fit instruments in the hands of power, to reduce the ancient free Protestant Colonies to the same state of slavery with themselves."[11]

The "Address" goes on to menace British readers. For once the colonies are reduced to "perfect humiliation and slavery. . . . May not a Ministry with the same Armies enslave you?" The author expresses (or perhaps feigns) astonishment "that a British Parliament should ever consent to establish in that country a religion that has deluged your island in blood, and dispersed impiety, bigotry, persecution, murder and rebellion through every part of the world." Might this be evidence that the same might take place in mainland Britain itself? "In a word, take care that you do not fall into the pit that is preparing for us" the author concludes.[12]

Paul Revere, ever a man with things to say (or to visually demonstrate), also leapt into the fray surrounding the Quebec Act. In his "The Mitred Minuet" four Anglican bishops join hands in a minuet dance over a document marked "Quebec Bill." On the sides of the image, British officials Lord Bute and Lord North, prominent figures associated with the Stamp Act, are accompanied by the Devil. In this way, the engraving connects the two Acts together and lends the second an apocalyptic tone. Congregational minister Judah Champion, in a sermon given to the General Assembly of Connecticut in 1776, connected pope and king even more clearly, asking, "Is not the King of *Great-Britain*, by the Quebec Bill, set at the head of the Romish church in *Canada*?"[13]

Another Congregational minister, Daniel Barber, later recalled these apocalyptic overtones in his memoir *The History of My Own Times* (1827). The colonies, in Barber's memory, were "in danger of being brought into bondage by the uncontrolled and arbitrary power of George the Third and his armies. . . . This same George, by granting the Quebec Bill . . . had thereby become a traitor; had broke his coronation oath; [and] was secretly a Papist."[14] According to Barber, George risked putting an end to the colonies, leaving them "destroyed, soul and body, by that frightful image with seven heads and ten horns."[15] As a supposed crypto-Catholic, George was believed to have fallen in league with the Beast of the Apocalypse, and all of the colonies were perceived to be suffering for it.

George III, Beast of the Apocalypse

But the problem went beyond George's supposed secret affinity for Roman Catholicism. Barber goes on to say, "the common word then was, 'No King, no Popery.'"[16] By the start of the Revolutionary War, the two figures had become somewhat synonymous in people's minds. This meant that, in the public imagination, George III was in league with the Papal Beast.

Yet the association did not end there. As the conflict between the colonists and Britain intensified, the notion that George was not just sympathetic to the Papacy but was himself demonic began to take shape. In June 1775, *The Crisis*, a weekly publication in London that addressed the emerging conflict in the colonies, printed a letter addressed "To his Tyrannic Majesty—the Devil" and using the salutation "Most infernal Sir," before launching into the litany of crimes that George III and "your Majesty's best beloved spirits, Bute and Mansfield [another Stamp Act figure] . . . the blackest imps in all your train" had perpetrated.[17]

While the letter is most certainly evoking an image of George as the Devil satirically, this humorous approach to the topic is not echoed in other sources. For instance, the *Maryland Journal* published a story noting that a group of New York soldiers had decapitated "the IMAGE of the BEAST," meaning an effigy of George, when independence was declared in 1776.[18]

That understanding of George was not limited to the former British colonies. In 1778, the Scottish religious reformer James Purves declared in his *Observations on Prophetic Time and Similitudes*, an exploration of biblical symbolism and prophecy, that "some have thought that a combination of *Hebrew* or *Greek* letters, the corresponding of which will make 666, should shew the *Beast's* name." Though Purves agrees that it is clear that this number could point to a "*Roman* or *Latin Beast* . . ." he further says, "I shall by the same mode of explanation, show, that . . . [the letters] point out (at least) as clearly that the *Royal Supremacy* in *Great Britain*, is the *Beast* there described."[19] In other words, the two conclusions—a Papal Beast or George as the Beast—carry equal weight based on numerology.

In fact, the idea that all British were demonic quickly spread as the Revolutionary War began. The idea that the British were ubiquitously demonic removed the need for the Papal Beast as an intermediary for their wickedness. As Ruth Bloch notes:

> Once the bloodshed began, the influence of Rome no longer remained crucial to this symbolic connection: The British alone became the target of extreme vilification as the agents of the Antichrist. The patriot clergy and laity of varying degrees of religious orthodoxy repeatedly described the American patriot forces as the soldiers of Christ doing heroic battle against "all the powers of Hell," "the prince of darkness," "the serpent," "the dragon," "the antichristian beast" of biblical prophecy.[20]

That is to say, Britain was overrun with demons, and they were coming to America.

This image of Americans fighting against the forces of the Devil and the Apocalypse increasingly cast the United States (at least to itself) in a utopian light, and its people as God's chosen people. To these Americans, the millennial reign of the saints had begun, and the descent of the New Jerusalem would not be long.

American Apocalypse

The Papal Beast. The French and Indian War. The Revolution. All of these events were perceived by British colonists as being interrelated, and this interpretation built toward one inescapable conclusion for early Americans: The Apocalypse would be an American phenomenon.

Though, it was not precisely clear how this would occur. That might mean that the events of Revelation would happen upon American soil and ripple outward, that the demonic figures in that book would directly impact American politics, or that the final battle depicted in it would be one that was predominately fought by God-fearing Americans. All of these possibilities were entertained.

For instance, Samuel Sherwood, a US congressional representative from New York, speculated about the Continental Congress's role in the Apocalypse in his book *The Church's Flight into the Wilderness: An Address on the Times* (1776). Interpreting the portions of Revelation focused on the Beast from the Sea, Sherwood suggested that:

> Should our honourable Continental Congress, see fit, in their great wisdom, at this difficult juncture, to open a free trade, and correspond with that nation, in a way in which our threatened rights and liberties might have such security and indemnification, as to be in no hazard or danger of any future encroachment on them, the spirit of liberty might spread and circulate with commerce; and from small sparks, kindle up into a bright and inextinguishable flame, in that, and in other kingdoms of the earth; and so hasten the fulfilment of this prophecy, in the entire destruction of the beast, or man of sin, and in the complete and glorious salvation of God's afflicted church.[21]

In other words, according to Sherwood, the Congress should put aside its differences with France to fight the new emissary of the Papal Beast, England. Doing so, he believed, would result in the destruction of the Beast and the salvation of American Protestants. Then, through politics and trade, the sparks of reformation would engulf the world. Though Sherwood does not specify a desired end result, it is likely that he was imagining the idea of the New Jerusalem that descends to earth in Revelation 21.

The Congregational minister Samuel West echoed this sentiment a year later in a sermon delivered at Plymouth, Massachusetts. He began with an exposition on Isaiah—another text that is often allegorically combined with Revelation to create further apocalyptic details, exhorting his listeners with these words from Isaiah 66:5–9:

> Hear the word of the LORD, ye that tremble at his word: your brethren that hated you, that cast you out for my names sake, said, Let the Lord be glorified; but he shall appear to your joy, and they shall be ashamed. A voice of noise from the city, a voice from the temple, a voice of the LORD that rendereth recompense to his enemies. Before she travailed she brought forth; before her pain came, she was delivered of a man child. Who hath heard such a thing? Who hath seen such things? Shall the earth be made to bring forth in one day, or shall a nation be born at once? For as soon as Zion travailed she brought forth her children. Shall I bring to the birth, and not cause to bring forth? Saith the LORD; shall I cause to bring forth, and shut the womb? Saith thy God.[22]

West goes on to claim that "I have been fully persuaded in my own mind for several years, that this text does contain in it, a prophecy of the dispensations of divine providence toward his church and people in New-England"[23] and that much of these words had already been fulfilled.

How those hearing this must have felt! A hundred and fifty years before, those who had been "cast out" by the "brethren that hated" them in England had landed on those very shores. And despite all of the "travail" that the colonists and their descendants had born, Scripture promised that the earth would bring forth Zion, the heavenly city, if they could just hang on a little while longer. After all, according to these verses, a nation was "being born" from the conflict. The remainder of West's sermon was devoted to proving "that a great part of this text has already been remarkably fulfilled in our Land."[24]

And there it was: West's proclamation, which was becoming a dominant way of thinking in the newly born United States of America. In the eyes of those living in the brand-new nation, New England—and eventually, the newly established, United States of America—had proved itself to be the land of prophecy. And its people, the chosen of God.

The Modern Takeaway

American Apocalypse

THIS IDEA OF an American Apocalypse has had two significant effects upon the United States that continue to this day. The first effect is easy to see: Perhaps more than any other group in history, Americans have been, and continue to be, obsessed with the immediacy of a coming Apocalypse. We saw this in the historical events that led up to the Revolution, but the dynamic didn't end there. After the Revolution, pronouncements by Americans regarding the Apocalypse kept on coming; many were small-scale claims, but others grew into sweeping movements.

William Miller, an American farmer and Baptist preacher who became a key figure in a religious movement known as Millerism, predicted that Christ would return before 1843. What started off as a private disclosure among close confidants soon swelled to a larger audience, drawing in more and more people until belief in this prophecy had swept the nation. The subsequent "Great Disappointment"—Christ's failure to return as expected—affected tens of thousands of Americans who identified as "Millerites." While the vast majority of Miller's followers abandoned his ideas, others reinterpreted his views and went on to become the Seventh-day Adventist Church.

Another group, the Jehovah's Witnesses—a now-multinational but originally an American Christian denomination—predicted numerous apocalyptic dates ranging from 1799 to 1925. In 1920, this final date was heralded as "the resurrection of the faithful worthies of old"[1] in a pamphlet authored by Joseph Franklin Rutherford of the Watch Tower Bible and Tract Society, who was so sure of his proclamation that "millions now living will never die!" that those words became the title of the publication.

The early American Christian radio broadcaster and evangelist Harold Camping, one of the founders of "Family Radio," a Christian broadcasting network founded in the 1950s, made several predictions about the timing and details of the Apocalypse as well, claims that netted him first national, then international fame (not to mention millions in listener donations). Billboards and airwaves loudly proclaimed his changing predictions about the coming Apocalypse, ending in a final date in 2011, after which Camping ceased making predictions.

As part of its unique obsession, our nation has adopted or produced interpretations of the Apocalypse that originated in the past two centuries. Often, we don't realize that these are much more modern than they at first appear. For example, I have been asked several times by students in my medieval studies courses what medieval people thought about "the Rapture." My response is simple: "Nothing, the Rapture is an invention of the modern world."

John Nelson Darby (1800–1882)—an English reverend who founded the Exclusive Bretheren, an evangelical group founded in London—is generally credited as the founder of Rapture theology, but it wasn't until the Scofield Study Bible of 1908 that the idea was popularized and found a wide audience, an American audience. Yet, the Rapture is firmly ingrained in the contemporary American mind as an idea that has been believed in and accepted since biblical times. This is likely due in part to the astounding success and influence of the *Left Behind* series of novels written by authors Tim LaHaye and Jerry B. Jenkins, which depict fictional accounts of the end times and whose volumes have sold upwards of eighty million copies.

Popular media further plays into this perception of an American Apocalypse by frequently making the claim that the Apocalypse will occur on American soil. The television show *Supernatural*, which ran for *15 seasons* (2005–2020) and resulted in several spinoffs, told the story of Dean and Sam Winchester, two simple Midwestern boys who faced apocalyptic threats while driving around in a beat-up Chevy Impala. The rather quirky *Sleepy Hollow* series (2013–2017), which blended events from Washington Irving's tale with Revelation, netted 10.1 million viewers on the night of its debut. Hollywood has seemingly been more hesitant to portray apocalyptic allegories, but it has still dipped its toe in the water with films such as *Knowing* (2009) and *Left Behind* (2014), both starring Nicolas Cage. Capitalizing on Hollywood's tentativeness, smaller, "faith-based" companies such as Affirm Films and Cloud Ten Pictures have offered more explicitly biblically focused films like *Left Behind: The Movie* (2000) and *The Remaining* (2014), catering to America's desire to see itself in the end. The Apocalypse, it appears, is big business.

The second effect of an American Apocalypse on the United States is harder to see. While the belief I'm referring to is complex, the main idea can be summed up as the concept that America is a special place inhabited by a special people. We often refer to this idea in scholarship as "American Exceptionalism," but we often forget that this has an apocalyptic context.

Consider the following biblical passages. Revelation 21 depicts a holy city, the New Jerusalem, which descends from Heaven. The idea of a holy city can likewise be found in Jesus's exhortation in Matthew 5:14: "You are the light of the world. A city that is set on a hill cannot be hidden." Likewise, the idea of "Zion," often synonymous with Jerusalem but also allegorically as the land of Israel, from biblical verses such as Revelation 14:1, Hebrews 12:22, and Isaiah 33:14. All of these conceptual frameworks carry an apocalyptic connotation: a land or people that stand in a future state of perfection.

Taken together, these verses paint an image of holiness and a virtuous exemplar, the New Jerusalem, the holy city of Zion, is a divine ideal. This is the future of America that has existed in the minds of many Americans throughout our nation's history. For instance, John Winthrop, the first governor of the Massachusetts Bay Colony, described the New World of the colonies as a "citty upon a hill,"[2] quoting Matthew 5:14 and invoking ideas of the city at the End of Time. Three hundred and thirty years later, in 1961, John F. Kennedy invoked Winthrop's idea and, building upon it, argued that America must serve as a moral example to the world, claiming that the "eyes of all people are truly upon" the "city upon a hill."[3] In his farewell address at the end of his second term as president, Ronald Reagan too referenced the "shining city upon a hill," describing the United States as "still a beacon, still a magnet for all who must have freedom, for all the pilgrims from all the lost places who are hurtling through the darkness, toward home."[4]

Inspiring words, but words that come at a cost: because if America is a light to the world, then the implicit expectation is that it needs to act as such. This idea has led to two problematic myths in American politics: the myth of American Exceptionalism and the myth of American Exemplar. The first myth tells us that as the chosen of God, the city on the hill that is the light of the world, America is an exceptional place, a divinely significant land with divinely significant people. The second insists that as such, it must stand as an exemplar, the best model, of how countries ought to be.

On the surface, both sentiments may sound inspirational. However, both are also open to interpretation, and it is here that we as a nation have repeatedly gotten ourselves into trouble and caused great harm. That is because these ideas have led to a slew of disastrous political consequences, both within the United States and without. Consider, for instance, the idea of "manifest destiny," the notion that the United States was divinely ordained to extend across North America for the purpose of spreading Christianity and democracy. In 1847, the Unitarian minister Rev. Henry Whitney Bellows wrote of manifest destiny in the *American Whig Review* and what the ideology had in store when he claimed in "The Destiny of the Country" that, "It becomes a simple calculation, how soon, at this rate, we shall reach the Pacific ocean."[5] More disturbingly, he promised joyfully

> . . . the final extinction of the Indian races, to which the mass of the Mexican population seem very little superior; and we have no reason to doubt that this country will not have doubled its three centuries of existence, before South America will speak the English tongue and submit to the civilization, laws and religion of the Anglo-Saxon race. [6]

The idea of manifest destiny would result in the "Trail of Tears," a government-forced relocation of thousands of Native Americans in the southeastern United States to so-called Indian Territory west of the Mississippi River, which saw the death and displacement of over sixty thousand Indigenous Americans.

When it comes to actions taken by our country outside our own borders, the notion of the United States as an exemplar of divinely ordained order has turned us into an empire in everything but name. In 1783, Ezra Stiles, then-president of Yale, delivered a sermon entitled "The United States Elevated to Glory and Honor" in Hartford, Connecticut at the annual election in which he extolled the virtues of "God's American Israel" and argued that it had been destined by God "to prosper and flourish into a great American Republic; and ascend into high and distinguished honor among the nations of the earth."[7] This development, Stiles claimed, would eventually lead to the flowering of the United States, "under a truly patriotic, upright, and firm administration, the beautiful superstructure of a well governed and prosperous empire."[8] After George Washington gave his first inaugural address in 1789 in New York City, David Humphreys, a former Continental Army colonel who'd been Washington's *aide-de-camp* during the War, wrote in his poem titled "A Poem on the Happiness of America": "Our constitutions form'd on freedom's base, / Which all the blessings of all lands embrace; / Embrace humanity's extended cause, / A world of our empire, for a world of our laws."[9]

The sentiment here was that the newly formed United States would transform the world around it, making the unclean, clean; the unholy, sacred. This idea of identity became what the early twentieth-century American scholar and author Ernest Lee Tuveson would later refer to as a "Redeemer Nation" in his book of the same name. According to Tuveson, the United States, marked by the belief that "Providence, or history, has put a special responsibility on the American people to spread the blessings of liberty, democracy, and equality to others throughout the earth, and to defeat, if necessary by force, the sinister powers of darkness,"[10] would transform the world by offering it redemption from tyranny, despotism, and inequality.

These ideas of America as a divinely anointed nation have not just affected the way we've turned our influence outward. The idea of the United States being a New Jerusalem also impacts whom we accept into the holy "city." In Revelation 21, the New Jerusalem is described as a beautiful location that shines with the glory of God, but it is also one that has "a great high wall with twelve gates" (Revelation 21:12). These gates admit people into the heavenly city who are meant to be there—the best and brightest, those who are the "glory and honor of the nations" (Revelation 21:26). Yet, they also are there to keep undesirable populations out such as "those who refuse to believe, who do evil things, who kill, [and] who sin sexually" (Revelation 21:8). Whether or not President Donald Trump and his advisors consciously had this verse in mind when speaking about "migrant criminals" who are "killers" and "rapists" who wanted to cross the border into the United States, the only policy solution for which was to "build a wall," the alignment between his language and these verses, with America in the position of the heavenly city, are hard to miss.

As Yii-Jan Lin, a New Testament professor at Yale Divinity School, brilliantly argues in her work *Immigration and Apocalypse: How the Book of Revelation Shaped American Immigration* (2024), Revelation serves as an invisible guide to immigration policies in the United States. "Revelation remains a text uniquely important to the American origin myth and to arguments against the inclusion of certain immigrant groups,"[11] she writes. And the interpretation of this text as a document to lead immigration has "been used to incite hate and fear against any number of unwanted peoples, whether the Antichrist-serving Irish, the locust horde of Chinese, the criminal Mexican or the infidel Muslim."[12]

The Papal Beast still rears its ugly heads in contemporary America. Not just in claims that are still made (surprisingly frequently!) that the Vatican is an apocalyptic actor, but also in the history of our interpretation, a history that continues to impact us in the present. This history tells us, both consciously and unconsciously, that the United States is a special actor on the world stage, a providential nation that heralds the "end of history." It is a force that turns every war into a crusade, and immigrants into demonic presences that must be excluded from the City of God.

Part III

Spiritualism to the Civil War

The Nineteenth Century

CHAPTER FIVE

Speaking with the Dead

In New York State, there is a quaint, little town that sits on the edge of a picturesque lake. Rows and rows of Victorian houses with neatly manicured lawns and gardens give the impression that one has stepped back in time. If you arrive in the dead of winter, the lake is frozen over, and the town harbors a population of no more than three hundred living souls. Yet, every summer, the population swells as tens of thousands of visitors stream through the entrance gate to the town in the hopes of speaking with the souls of those who are no longer living through the individuals that occupy the town. This is Lily Dale, New York: one of the last bastions of Spiritualist belief and practice in the United States.

At present, there are about a quarter of a million people in the United States who subscribe to Spiritualist beliefs, a fraction of a fraction of the total population. Yet, once upon a time there were millions of ardent Spiritualists, and many times more individuals than that who attended séances and other performances by mediums (individuals who claimed to speak with the dead) out of curiosity or for fun. Cathy Gutierrez, a noted expert on Spiritualism, writes that "scholars have estimated that half of Americans experienced Spiritualism in some manner" in the mid-nineteenth to early twentieth centuries.[1] Its popularity in that era is difficult to overstate.

Though Spiritualism is considered a distinct religious movement in itself, its core doctrines may be described as a potpourri of different ideas about the world drawn from a variety of influences from the eighteenth and nineteenth centuries: from the theology of the Swedish scientist and philosopher Emmanuel Swedenborg to the magnetic practices of the Austrian physician Anton Mesmer and his follower, the French aristocrat and hypnotist Marquis de Puységur, to the experiences of the nineteenth century American clairvoyant Andrew Jackson Davis. It is a complex system of belief that has been addressed in the work of numerous scholars. Literally thousands upon thousands of pages have been written on the subject.

Luckily, its core premise is easy to summarize: Spiritualists believed (and continue to believe) that they could contact the dead. And conservative Christian circles of the nineteenth and twentieth centuries condemned them for it (and also continue to do so). In this chapter, I'll offer you a brief overview of the movement as a whole—fascinating in its own right—as well as lay the foundation for why Spiritualist practices are still so reviled by conservative Christians today.

Clever as a Fox Sister

It was demonstrations by the Fox sisters in the mid-1800s that galvanized Spiritualism, a loose set of beliefs and practices, into a movement. In 1848, Margaretta (called Maggie) and Catherine (called Kate) Fox had just moved with their family into a new home in Hydesville, New York. According to the testimony of Margaret Fox, the girls' mother, she and her daughters heard a mysterious noise at night that "sounded like some one knocking in the east bed-room . . . The whole family slept in that room together, and all heard the noise."[2]

The Foxes reported that the family eagerly sought out the noise by candlelight. But no matter where they searched, they came up empty handed, and the noise persisted.

Weeks passed and the knocking did not let up. By the following March, the youngest girl, Kate, had figured out that the noises appeared to be responsive: When she snapped her fingers, the noises would seemingly respond by imitating the sounds of her snapping. Maggie then began to talk to the noises, encouraging them to mimic her patterns, which they did. At this point, the mother took over, asking the noises to respond to questions through sequences of knocks. Through this method, she determined that the knocking was caused by the disembodied spirit of a thirty-one-year-old man who had died in the house.

The Foxes invited their neighbors over to witness the phenomenon, which repeated. Word of the "mysterious rappings" soon spread to inhabitants of the surrounding towns and villages, and gradually a phenomenon was born. Two of these early adopters were Amy and Isaac Post, Quakers who were close with the Fox family.[3] Given the alignment of Quakers with a number of liberal political causes (such as abolition), this may be where Spiritualism begins to acquire its progressive bent.

In 1849, the Fox sisters held a public demonstration of their ability to communicate with the dead. The Corinthian Hall in Rochester was packed with New Yorkers interested in watching the sisters perform their unearthly communion. Hundreds in attendance heard the infamous rapping sounds, and many left with the firm conviction that the Fox sisters had heralded a new age, a time when the living and the dead would hold community with one another. By the end of the 1850s, terms like "Spiritualism" and "Spiritualists" were commonly used to denote the movement and its participants.

As the years wore on, the Fox sisters became household names. The younger sisters had careers as spirit mediums and were managed by their eldest sister, Leah, as well as the founder of the *New-York Tribune*, Horace Greeley. The former was responsible for their day-to-day care while the latter used his influence to help them move in circles of wealth and influence far outside what they would otherwise be capable of. High status marriages, transatlantic tours, and frequent press coverage emerged from these liaisons.

As so often happens when fame and fortune coalesce, however, conflict arose. Behind the scenes, the younger sisters were not faring well. According to Arthur Conan Doyle, the creator of Sherlock Holmes and an avid Spiritualist, "when the girls were all the rage among those who had no conception of the religious significance of this new revelation, and who concerned themselves with it purely in the hope of worldly advantage, the sisters exposed themselves to the enervating influences of promiscuous séances in a way which no earnest Spiritualist could justify."[4]

It's not entirely clear what all Doyle was referring to in voicing this concern. Arguably, many potential activities could fall under the rubric of a "promiscuous séance." However, it's likely his critique includes at least one clear influence whose effects they would feel later in their career: Despite not being of age, they were allowed to drink alcohol. This practice, possibly compounded by a familial predisposition to addictive behavior, eventually resulted in the younger women becoming alcoholics. This and other occurrences appear to have created rifts between the three sisters, eventually resulting in estrangement between Leah and the younger two.

This was not the only trouble that arose. In 1888, Maggie published a retraction of her claims to mediumship in *New York World*. In the confession, she claimed that the rappings purportedly produced by the spirits had been, in fact, produced by her body. She explained, "With control of the muscles of the foot, the toes may be brought down to the floor without any movement that is perceptible to the eye. The whole foot, in fact, can be made to give rappings by the use only of the muscles below the knee. This, then, is the simple explanation of the whole method of the knocks and raps."[5] Shortly thereafter on the stage of the New York Academy of Music, Maggie demonstrated her ability to create these rapping sounds for the public.

People's response to the confession and demonstration was mixed. Some saw the two as evidence of the fall of Spiritualism, a reveal of a long-awaited truth that the skeptics had always known. Critics of the movement sounded out "Told you so!" about the mediums in books, pamphlets, and newspapers. Ardent Spiritualists on the other hand saw this shocking development as nothing more than signs of Maggie being led astray by promises of money for her false claims or influenced by the pernicious actions of the Roman Catholic Church, to which she belonged. In their minds, a single confession did not prove that the revelations of the movement as a whole were false. And in fact, a year later, she would go on to retract her retraction, muddying the waters even further.

No clear verdict was reached. And regardless of what was true, Maggie's recanting was not the death knell of Spiritualism. The movement did gradually lose influence and members over the course of the twentieth century. Spiritualism, however, is still very much alive, if not particularly well, in the United States.

No Hell Below Us

The Fox sisters' story and demonstrations were dramatic and attention-grabbing, but what were the tenets of the movement they inspired? What, exactly, did Spiritualists think was going on to cause the knocking? What did the movement's followers believe? And why did they, as we shall see come to pass, draw such fire from conservative Christian circles for their practices?

Part and parcel to these questions was the political orientation of Spiritualists. While Spiritualists claimed to speak for the spirits, it was hard to miss the fact that many of the dead maintained politically liberal views. The vast majority of Spiritualists were abolitionists, in favor of marriage reform and women's rights, all of which appeared to be supported by the doctrines given to them by the spirits (something we will talk about more in chapter 8).

As previously noted, Spiritualism as a belief system drew from a wide range of cultural, scientific, social, and religious ideas. But while most Spiritualists were generally too individualistic to embrace things like faith statements or "denominational" approaches, there are some mainstays of the movement that consistently emerged both in terms of philosophy and practice.

First and possibly most importantly, Spiritualists rejected the idea of Hell as a place of permanent suffering. Instead, their teachings frequently depicted the afterlife as a tiered system, in which the dead were capable of climbing, with progressive effort, from the bottom to the top. That is, when a person died, they were assigned to one of a number of spheres of Heaven. From there, they would learn and improve their souls, slowly but surely moving from one heaven to the next until they reached the top.

This belief had two major ramifications to the Christian doctrine upon which Spiritualism was loosely based. First, in what we might consider the "typical" or "popular contemporary" narrative of Hell, people are consigned to the Pit upon death due to their performance of sin while they were alive. In this understanding of Hell, God has proclaimed right and wrong courses of action, the latter of which, if left unabsolved, will lead to a soul's permanent descent upon death.

Spiritualists, however, did away with sin. In their minds, it was ignorance to cosmic truth, not sin, that was humanity's primary fault. They believed that those who were most ignorant would be sent to the lowest sphere of the heavens. Truth be told, this lowest level might seem indistinguishable from a typical Christian Hell to the untrained eye: It was filled with all the usual culprits, from the sexually immoral to the intemperate to murderers. Yet, there was one key difference: All the inhabitants of this sphere inflicted tortures upon each other and themselves.

Not a Devil or a demon in sight.

Heaven for All

Perhaps an even more striking difference between Christian doctrine and Spiritualist philosophy is that in Spiritualist thinking, since the only destination available was Heaven, all human souls were bound for it. In theory, this allowed for all people, regardless of ethnicity, culture, skin tone, creed, or sex to enjoy the possibility of merging with the Godhead at the end of their spiritual journey. It also served as a jumping off point from which one could radically question the treatment of slaves, indigenous peoples, and women.

In this model, instead of existing as places of celestial enjoyment, the spheres of Heaven served as places of learning. If the dead were to advance, they must be in a constant state of improvement, neither perfected at the moment of death nor condemned to remain in place for eternity. This learning was not limited only to the heavenly spheres: When called to a séance, the dead might impart the fruit of their improved state to the séance's participants, commonly called sitters, through advice or knowledge, and they also might benefit from the advice or guidance of the sitters.

The dead also held community with one another in heaven, continuing forward with those practices and relationships that they held in life. For example, one particular spirit, Nannie, related to a medium in 1899 that in the spirit world where she resided, a temple was to be erected. "The purpose of this edifice was to 'Mother' little children who had been waifs and castaways on earth, and who would be taken to the immortal world by tender caretakers and teachers, and gently cared for and taught. The Temple in Spirit-life would be known as the 'Great Mother,' whose sheltering arms would shield and protect the little ones, but to us and others it should be called 'The Temple of Vesta.'"[6] Thus, the spirit world not only continued the practice of the living to coexist in community, but it also similarly allowed for provision for unfortunates and used titles and names (e.g., "Great Mother;" "Vesta") which the spirits remembered from their lives on earth.

Spiritualists believed that all spirits who wished to progress through the spirit world must come to terms with their memories and begin a spiritual life anew. For instance, one medium spoke to a "Scrooge"-type character who had exploited his poor tenants. As a result, he said, he had to experience their poverty—the poverty he was partly responsible for—in the afterlife because it was "good for him to wear threadbare clothing for a while, and to learn what poor mortals suffered through his greed and selfishness."[7] Likewise, one vain woman was reduced to wearing unattractive clothing and given "unpleasing marks of countenance" with the goal that she unlearn her attachment to physical beauty and instead cultivate a "desire for more enduring and spiritual conditions."[8] As Gutierrez puts it in her book *Plato's Ghost: Spiritualism in the American Renaissance*, the dead are forced to "unpick" their lives and do them over, just as a poor seamstress is forced to "unpick" their work and begin again.[9] Rather than bound for eternal flames, the dead were bound for rehabilitation and betterment.

Voice for the Voiceless

Due in part to this heavenly equity, the Spiritualist movement also empowered some women in ways not often seen in the nineteenth century. As a general rule, in US society women were seen as men's intellectual inferiors. Men generally enjoyed dominance in commerce, politics, education, and a host of other empowering activities.

However, when a female medium spoke for the spirits, she did not speak as a human woman; she spoke as a representative of the spirit world. In this way, she was free to offer advice, to speak on a variety of topics with authority, and even to admonish her male listeners for their ignorance. And they would listen, because "she" was speaking as a more enlightened spiritual being at that moment. Certainly, the scope of the empowerment made possible under these conditions was limited. Women were only allowed to speak *for* the spirits rather than for themselves. Still, this role offered some women a degree of power and agency that had not heretofore been afforded them.

Another benefit for female mediums is that they were allowed to act in an "unfeminine fashion" when certain spirits descended. For instance, if a spirit predisposed toward violence or insanity were to act through a medium, then the medium herself was partially or totally absolved from the violence or odd behaviors that the spirit might perform. Likewise, if the spirit of a sailor were to enter the circle, it was perfectly natural that a medium would then be prone toward swearing and drinking.

Séances that were held within the home often had a sexual aspect to them as well. Spirits acting through a medium might kiss or fondle those in attendance or ask for the same to be done to them. Modern day scholar of Spiritualism Marlene Tromp writes of one such encounter in which T. P. Barkas, a nineteenth century British writer and investigator of Spiritualist encounters, meets a spirit, "Pocka." Pocka began to touch Barkas's knee, but Barkas "in hopes of producing greater intimacy" did not acknowledge the touch. When Pocka, perhaps, somewhat poutily, asked Barkas why he failed to acknowledge her, Barkas "said, in an almost inaudible whisper, 'Will you kiss me, 'Pocka,'?' Remarkably, Barkas described how, in this darkened Victorian drawing room, 'hands took hold of the front collar of my coat, one on each side, and I was drawn forward, and gently and softly [kissed].'"[10] Sexual acts like these, even in a private space such as this one, initiated on the part of women in the nineteenth century United States would have been profoundly scandalous. But for the spirits, such behavior was expected and even encouraged.

The Anatomy of a Séance

This encounter raises the questions as to what someone might expect when attending a séance or other event intended to provide evidence of communication between the living and the dead. Let's start with the question: What exactly did nineteenth century Spiritualist demonstrations look like?

Generally speaking, performances would vary significantly from medium to medium. Location also played a role, with some demonstrations taking place in large lecture halls. The most common form of demonstration, however, was a private sitting, which would take place in a private home and generally be attended by friends and families of those who had contracted the medium's services. They might gather in a parlor, around a large table, or another large space that could accommodate a number of people.

From here, the "action" would largely depend upon the audience. Some sitters would ask spirit mediums to contact specific spirits, those of deceased loved ones, for instance. Other sitters might seek out a discourse on philosophy or another subject from spirits. The forms of communication the mediums used included everything from rappings similar to those produced by the Fox sisters; to automatic writing, the practice of allowing spirits to write "through" the medium's hand; to speaking on behalf of the spirits, sometimes with changes in pitch, vocal quality, and even language.

At other times, sitters attended hoping to see more visceral phenomena, proof of the continued existence of the spirits and their capabilities. They might want to see tables tip of their own accord, to watch ghostly lights—cold to the touch—float around the room, or to gape in awe at ectoplasm streaming from the orifices of the medium. Alternatively, ghostly instruments might produce music, spiritual hands might be seen manipulating objects, or the objects themselves—or even the medium—might levitate or fly through the room. Arguably, one of the most sought-after forms of spiritual contact in these séances was a manifestation in which the spirit conjured would produce an ectoplasmic body to interact with the sitters, appearing in the air or even touching them.

The abilities of the spirits seemed almost too spectacular to be true!

Exchanging Demons for Ghosts

Certainly, there were some who thought they *were* too good to be true. Almost immediately after the legend of the Fox sisters began to grow, theologically conservative Christian groups began to push back. Where Spiritualists saw the work of the revered dead, these Christians saw the work of the Devil. The messages that Spiritualists received were real enough, these Christians reasoned, but they were neither true nor offering redemption. The intention of the message was, instead, these Christians believed, to damn those hearing them. When ghosts manifested in the parlors of nineteenth century Americans, these Christians understood that it was because the séance had opened a gate to Hell that invited demons to play.

For them, Spiritualism was not a new mode of thought or a new practice. Instead, it was a variation on a very old method of demonic manipulation, one which had been attested to in the Hebrew Bible in 1 Samuel 28.

This was the work of the "Witch of Endor."

CHAPTER SIX

The New Witches of Endor

THE SO-CALLED WITCH of Endor is a figure who appears very briefly in the Bible in 1 Samuel. Samuel is the prophet whom God has chosen to be leader of his people. At this time, the Israelites are being oppressed by the Philistines while they live in the land of Canaan (an area that occupies portions of modern-day Israel, Palestine, Jordan, Lebanon and Syria), and Samuel leads the Israelites to victory against them. In his old age, Samuel installs his sons, Joel and Abijah, as the new judges to lead Israel. However, the two men prove to be less than ideal rulers, prompting the Israelites to demand that a king, instead of a judge, be appointed to lead them.

After much hemming and hawing, Samuel appoints Saul. But Saul turns out to be less than ideal as well, with a reign that's marked by his disobedience to God. Eventually, the Philistines return, and Saul is terrified. Unfortunately, by then Samuel is dead and buried, and God refuses to speak with Saul.

In desperate straits, Saul commands his men to find a *ba'ălat-'ôb*, literally, a "mistress of the/an 'ôb" (1 Samuel 28:7). I use the precise term from the original text here, because it presents significant difficulty to both historical and modern-day translators of the Bible. Although it is often translated as "familiar spirit," we're just not really sure precisely what an "ôb" is. Whatever it happens to be, however, the effect of the woman's mastery is clear: She can speak with the dead.

Saul has, ironically, banned all spiritual mediums from Israel (1 Samuel 28:3). However, his men find such a woman in the village of Endor, and Saul quickly goes to her in disguise to get the answers he needs. During his meeting with her, she conjures the spirit of Samuel, she recognizes Saul for who he is (a proof of her otherworldly powers), and Samuel proclaims Saul's doom through the woman. Shortly thereafter, this prophecy proves genuine: Saul falls on his sword (literally) after the Israelites are routed by the Philistines.

The "ôb"—whatever it is—seems to tell the truth.

From Mistress of the "ôb" to Necromancy

For our purposes, it doesn't really matter what an "ôb" is. Instead, the important element is the history of where that term leads us. That is, how do we go from that weird Hebrew term to the "Witch of Endor" or the "Medium of Endor?"

In the perspective of ancient Israelites, speaking with the dead was very possible but forbidden. In their worldview, the dead were basically just slumbering in the earth or consigned to an underworld-type realm, so speaking with them was simply a matter of "dialing" the right number. The authors of the book of Samuel, then, would not have raised any eyebrows when they wrote down this account centuries before the birth of Christ.

When early Christians got ahold of this passage (1 Samuel 28:7–25) and began to interpret it, however, a disconnect emerged. As Christian theology developed over the first few centuries of the Christian era, Heaven and Hell generally came to be perceived as closed systems, with the dead locked away from the world in a way that differed from earlier Greek and Israelite religious thought.

Due to this shift, early Christian theologians generally had the option of choosing from three possible interpretations of this passage. The first accepted at face value the traditional reading of the text and ignored the developing cosmological issues, that is, issues related to the way a religious system makes sense of the universe and the way its different parts relate to one another. This type of reading says that the woman could and did conjure Samuel successfully and that in that story, Saul really did speak with Samuel. However, as mentioned, it was difficult for many early Christians to imagine a mere human conjuring the dead from behind doors that God had locked.

This problem led to a second interpretation. This theological camp argued that *ordinarily* human beings are not able to conjure the dead out of Heaven or Hell, but that God allowed this specific instance to occur. Thus, the woman could not have conjured Samuel herself, but through God's aid, she was able to connect with the spirit of Samuel in order to pronounce doom on Israel's errant king.

Still other theologians ventured a third option: The woman had not conjured Samuel at all; rather, she had summoned a demon who'd disguised itself to look like Samuel. In this understanding of God and the universe, every time someone spoke with the dead, they were actually speaking with deceptive demons who only *pretended* to be the dead.

This interpretation provided a useful explanation for how a person could look like they were communicating with the supposedly closed system of the dead. But it proved to be somewhat useful in other ways as well. For centuries, non-Christian Greeks had been practicing "necromancy"—the art of predicting the future through discussions with the dead—as well as many other forms of divination. By reimagining all of these practices for predicting the future as communion with demons, Christians acquired a powerful means by which to curb acts that they saw as distinctly non-Christian: *You think you have power in the world, but this is really just demons trying to lead you astray. Reject the demons and believe in God!*

The problem was, many times, these prophecies could seem incredibly accurate to the practitioners. Yet, God was supposedly the only being who knew the totality of the future. Many wondered: How could mere demons produce such startlingly accurate proclamations of the future if they had no power to foretell it?

Well, the early Christian theologians responded, demons are a crafty lot. They explained: Since demons had been around for thousands of years and their aerial bodies could flit from place to place as quickly as the wind itself, they could often produce what *seemed like* accurate readings of the future that were instead based on experience.

Here's an example of what that might look like in today's terms. Let's say a Greek magician is paid to discern whether it is safe to take a particular ship from Egypt to Rome. The demon simply flies into the upper atmosphere to observe the weather. From this vantage, it can use its vast knowledge to predict the weather in somewhat the same manner that a meteorologist might use. It then returns to the magician to deliver its verdict.

Could a sudden squall kick up and sink the ship? Sure, but in this scenario, the demon is probably correct more times than not.

From Necromancy to the Witch

By the Middle Ages, Christians suspected most forms of divination to be demonic. At that point, necromancy had fallen into such disrepute that the word had transcended its original meaning—performing divination by communicating with the dead—and come instead to mean something closer to *bad magic worked through demons*.

At the same time, a new discourse began to rise around those who practiced bad magic (that is, magic worked with the intent to harm). In the late fifteenth century, a German clergyman and inquisitor named Heinrich Kramer published a treatise on witchcraft titled *Malleus Maleficarm* (The Hammer Against Witches), which presented a new way to view people who practiced bad magic. It posited that some women were in league with the Devil. According to Kramer, they entered this league by accepting a demonic pact (one that they sealed through sexual intercourse with demons), which enabled them to work dangerous magical acts that could destroy the Christian communities they belonged to from within by turning neighbor against neighbor, causing miscarriages, or spreading illnesses.

It may come as a surprise, but the fact is, before Kramer's work, people weren't all that concerned about witches. No one really doubted that there were people who practiced bad magic and that most of these people were women.[1] But very few people read Exodus 22:18—the famous "Thou shalt not suffer a witch to live" line—as an actual directive about putting witches to death.

The *Malleus*, however, changed that. In it, Kramer claimed that witches were a threat to people's lives and salvation in a way they never truly had been. He further insisted that they needed to be stopped. His text advises that women identified as witches should be understood to be heretics. And heresy was at the time a capital offense in Europe. Heretics at that time were often sentenced to death by burning at the stake. Over the next three centuries, between forty thousand and sixty thousand individuals were executed for practicing witchcraft during the European witch hunts.

This was a wildly different approach than had previously been taken with those who used harmful magic, one that allowed for the use of torture to extract witchcraft confessions and brought a new, literal reading to the verse "Thou shalt not suffer a witch to live."

Thus, while the language of "witches" and perhaps even the "Witch of Endor" is familiar to us today, our understanding of those terms is the end result of a long historical process. It would take centuries for a discourse around the woman at Endor and divinatory acts in general to produce the idea that all such divination is manifested by demons. It would take even longer for Christians to develop an idea of witches as a hidden force that threatens the totality of the Christian body. However, by the time that Spiritualism starts to rise, both ideas are firmly rooted in the minds of Americans.

From Witch to Medium

It is unsurprising that the opponents of Spiritualism would use these ideas in their criticism of the movement. After all, the new mediums appeared to be doing exactly what the old "Witch of Endor" once had: conjuring up the spirits of the dead to obtain information and comfort. And the critics of the day were not shy about saying so.

James Porter, a nineteenth century Methodist who critiqued Spiritualist practices, wrote in the lengthily titled work, *The Spirit Rappings, Mesmerism, Clairvoyance, Visions, Revelations, Startling Phenomena, and Infidelity of the Rapping Fraternity Calmly Considered, and Exposed* (1853), "said the witch of Endor to Saul, 'Whom shall I bring up?' And the medium inquires, 'What spirit shall I call for?,'. . ."[2] Porter goes on to say that the revelations provided by these spirits are often contradictory or childish, or even of an evil character. He concludes that, clearly, these are not the souls of the dead, but rather "familiar spirits" who speak in place of the dead. Put simply, Spiritualists were consorting with demons, and their practices were nothing but the "witchcraft of old."[3]

In an 1853 critique titled *The Spiritual Telegraphic Opposition Line*, author Z. Campbell goes a step further invoking not only the idea of witches but necromancy as well in his description of Spiritualism:

> That the witch of Endor was what is now called a medium, cannot be doubted. Hear the language addressed to her by Saul: "Divine unto me by the familiar spirit, and bring me him up whom I shall name unto thee." (1 Sam. xxviii. 8.) And for this sin Saul died. (1 Chron. x. 13.) At the present time, people are going to persons called mediums, and saying, "Bring me up those I shall name." And the spirits of such are said to be brought up. No matter by what agency it is said to be done, whether by witchcraft, electricity, odyle, necromancy, or mesmerism, it is the same thing.[4]

Speaking at the Mormon Tabernacle in Salt Lake City in 1854, Elder Jedidiah Grant offered a similar view of the phenomenon. Grant claims that the spirits who attend mediums are "wicked spirits" and that the fact that they come when summoned is just what one should expect: "I would ask you if Jehovah has not in all ages tried His people by the power of Lucifer and his associates; and on the other hand, has He not tried them and proved them by His Prophets?"[5] Here, Grant is painting Spiritualism as a kind of demonic challenge, a demonic challenge that he is confident the faithful of his community can surmount. To his fellow Latter-Day Saints, Grant declares, "Let the Rappers [the Spiritualists] go ahead, then, for it is not possible for them to deceive the elect of God; and let the witch of Endor, and all other witches and wizards, with the prince and power of the air at their head, do their best."[6]

Likewise, when confronting a proponent of Spiritualism in a public debate that was originally published in 1855, Isaac Errett, a reverend and leader in the Restoration Movement, invoked the "Witch of Endor" as a model for understanding Spiritualism. He condemns it as "modern necromancy," and reminds his audience that Isaiah 8:19–20 encourages God's people to reject "them that have familiar spirits, and . . . wizards that peep and mutter."[7]

Conservative Christians of the day were quick to pick up this view of the new mediums as successors to the old Witch of Endor, and the comparison enjoyed a long life. Two decades after Errett's proclamation that Christians should avoid the new "Witches of Endor," the Reverend John Rose echoed the same ideas in a lecture that was later reprinted in the *Local Preachers' Magazine* of the Wesleyan Methodists. "The spirits of witchcraft and necromancy are again on the wing," Rose claimed, "[For] what is spiritualism but renascent necromancy and witchcraft?"[8]

And this "necromancy and witchcraft" is clearly the same practiced by the Witch of Endor centuries before. Spiritualists carry on with the same "familiar spirits" of 1 Samuel, beings who are actually "*demons*, as the Bible proves."[9] While Spiritualists might seek to deny it, they are obviously "related to the witch of Endor."[10]

Over three decades after Rose's writings, the Seventh-day Adventist minister Carlyle Boynton Haynes devoted the entirety of his tenth chapter in *Spiritualism Versus Christianity* (1918) to the subject of the Witch of Endor and her supposed demonic associations. Haynes feels this extensive coverage is required since "in ancient times it was not called Spiritualism, but witchcraft, sorcery, wizardry, necromancy, and consulting with familiar spirits. Under these names it is spoken of in the Bible and strongly denounced, condemned, and prohibited."[11] With such a long pedigree, there is considerable ground that Haynes needs to cover, and plenty of material to prove that modern day Spiritualists were nothing more than "witches."

Cohesion in Condemnation

And yet, there seems to be an understanding shared between both Spiritualists and their opponents that the term *witch* just didn't quite fit. Spiritualists rejected the term on the grounds that they were not "witches" but instead something categorically more positive. They acknowledged the similarity between what they and the woman at Endor did, but referred to her as the "Lady of Endor," the "mother of all mediums," or, more simply, as a seer or prophetess.[12] Their rejection of the term *witch* was on moral grounds: as Robert Hallock declared in *The Medium and Daybreak*, "the woman of Endor practiced the noblest of Christian virtues before Christianity was born into the world."[13]

On the other hand, anti-Spiritualists came from a Christian intellectual tradition that taught that witches were intentional bringers of harm and woe. While anti-Spiritualists saw demons at work in séances, it did not appear that Spiritualists were intentionally causing harm or working magic whose intention was evil.

This required an evolution of thought surrounding the idea of the "Witch of Endor." Spiritualists, these anti-Spiritualist thinkers reasoned, clearly were not traditional witches, that is, they did not intend to cause harm to others through magical means or understand themselves to be holding congress with demons and devils. No, they seemed overall too sincere in their belief for such things to be true.

Instead, these groups concluded, it must be the case that Spiritualists were being deceived. Moreover, this deception must be so subtle and overwhelming that they were unable to see the "plain and clear" truth of the Bible that was repeatedly slipped under their noses. Looking for answers, these Christians began casting their eyes toward the Bible and soon viewed the "casting out" of demons spoken of in the New Testament in a new light.

Perhaps, they theorized, the mediums were not *just* speaking to demons. Perhaps the demons were entering the mediums, possessing them in a fashion that had heretofore gone unnoticed.

If that was the case, then perhaps demons were also using them as political mouthpieces, spreading anti-Christian positions far and wide.

CHAPTER SEVEN

The Wages of Sin Is Death

LET'S RETURN TO the Gerasene demoniac from chapter 2, the one occupied by "Legion." Remember him? He caused such a ruckus that he had to be chained up, and even then would burst from the chains on a regular basis. This was a key biblical image by which many Christians understood what it looked like when a person was possessed by demons.

Before the rise of Spiritualism in the United States, and conservative Christian pushback against it, demon possession was not a big topic in this country. In medieval Europe, on the other hand, exorcisms had featured regularly in Saints' Lives literature and other religious accounts, often described in terms of demons that jumped from one body to another, long demonic speeches, and shocking supernatural phenomena such as levitations, the production of illusory phenomena, and extreme behavioral or personality changes.

Exorcisms also appeared in art. For example, an exorcism is one of the forty-seven miracles depicted in the Small Miracle Altar of Mariazell in Austria. A flock of black-winged demons surrounds a woman who seems to cry out as a monk performs the exorcism. The butchered remains of what presumably are her family lie on the floor next to her, apparently killed by the woman while she was possessed.

Exorcisms had also long been reported to have occurred in real life. One well-known example was the women in the Loudun affair—in which a convent of Ursaline nuns in 1634 France, who were believed to be possessed by demons, swore like sailors, curled their bodies into *O* shapes while lying on their stomachs, and spoke clearly despite having blackened tongues that were swollen and covered with pimples.

In all of these cases, possession was not subtle; demons demonstrated no need to hide.

Yet, those who opposed the Spiritualists reasoned that this could not always be the case. It seemed obvious to them that what these women (and a few men) were doing was demonic, as demonic as what the "Witch of Endor" had done in her encounter with King Saul centuries before. And yet, the Spiritualist mediums displayed none of the bravado that their critics believed typical demons might. There were no clear indications of possession, and the women were able to pass off their demonstrations as the comings and goings of friendly spirits rather than the horror shows of demonic possession.

Eventually, this Spiritual opposition concluded that there must be another way that these demons were possessing these women. One that was infinitely more subtle than any methods that had been utilized before.

The Beginning

Those who opposed Spiritualists began to develop an idea of possession that would, in time, powerfully influence the minds of Americans. As the anti-Spiritualists grappled with how to understand Spiritualist phenomena as demonic, they began to form a new idea of the "rules" of demonic possession. These rules allowed them to explain Spiritualist manifestations as the result of subtle and gradual demon possession, a subtle and gradual possession that had the potential to shift the very political fabric of the nation. Here is the general explanation they came up with, and which they circulated through the distribution of anti-Spiritualist tracts.

According to the anti-Spiritualists, this gradual possession begins with the opening of a kind of gateway through which a demon could enter into a person. This act of opening oneself up could take a variety of different forms, but most often it required engaging with Spiritualist practices. For example, someone might become curious about the afterlife, seeking out confirmation of life eternal and the state of continued existence on the Other Side. As a result, they might attend a séance or watch a medium perform in a public show in order to acquire more information to sate their curiosity. The demons would happily oblige their curiosity through the medium, offering up lies and half-truths intended to deceive the person and drag them away from God.

If the person proved receptive to these messages, the demons might next encourage them to begin Spiritualist practices themselves. The individual might begin to develop their abilities as a medium, such as through automatic writing or by conjuring the dead in séances. All these activities required the budding Spiritualist to adopt a "passive" frame of mind in order to receive messages from the spirits, a frame of mind that they would need to actively practice and develop. As their minds grew increasingly used to this passivity, the theory went, the demons would be able to slip through the natural defenses of the human brain and begin to gradually possess the new medium. In the same manner that an interior decorator might make spaces more livable or appealing to potential occupants, the demons would carefully curate the brain of the medium to make an attractive living space for themselves. That is to say, by encouraging the medium to train themselves to be passive and practice passivity again and again, demons cultivated a vessel that they could easily manipulate.

The End

Once more, let us return to chapter 2 and to the idea that largely predominated through history to this point, namely that demons occupied the same space as human beings. That is to say, whenever demons roamed the earth, they literally occupied the same space and terrain that human beings did. If a demon wanted to possess someone, it would compress its aerial body into the orifices of a person and work the air inside of the body and brain to produce a variety of effects from hallucinations to supernatural strength. Put another way, demons were invisible (due to their wind-like nature) but remained physically present in the world.

Our anti-Spiritualist authors were still firmly positioned within this world view. Although they no longer thought of mental processes as being created by spiritualized air moving through the body, they did still think of demons as having to physically interact with some element of the human body in order to produce adverse effects. Thus, when what amounted to demonic interior decorators were manipulating the brains of mediums, it was via a largely physical method: They were simply pressing "buttons" inside of the person's brain to elicit effects. And according to their theory, just like any button that is pressed too often, those portions of the brain eventually became worn down or broke.

Carlyle Boynton Haynes summarized this idea nicely for his readers when he wrote:

> Thus through all the ages of the past, from the time of the first spirit medium, the serpent in the garden of Eden, Spiritualism

> has been beguiling and deceiving unwary souls until they have yielded themselves both soul and body to the control of evil and unclean spirits. These spirits have then taken possession of their victims even to the deepest centers of their mental, nervous, and vital action, and have so disarranged their nervous systems, disturbed their physical nature, subverted their wills, unhinged their judgment, and disordered their minds, that the first slight control of the spirits has developed into the permanent madness of demoniac possession, wrecking both the mental and moral constitution of the victim, until this perfect work of Spiritualism is concealed from the world either by the grave of the suicide or the madhouse of the lunatic.[1]

Haynes, writing in 1918, is to one extent or another synthesizing the conclusions of the anti-Spiritualists toward the end of Spiritualism's heyday. As such, his writing contains some key takeaways that can help us to understand this uniquely American take on demon possession that powerfully shapes our political landscape today.

Demons as Electric Beings

The first takeaway is the notion that demons are themselves beings made of electricity or beings whose nature at least shares enough of the electric to be able to manipulate the action of a medium's nervous system.

These possibilities are explored in *The Mystery Solved*, an anti-Spiritualist tract published in 1853 shortly after Spiritualism began to spread. In it, the author grapples with the idea of the electric nature of evil spirits. Quoting the work of a physician—a Mr. Taylor who published in the *Boston Medical and Surgical Journal*—the author of the tract, one John C. Bywater, notes that Taylor chalks up the phenomenon of automatic writing to the presence of electrical feedback in the human brain that has taken on a kind of life of its own.

Bywater rejects this idea, claiming that this would mean two things: that such electricity had both "life and intelligence" and that this electricity was still a part of the brain that created it.[2] Both cannot be true, Bywater claimed: the electricity cannot be both part of the brain and also hold a separate intelligence. Instead, Bywater argued, one of the two conclusions of the theory must be discarded. Since Taylor appeared to be able to reproduce accurate signatures of those long dead, Bywater determined that the conclusion that needed discarding was the one that credited Taylor's brain with playing a part in the production of such writing. Instead, he determined, it must be that this "electricity" was itself a sentient being.

Returning to the idea of electricity later in his work, Bywater claims: "We may grant that electricity is the agent by which these things are done; and we presume it is so; yet it by no means follows, that either human beings, or the spirits of the dead, excite the electricity in such cases. It is more reasonable to suppose that it is done by the devil, or some of his invisible angels, called unclean spirits or demons."[3]

And if demons were an electrical phenomenon or manipulated the electricity in the brain, then it stood to reason that healthy human brains could fight their influence.

The Necessity of Human Passivity

Ideally then, demons would want human brains that had been trained not to fight back. Thus, the second key element about this then-developing American understanding of demons is the cultivation of neural passivity. This passivity would make it easier for the demon to move through the brain or to manipulate the electricity in the brain as it desired. While Spiritualists did not cite this as the goal, they themselves, in their own publications, extolled to mediums and sitters the virtue of cultivating a passive nature. For instance, in *The Medium and Daybreak*—one of the most popular periodicals for Spiritualists—the frequently reprinted "Rules and Conditions for the Spirit-Circle" indicate that "the minds of the sitters should be in a passive rather than an active state, possessed by the love of truth and of mankind."[4] Likewise, in the same periodical, a writer going by "Omega" elaborates on the ideal characteristics of a medium saying that such a medium is "meek, devout, and eminently Christ-like; perfectly passive (a very essential matter)."[5]

From an anti-Spiritualist perspective, this passivity was what allowed the demons to manipulate mediums and sitters, a manipulation that these critics believed could not occur if either party actively resisted the demonic influence. In this view, passivity allowed demons to root around in people's brains for the answers to questions they were asking and allowed the demons to more easily manipulate their physical bodies.

As a medium's passivity grew, their mind would become even more predisposed to the demon's influence, allowing the demon to commandeer their body's functions even when the person might try to resist.

As the communication became sinister, the medium might try to prevent it, but such efforts were often too little, too late. As the *London Chronicle* reported regarding British author and psychical investigator J. Godfrey Raupert's research into the phenomenon of Spiritualism:

> Through the whole of his experience, he obtained proofs that the character of these spirits is immoral, and, of a blighting influence upon their victims. Although for a time they dictate high moral principle, especially to those who indulge in automatic writing, these invariably degenerate into sinister, blasphemous, or obscene suggestions. Hints are thrown out that morality is a matter of conventionality, that certain instincts are implanted in us in order to be gratified. Mr. Raupert asserts that he has known many women ruined utterly in body and soul by these debasing immoralities, urged upon them when their will power had been destroyed by opening the doors of their mind to evil suggestions.[6]

Thus, once the mind was made sufficiently passive, the communication Spiritualists previously enjoyed became a terrifying ordeal. It became readily apparent in this transition that the doting dead were actually degenerate demons.

Death and Insanity

Haynes's final takeaway regarding the influence of demons is death and insanity. As suggested by authors such as Haynes and Raupert, the eventual result of such neurological distress described above was institutionalization or death. Raupert relates another experience by a medium that reportedly began with failing neurological health and led to an eventual attempt at suicide:

> About this time she began to experience pains at the base of the brain, and these gradually increased until they became almost unbearable. Her step was interrupted and her health

> began to fail perceptibly. It was at this time that she announced that she was obsessed; that the intelligence that had communicated through her had taken full command of her body, so that she was no longer a free agent. Treatment of every kind was tried- all to no benefit. And now a new and more terrible feature developed. Hitherto the impulse had been to write. Now it was voices that sounded in her head, sometimes one, but more frequently two, three, or even four voices, talking to one another and freely conversing about her. Some would commend her conduct; others would blame her. Some would swear and curse and call her names -names so vile that she could scarcely have heard them in her normal state, while others would try to defend her from the grosser and coarser forces. In the early stages the things which the voices told her to do were practically harmless, but before long, they commenced to urge her to commit suicide, and she sought to obey them.[7]

This idea of the madness of mediums seems to be similarly echoed in a statement by the English Jesuit priest Bernard Vaughan, who claimed, "I have come across, abroad as well as at home, men and women devoted to spiritism. I have not found them improved by it, and in more instances than one spiritism has unhinged their minds, shattered their nerves, broken their spirit, and left them fit for nothing."[8] Likewise, the nineteenth century American Methodist minister James Porter writes in *The Spirit Rappings*, a critique of Spiritualism, that

> ... To become a medium is dangerous. The physical influence of the operation, particularly upon the nervous system, is manifestly of the most alarming character. It may be endured for a time, but, like other unnatural excitements, it will prey upon the system it convulses until it can no longer perform its proper functions, when disease and premature death will ensue.[9]

In the eyes of anti-Spiritualists, this was the inevitable end of a Spiritualist's career. Slowly but surely, the demons that they engaged with would manipulate their brains, brains made passive by Spiritualist practices. Once the demon had sufficiently subjugated the medium, it would begin to bombard them with unwholesome commands and communication.

This repeated neural activity would eventually render the medium mad or send them to an early grave.

Between the Beginning and the End

Involuntary movements, voices in one's head, suicidal ideation, spontaneous death: The anti-Spiritualists certainly gave prospective mediums plenty of reasons to reconsider adopting Spiritualist practice! While automatic writing or table-tipping could seem innocent enough to the curious, the opponents of Spiritualism argued that all of these practices imperiled mind, body, and soul. Little by little, bit by bit, the medium who adopted them would descend down a slippery slope into the maw of Hell itself.

And while anti-Spiritualists were clearly concerned about these lost souls, much concern was also focused on what the demons were saying before the medium faced death or the asylum. Mediums, after all, had an audience: People believed they spoke with the authority of the spirits. Between large venues like concert halls and uncountable private sittings, mediums and the spirits they spoke with had the ear of the nation.

Yet, this meant that the nation was really listening to the proclamations of demons. They were accepting the things the mediums told them, and some of these things were clearly political in nature. This represented a significant concern for anti-Spiritualists, who understood the demons influencing mediums to have political goals and the beliefs they spread to have political ramifications.

On an individual level, Spiritualists believed in what we might term in the present day "progressive" causes and ideas. It may be that this was due to most mediums being women, the influence of Quakerism on its early roots, or the egalitarian nature of the afterlife that they espoused. Regardless, the anti-Spiritualists saw these progressive causes as demonic agendas. In the next chapter, we'll look at three of these ideas that predominated in Spiritualism, and the way in which anti-Spiritualists saw the work of the Devil in each.

CHAPTER EIGHT

Abominable Beliefs, Abominable Politics

ANTI-SPIRITUALISTS WERE CONCERNED with the gradual possession of mediums, and they were horrified that death and insanity could strike those who were so afflicted. However, many found what was brought *out of* the séances just as troubling as what happened *inside* of them.

As I've suggested, Spiritualists were almost universally aligned with several progressive political causes, and anti-Spiritualists saw these political alignments as a direct result of the demonic influence that was exerted over their brains. While many Spiritualists also considered themselves to be Christians, anti-Spiritualists, who generally adopted a more conservative approach to Christan belief, did not see the two systems as compatible. Anti-Spiritualists believed that as the medium became more passive and subject to a demon's control, the demon would begin to suggest ideas and philosophies that would drag the medium further and further away from what the anti-Spiritualists regarded as "Christian truth."

While this trickery could take a variety of different, supposedly dangerous forms, there are three political ideas in particular that the opponents of Spiritualism targeted: the Free Love movement, women's suffrage, and abolition. Although these three political notions were not exclusively Spiritualist, Spiritualists trended toward all three of these ideas with much greater frequency than non-Spiritualists. For that reason, these three ideas came to be strongly associated with the movement.

Free Love

The idea of "free love" is widely understood to be the belief that love and sexual relationships should be based on choice and consent and not governed or enforced by law or religion. Modern readers might associate the idea of "free love" with the sexually libertine American hippies of the '60s, but European authors had already begun to formulate the idea by the eighteenth century! However, whereas we might be tempted to think of free love purely in terms of sex (and possibly, in some circumstances, sexual immorality), these authors who wrote about the Free Love movement were largely making early feminist political statements. For these authors, the Free Love movement was really about women being able to make free choices about their education, marital status, and other social realities.

Consider, for instance, the lot of women in the eighteenth and nineteenth centuries (along with, arguably, a fair portion of the twentieth). During this time, most people in the West did not think to formally educate girls or women, and schools that welcomed them were rare. As Mary Wollstonecraft points out in *A Vindication of the Rights of Woman* (1792), "girls . . . receive only a disorderly kind of education."[1] That is, instruction for men is more methodical in nature and their instruction more rigorous. Conversely, women must learn "by sheer observations on real life" rather than comprehensive instruction.[2] This oversight is attributable to widespread preconceptions of women's intellectual virtue in that time, which were formed largely because, as Wollstonecraft claimed, "all the writers who have written on the subject of female education and manners from Rousseau to Dr. Gregory, have contributed to render women more artificial, weak characters, than they would otherwise have been; and, consequently, more useless members of society."[3]

This perceived "uselessness" and related lack of education presented a significant problem for women. In many cases, women were obliged to marry or rely upon the good graces of their male relatives in order to acquire financial security. That does not mean that women could not marry for love. They could, and some certainly did. But there also were many women who were forced, by necessity or coercion, to marry simply so that they could survive.

Such marriages provided some stability. However, once women were married, they also forfeited certain rights that they would have had if they had remained unwed. For instance, upon her marriage, all property owned by a woman passed from her control into the hands of her husband. Likewise, if she were to find a job to work, her wages would legally belong to her husband. Nor could she benefit from most forms of financial investment since she was unable to act as a legally separate entity from her husband. Women's bodily autonomy was also all but eliminated, as: "men were allowed to treat their possessions, or 'chattel,' in nearly any way they wanted,"[4] including spousal rape or beatings. (Needless to say, "no fault" or "unilateral" divorces did not exist, and their invention was still decades away.)

The proponents of the Free Love movement argued that such an oppressive system could be changed by simply getting rid of marriage. In their view, by setting up a social system in which women and men were allowed to move in and out of relationships as they saw fit, a marital system that was oppressive and tolerant of violence could be eliminated. As Victoria Woodhull, a Spiritualist herself and a woman of firsts (first female presidential candidate, first woman to run a Wall Street brokerage, and the first woman to own and publish a national newspaper), declared in 1871 in "The Truth Shall Set You Free," a speech she made in defense of freedom to love and of sexual autonomy:

> Yes, I am a Free Lover. I have an inalienable, constitutional and natural right to love whom I may, to love as long or as short a period as I can; to change that love every day if I please, and with that right neither you nor any law you can frame have any right to interfere. And I have the further right to demand a free and unrestricted exercise of that right, and it is your duty not only to accord it, but, as a community, to see that I am protected in it. I trust that I am fully understood, for I mean just that, and nothing less![5]

At the risk of editorializing, I feel compelled to reply: *Good show, Ms. Woodhull!*

Unfortunately, there was the small matter of biblical precedent that stood in her and other Free Love proponents' way. For centuries, the standard for most Christian denominations had been to accept sexual intercourse as a moral act only within the confines of marriage. Since Free Lovers were suggesting that women should be able to have sexual intercourse within their non-marital relationships and even to have children with their sexual partners, it seemed clear to critics that these teachings clearly fell outside the biblical bounds of acceptable sexual practice. Thus, the anti-Spiritualists reasoned, this doctrine of free love must emerge from a demonic source; efforts to convince people of free love's merits then must be attempts to lead men and women astray from the roles they play in God's plan.

Thomas Nast, often regarded as the father of American political cartooning, offered an interesting visual representation of the issue. In his political cartoon entitled "Get Thee Behind Me, (Mrs.) Satan!," published on February 17, 1872, in *Harper's Weekly*, Nast depicts Woodhull as an austere diabolical figure, complete with menacing bat wings and horns.

In the illustration, Woodhull holds a poster whose text suggests that salvation can be found in Free Love, salvation which is being offered to a haggard wife carrying multiple children and a drunkard husband shouting at the heavens. Yet, descriptions and annotations of the cartoon in digital archives frequently focus on the, admittedly striking, appearance of Woodhull-Satan, usually failing to note how the figure of the wife, in whose life the demonic looking Woodhull has appeared, encourages women to accept their subjugation in marriage as a holy duty. The wife wears simple clothes and shoes and carries a strong walking stick, typical clothing choices for medieval pilgrims. Her response is couched in conservative Christian ideas. To the Woodhull-Satan, the "Wife (with heavy burden)" replies "I'd rather travel the hardest path of matrimony than follow your footsteps."[6]

While her way up the mountain depicts a genuinely difficult path, the language of "the hardest path" was not unique to the wife's lot and was in fact used frequently in sermons and interpretations of Christ's life around the time of Nast's cartoon. For instance, in a sermon on Romans 8:32, Charles Pettit McIlvaine, an Episcopal Bishop and a chaplain of the Senate, directed his listeners to be "always ready—when temptation assails, to stand in the whole armor of God; when duty calls, to be first about with truth, for its longest and hardest path."[7] In an article entitled "The Moral Character of Jesus," in the literary and philosophical journal *The Dial*, which featured a series of articles on "The Christianity of Christ," the author proclaims that Jesus conquered "passion by sheer force of a consecrated will,—to choose the hardest path, the crookedest, the thorniest, and to walk it firmly with bleeding feet to the end."[8]

This hardest path that Christ followed with bleeding feet also frames the wife's refusal to Woodhull-Satan to "follow your

[Woodhull-Satan's] footsteps." The wife has chosen instead the path of submission described in 1 Peter 2:20–21: "For what credit *is it* if, when you are beaten for your faults, you take it patiently? But when you do good and suffer, if you take it patiently, this *is* commendable before God. For to this you were called, because Christ also suffered for us, leaving us an example, that you should follow His steps." In the mind of Nast and his readers, the Free Lovers had abandoned Christ's hardest path; better, they believed, to subjugate oneself to marriage than to the Devil.

And this Devil, they understood, was far less figurative than he appeared in political cartoons. In *A Hand-book of Christian Evidence* (1880), a book focusing on offering proof of the claims of Christianity, the Restorationist preacher and author Laurence W. Scott devotes one section to the topic of Spiritualism and Paul's supposed anticipation of this Satanic formation. Here, the author cites the words of several former Spiritualists-turned-critics and lays out the accusations of sins that they had levied against the movement. For example, a "Dr. P. B. Randolph, a noted Spiritualistic lecturer," claimed that "for seven years I held daily intercourse with what purported to be my mother's spirit. *I am now firmly persuaded that it was nothing but an evil spirit and infernal demon, who in that guise gained my soul's confidence, and lead me to the very brink of ruin.*"[9] The same individual claimed that "I have a volume of sixty closely written pages, of names of those who have been drawn down from respectability, morality, wealth and intelligence, to the filth of free love, poverty, and to insanity itself."[10] Evidence like this, the anti-Spiritualists claimed, proved that Free Love was the way to ruin.

In the eyes of Spiritualism's detractors, to support the Free Love movement was not to be in support of women's rights; rather, it was to become mired in a libertine lifestyle of sexual excess. In his work of critique, *Spiritualism Versus Christianity: Or, Spiritualism Thoroughly Exposed*, published in 1856, author J. W. Daniels takes aim at *Nichols' Monthly*, a Spiritualist affiliated publication edited by T. L. Nichols and Mary S. Gove, which advocated abolishing "every law which renders the marriage tie sacred and inviolable, and the immediate practice of Free Love principles, in utter contempt of all law, human and Divine."[11] And here, again, we return to the idea of the demonic, as Daniels argues that the magazine is "chiefly devoted to the very doctrines noticed by the Apostle as *the doctrines of demons*"[12] and that the Bible connects free love practices with "heathen gods . . . [which] warrants the conclusion that this doctrine was the inevitable result of necromancy."[13]

Where Free Love was practiced in a specific setting, some authors depicted that setting as nothing more than a location for facilitating a sex cult. For instance, in *Spiritualism Unveiled, and Shown to Be the Work of Demons* (1866), Miles Grant writes about the creation of a Free Love community in Berlin Heights, Ohio, which he refers to as an "institution."[14] According to Grant, a young woman had been encouraged to abandon her husband and join this community, and her husband was unable to discover her whereabouts for several weeks. When she eventually returned home, he heard tales of her experiences that reportedly included:

> all that is degrading and loathsome to a virtuous and high-minded woman. Low-bred familiarities with vulgar, fanatical men; companionship with women who deemed themselves elevated above humanity in becoming the victims of their own and their companions' lusts, and a close familiarity with a brutish, criminal enjoyment, which was the highest sphere aimed at in this delectable community, were what she was obliged to submit to.[15]

Grant was further concerned that even women who properly submitted to their husbands would be harmed by the existence of Free Love. For instance, he cites a "Mrs. Annie Hunter," who relates the story of her husband who she alleges began the Berlin Heights institute. According to her letter, Hunter's husband claimed to be away on business for a year, but during his time, he instead "roamed around in search of free-love companions." Once he located enough companions, he "founded the infamous den of lust," the Berlin Heights institution previously mentioned above. She herself was left to care for their three children and, with no means by which to do so, she become a washerwoman.[16] To the woman who escapes the influence of such a movement, Mrs. Hunter advises: "Let her thank a kind Providence that she is restored to the arms of a loving and kind-hearted husband, and is not this moment, as I am, a deserted and heart-stricken wife and mother."[17]

I was not able to locate any evidence that any figure named "Hunter" helped found the Berlin Heights Free Love community. Nevertheless, this woman's testimony, along with other critics' testimonies and arguments, further shored up the claims by critics that Free Love was both demonic in nature and harmful to the general public.

Women's Suffrage

Another issue that was related to the rights of women in marriage was the right of women to vote. Both issues revolved around the idea that women were autonomous human beings who functioned separately from the men with whom they lived or kept community. Women's suffrage was one of many causes championed by powerful and outspoken women of the period banding together for the purposes of social reform.

Often these organizations were based upon applied biblical principles, an origin that meant that many such groups were comfortable supporting causes other than what they were established for. For example, the Women's Christian Temperance Union (organized 1873) was established to curb the consumption of alcohol (something the Bible warns against in passages such as Proverbs 20:1 and Ephesians 5:18). Nevertheless, the group did not limit its goal of reform to temperance; the organization was a significant supporter of the women's suffrage movement as well.

The story of women's suffrage in the United States is frequently told, to one extent or another, through the figure of Susan B. Anthony, one such powerful and outspoken woman. Arguably the most famous suffragette in American history, Anthony would be inducted into the Hall of Fame for Great Americans in 1950 and the National Women's Hall of Fame in 1973. Statues commemorating her would appear throughout the United States, her image would grace stamps and coins, and her grave in Mount Hope Cemetery would be regularly obscured by "I Voted" stickers on election day pilgrimages.

There is, however, another woman who often appears on some of these same monuments and images alongside of Anthony. She was the primary motivating force behind the Seneca Falls Convention and the Declaration of Sentiments, the opening salvo of the women's rights movement. She worked closely with Anthony to publish the newspaper *The Revolution* and to create the American Equal Rights Association, and she was the president (and cofounder with Anthony) of the

National Woman Suffrage Association and president of the National American Woman Suffrage Association. That woman was Elizabeth Cady Stanton.

So, why do we know generally less about this massively influential figure than the just-as-influential Anthony? One reason may be that Stanton took aim at the religious structures that served to prop up inequality. Since Christianity, broadly construed, was and is a considerable force in American politics, idolizing a figure who took such a clearly antagonistic stance toward it would meet considerable resistance.

While many in the women's suffrage movement were cautious to confine their critique of misogynist practices, that is, those practices that reinforced prejudice against women and limited their rights and dignity, to those embedded in contemporary society, Stanton isolated and called out a thread in these misogynistic social structures that she saw as significantly contributing to women's suffering: peoples' problematic readings of the Bible and the precedents those readings set. Scholars today recognize as a given the effects that patriarchal and even misogynistic interpretations of certain Bible verses have had on society; but at that time, the idea was relatively new. Stanton worked with a group of women from the women's rights movement who also studied the Bible seriously to create a corrective to these harmful interpretations. In 1895 and 1898, the two volumes of *The Woman's Bible*, which added feminist commentary to already established translations of Scripture, were published.

In her introduction to this work, Stanton offers a blistering observation that is worth quoting in full:

> From the inauguration of the movement for woman's emancipation the Bible has been used to hold her in the "divinely ordained sphere," prescribed in the Old and New Testaments. The canon and civil law; church and state; priests and legislators; all political parties and religious denominations have alike taught that woman was made after man, of man, and for man, an inferior being, subject to man. Creeds, codes, Scriptures and statutes, are all based on this idea. The fashions, forms, ceremonies and customs of society, church ordinances and discipline all grow out of this idea. . . . The Bible teaches that woman

> brought sin and death into the world, that she precipitated the fall of the race, that she was arraigned before the judgment seat of Heaven, tried, condemned and sentenced. Marriage for her was to be a condition of bondage, maternity a period of suffering and anguish, and in silence and subjection, she was to play the role of a dependent on man's bounty for all her material wants, and for all the information she might desire on the vital questions of the hour, she was commanded to ask her husband at home. Here is the Bible position of woman briefly summed up.[18]

Is it any wonder that the defenders of such a "Bible position" critiqued by Stanton might be inclined to see women's suffrage as inspired by demons? The fact that so many proponents of women's rights also turned out to be Spiritualists seemed only to further cement the idea of a demonic origin to the movement.

To some people, evidence that the spirits themselves were clamoring for women's rights was the final nail in the coffin. For example, many of the poems printed in the work *Astrea: Or, Goddess of Justice*, a book of poetry by E. P. Thorndyke and published in 1881, are credited as having been composed by the spirits and delivered through mediums. Several of these poems were unabashedly in favor of women's rights.

For instance, "The Grey Dawn of the Morn" was "Given through the mediumship of Miss HOUGHTON, and claiming to come from the Spirit of Milton."[19] That is to say, John Milton, the author of the epic poem *Paradise Lost*. Here, "Milton" seems to express a surprisingly progressive view regarding women's rights for someone who lived in the 1600s:

> *Thou did'st ask of man, thy brother,*
> *How can ye be true and brave,*
> *When to your caprice and passion,*
> *Woman lives, and dies a slave!*
>
> *Thou did'st say that peace would never*
> *Woeful human nature greet,*
> *Till beside her holiest altars,*
> *Man and woman equal meet.*[20]

While such sentiments were frequently expressed by Spiritualists, it is perhaps a stanza some lines down which expressed the rising danger that conservative Christians of the day feared:

> *Lo! man's ancient faith is waning,*
> *With his iron rule of might;*
> *Woman, from her slumber rising,*
> *Upward struggles to the light.*[21]

To its religious opponents, women's suffrage, alongside such threats as the Free Love movement, offered another way in which the "ancient faith" of Christianity was under threat.

It is perhaps in Orestes Brownson's *The Spirit-Rapper*, an anti-Spiritualist work of fiction published in 1854, that we can most clearly see an illustration of how some people transplanted the idea of demonic nature onto women's suffrage. The novel is a confusing one, beginning with its subtitle, *An Autobiography*, which is a misdirection, given that Brownson is not writing about his own life.

The unnamed protagonist of the novel is a mesmerist, a member of a movement that predates and overlaps with Spiritualism and whose practices may be best compared to modern hypnotism. In the story, this character forms in his mind the idea that he will "philanthropically" reform the world, philanthropy being the author Brownson's catch-all term for liberal political causes. To accomplish this goal, the protagonist decides to subject the population to mass hypnosis through strategically placed "mesmeric batteries": mysterious tools that will allow him to capitalize on mesmeric forces to manipulate the world.

While his intentions appear pure to begin with, it quickly becomes apparent that to accomplish his reform he must do away with Christianity as a whole. Intimated throughout the story, and made clear at the end, is the fact that his mesmeric powers, as well as the abilities of Spiritualists and the doctrines associated with them, are actually the works of clever demons.

Featured in the story is the recurring character of Priscilla, who serves as Brownson's straw man for women's rights. Priscilla is clearly brilliant, described as a new "Hypatia of Alexandria" after the famous female philosopher and mathematician.[22] Priscilla's rhetorical and philosophical chops are displayed several times throughout the novel. Brownson introduces her philanthropic quest in this way:

> She had been sent by the Abolition Society as a delegate to the great Anti-Slavery World's Convention at London, and being denied a seat in that illustrious body, because a woman, she had turned her attention to the question of woman's rights, and, after travelling a few months on the continent, had returned home well instructed in Godwin's *Political Justice*, and a devout believer in Mary Wolstonecroft [sic].[23]

Priscilla expertly organizes the efforts of other women's rights advocates, and her passion is enough to ensnare the narrator; first he develops one-sided romantic feelings toward her and then becomes convinced of the righteousness of her cause.

As the novel wears on, she begins to parrot the kind of revolutionary ideas that were growing in popularity around the world that would later be espoused in *The Woman's Bible.* In one conversation with Mr. Merton, the conservative Christian character who eventually liberates the narrator from his demonic views, Priscilla declares:

> "The Bible . . . is a genuine book, and faithfully records the real experience of prophets and seers of old times, and is of no value to us save as interpreted by the facts of each one's own inner life. Much of it is local, temporary, colored by the nation and age that produced it, and is no longer of any significance for us. . . ."[24]

In a later conversation in the story, she says, once more parroting Spiritualist claims:

> The world in its nonage was imposed upon, and induced to call evil good and good evil. The wisdom I assume, and am laboring to diffuse, is that which the priests have branded as Satanic. Satan is my hero. He was a bold and daring rebel, and the first to set the example of resistance to despotism and to assert unbounded freedom. For this all the priests, all rulers, despots, all who would hold their brethren in bondage, have cursed him. I take his part, and hope to live to see his memory vindicated. . . .[25]

To which Mr. Merton replies: "I suspect, that Madame Priscilla has listened or will listen to the modern spiritualism, which seems to me to be a revival of demonic worship."

Indeed, as the narrator falls deeper and deeper into the diabolical powers he works through mesmerism/Spiritualism, he begins to work his wiles upon Priscilla. He is able to impose his will to such a degree upon her that she had "no longer any will of her own. She had craved liberty, and had induced me to aid her in establishing it, and was now only my slave."[26] Slowly, Priscilla begins to lose her vitality, draining away before the eyes of everyone around her.

The inverse is true of her husband, James. Though he begins the story "an exceedingly meek and submissive-looking man, if man he could be called,"[27] once the narrator finally releases his mesmeric hold on Priscilla and she begins to deliver to James "the loaded affections of a lifetime" he begins to adopt a more commanding and traditionally masculine presence.[28]

"James was a man," the novel's author Brownson declares somewhat triumphantly in the narration. "A few months' practical experience served to cure him of a good deal of his philanthropy" (read: liberalism) "to damp the ardor of his zeal for reform."

Not only is James a man, but he is also a good Christian. The travels and experiences he had undertaken with Priscilla and the narrator "had opened his eyes to many things, and made him a staunch conservative . . . [he] had become sincerely converted to a real objective Christian faith."[29] Eventually, it is James who delivers a knife wound to the narrator that will result in a downward spiral of health and eventual death.

Through the fictional characters of Priscilla and James, Brownson makes his real-life argument that "philanthropy," of which women's rights plays a significant part, is the instrument of demons. As it becomes clearer and clearer that the narrator's best intentions are actually the paving stones to Hell, Priscilla and James undergo a remarkable transformation. Whereas before Priscilla is a suffragette unwilling to commit herself to her husband's love for fear of submission, she eventually realizes that she is only whole and happy when she *does* submit herself to her husband, abandoning her "philanthropic" goals entirely in favor of being a fully committed wife and mother. James, on the other hand, only becomes a "real man" when his wife gives up the ghost of women's rights and embraces her submission to him.

The reader sees clearly that these courses of action become possible only after they have mutually abandoned the demonic doctrines of Spiritualism and milquetoast, liberal Christianity.

Abolitionism

Despite Brownson's rejection of liberal Christianity, by the late 1850s, he had found agreement with one of the progressive political causes that Spiritualists and liberal Christians shared: abolitionism.[30] Most often these three ideas—abolitionism, women's suffrage, and free love—were connected through an idea of freedom. After all, if women were to be freed from submission to men, both in marriage and by the government, shouldn't all those who were enslaved be freed as well? In much the same way that the majority of Spiritualists were in favor of women's rights, so too were the majority in favor of abolition. (A smaller number favored the Free Love movement.)

Though he was not a Spiritualist himself, Gerrit Smith—a three-time presidential candidate, member of the House of Representatives, and abolitionist and Christian reformer—wrote about this trend in his collection of sermons, *Three Discourses on the Religion of Reason* (1859), claiming:

> . . . the Spiritualists I met in my tours through the State, last fall, were nearly all reformers. They had broken off from both political and ecclesiastical parties, and were earnestly and openly devoting themselves to the abolition of sectarianism, slavery, intemperance, and other wrongs. I have no doubt that, in proportion to their numbers, Spiritualists cast tenfold as many votes for the Abolition and Temperance ticket as did others. Surely such a fact is highly commendatory of the influence of Spiritualism.[31]

Even from the perspective of an outsider looking in, Spiritualism was clearly and overwhelmingly aligned with abolition.

And opponents of Spiritualism, once more, saw the work of demons in this political position. In an article titled "Steadfast, Unmovable" published in the June 1859 issue of *The Presbyterian Expositor*, an anonymous author claims that the world is in "a state of extraordinary excitement" and that more and more warnings of doctrinal errors are necessary as the time of prophecy approaches.

In that age, two things were clear to the author: (1) many churches had "departed from the faith of the Gospel" and (2) "great numbers of persons utterly ignorant of the whole subject of religion, have undertaken to be instructors of others." These latter fools, the writer claimed, appeared wise to some people and could lead many of the faithful astray because "whether Abolitionism, or Women's Rights, or Spiritualism be the hobby on which they ride, each, like quack doctors, has a nostrum which is the certain cure of the evils of society." And whence do these cures originate? "It is the express prediction of God's word, 'that in the latter times some shall depart from the faith, giving heed to seducing spirits, and doctrines of devils'—*demons* or spirits of deceased men and women."[32]

Earlier in that decade, *The Hartford Daily Courant* had published an article entitled "Anti-Bible Convention," which took aim at the Hartford Bible Convention that was held in Hartford, Connecticut in June 1853. The event had been organized by a group of reformers and Spiritualists and its speakers included the prominent Spiritualist Andrew Jackson Davis and abolitionist William Lloyd Garrison. The author of the article described the convention as an "infidel assemblage. . . . Of abolitionists, women's rights believers, spiritual rappers, and atheists, fathered for the purpose of spitting out their venom against all that this community hold sacred . . ."[33] According to the author, among other positions espoused by the speakers,

> Andrew Jackson Davis elevated the crude and undigested plagiarisms of his obscure philosophy above the teachings of Christ and his apostles, and held them as the gospel of the spiritualists. The ultra anti-slavery men, with Garrison at their head, denied the Bible for other reasons. With them, the abolition of slavery in this country is of more importance than the light of Christianity, or the salvation of souls through Jesus Christ. . . . Throughout the discussion, the opponents of the Bible filled the ears of the audience with the most revolting blasphemies, and made the convention a miniature hell, with demons spitting out the concentrated malice of their hearts in terms of "condensed damnation."[34]

Quoting the piece in its entirety, in his own 1853 critique of Spiritualism, the author Z. Campbell offers it to his readers as "a fair specimen of the evil tendency of 'spiritual disclosures'"—that is, of communications from the spirits—and promptly launches into a discussion of the role of the Devil in creating "advocates of false religion."[35] It is fascinating to think that these condemnations of slavery are considered part of the "evil tendency" of the communications given to Spiritualists. At the time, the idea of abolition occupied such an ambiguous intellectual space that it could be considered the work of the Devil!

Demons Get Political

In a book published a decade later, a pseudonymous author who identifies himself only as "A Citizen of Ohio" offers a short summary of how critics say all three political ideas—free love, women's suffrage, and abolitionism—collapse together for some anti-Spiritualists:

> The free-lover, who is always a woman's-rights man and an abolitionist, opens the door of suffrage alike to all sexes, kinds and colors, and because of the surrender of rights which attend the marriage relation, holds, that if the negro is enslaved by surrendering his liberties with his cares to a master, the wife is none the less a slave who makes the same surrender to a husband. [36]

The author rejects these ideas because, he says, all slaves are, at least from the author's perspective, "less" than their masters and proceeds to take aim at Spiritualists and their political ideas. He was far from the only person doing so. And such accusations had far-reaching ramifications.

That's because, for better or for worse, politics in the United States was, as it is at the time of this writing, a democratic system. That is to say, the citizens of the United States are to one extent or another responsible for the leaders who are elected and the choices that those leaders make. So, as the idea that people were increasingly understood to be possessed and influenced by demonic forces spread, it is perhaps unsurprising that some people began to ask: What might happen if a large portion of the electorate were unknowingly possessed by demons?

Authors such as the anonymous writer quoted above, in his 1863 book *Interior Causes of the War: The Nation Demonized, and Its President a Spirit-Rapper*, had a clear answer: Political tensions would mount until such time as those who knew what was "right" were forced to fight against demonic oppression. And as tensions built in the country between reformers and traditionalists, a fight is exactly what happened. This spiritual-political battle came to be known as "The Civil War" and in the eyes of some anti-Spiritualists, the primary Spiritualist responsible for it was Abraham Lincoln.

CHAPTER NINE

Abraham Lincoln's Pact with the Devil

It is difficult to overstate the impact that the Civil War, which lasted from 1861 to 1865, had on the United States. The bloody war resulted in loss of life on a greater scale for the United States than any other conflict to date. It drove a deep divide between the American people, a divide whose consequences for civil rights are still being dealt with to this day. In its wake, slavery—an institution which had deep roots in American history and the American mind—was dissolved.

While it is a relatively easy matter to demarcate which states were part of the "North" and "South" in the conflict, individual sympathies were far more diverse than geographic boundaries. For example, consider John Wilkes Booth, the assassin of then-President Abraham Lincoln in 1865. Booth was a native of Maryland, which was part of the North but a state of the Union in which slavery was licit. As a result, areas of Maryland had pockets of Confederate sympathy during the war. Nor was Booth's family composed uniformly of Confederate sympathizers: Some (like Booth) were deeply in favor of slavery while others rejected it wholeheartedly.

To transpose this onto our present concerns, it might be tempting to see the North as "Spiritualist" while the South was "anti-Spiritualist." This temptation could occur since Spiritualists were abolitionists and we associate the South as, well, not. The actuality is a bit more complex, and anti-Spiritualist sentiment coupled with pro-slavery stances were not geographically confined to North or South. Instead, individuals who occupied both the North and the South appear to have been interested in the influence Spiritualists might have had on the Civil War and eagerly sought a way to understand the "Great Rebellion" as the action of demons and the Devil through them.

"The Cause of the Great Rebellion"

In the collection of the Library of Congress, there is a pamphlet entitled "Pictorial History of the Cause of the Great Rebellion," which was published in 1865. The copyright is listed under the name of "Alfred Gale, Asbury, New Jersey," who may also be the creator of the piece. New Jersey, of course, would have been a Union state.

Titles of written works are important: They tell the reader what the piece is about, giving an initial clue as to the meaning they're supposed to divine from words and images. The term "Great Rebellion" here is a reference to what we now refer to as the Civil War, a term that was in common usage among Northern states to describe the conflict. Thus, the title leads us to assume that the pamphlet will tell the reader what factors the author believes led to the Civil War.

It is somewhat shocking then to find on the first page an explanation of Spiritualism. The text briefly sums up much of what you have read so far: the argument that Spiritualists are modern day Witches of Endor, that their séances amount to nothing more than summoning demons who masquerade as the dead, and that these practices are illicit according to the Bible.

The second page of the pamphlet then gets into the meat of the argument, that is, the promised explanation of the war's causes. First, a leering devil figure stands with his hand on the back of a white man and declares "Slavery is a national sin" under the date 1844. As the small print suggests, this was the date of the "Southern Schism" that divided the Methodist Episcopal Church: a split caused by tensions around the practice of slavery, which resulted in the formation of a new branch of the denomination, the Methodist Episcopal Church, South.

The cartoon's text adamantly declares: "Abolitionism divided the M.E. Church with its more than a million of membership, by introducing a new test of membership, although Mr. [John] Wesley [founder of the Methodist Episcopal Church], in 1784, when the Church was organized, did not make slave-holding a test. It never had been a test of membership from the Apostolic day until this time." In a second image, the "devil walks about like a roaring lion" (1 Peter 5:8), parroting the language of the failed Crittendon Compromise of 1860, which proposed that "Slavery may remain in the States where it now exists, but shall not be extended into the territories of the Union." The author clearly expresses, via these panels, frustration with the idea that the church should take a stand against slaveholding, as well as the prospect of the government limiting slavery in the new territories, painting both stances as demonic.

Text in small typeface goes on to condemn Lincoln for having been a "sectional President [elected] on a Sectional Platform," meaning that he won almost entirely from Northern support. The text then further identifies Lincoln's election as the act that "made the war." Finally, the last image features a hoofed Devil spearing a caricature of an African man with a trident. The text proclaims that the end result of the Civil War was "taxation without representation," a phrase that appears to suggest the overreach of the federal government unilaterally changing state laws and is an ominous invocation of the Revolutionary War.

The final image links the first two pages together. Here, we find two robed figures, seemingly representing spirits, in the process of smashing a miniature caricatured African man (likely representing abolition) into the head of a middle-class white man. While the second page only suggested that "Abolitionism" was to blame for the Civil War, the text on the third page goes one step further, condemning, in the lines of a lengthy poem that has not been reproduced here due to concerns about offensive language, the results of the war and blaming the war itself on the purportedly demonic spirits that some people claimed were Spiritualism's animating force. While anti-Spiritualism had previously blamed demons for filling Spiritualists heads with political issues, works like "Pictorial History" place the blame for the bloodiest conflict in American history squarely at the feet of Spiritualists.

Hell

The tract described is just one example of the liberal use of demonic imagery that was practiced during this time of upheaval—and not just in the years after the war. Works and images that make use of the Devil and his minions spread rapidly throughout both the North and South during the Civil War. For both parties, the Civil War was "Hell," plain and simple, and it would not be until the Vietnam War that another military event in American history would be painted as such.

Both during and after the Civil War, American engagement with the demonic rose to a fever pitch. Political cartoons from both sides of the political aisle branded members of the opposing party as demonic or accused them of consorting with demons; printers produced decorated envelopes that linked the seceded states with the Devil to use as stationary throughout the North. The phrase "Satan was the first secessionist" aptly summed up the North's perspective on secession. Southern white folks referred to their northern counterparts as "Black Republicans," invoking not only the idea of racial blackness but the blackness of demons as conceived by the popular mind.[1]

In *War Is All Hell: The Nature of Evil and the Civil War*, historians Edward J. Blum and John H. Matsui draw this conclusion about the perpetual presence of demonic imagery during the Civil War period:

> . . . some religious concepts were central, even pivotal to how Americans understood, experienced, and created the war. This appears obvious as we address questions like these: why was Lincoln's most famous speech from before the war, "A House Divided," based upon a biblical story involving devils; why did Americans produce, purchase, and mail envelopes that featured demons by the thousands throughout the war; why did the most memorable musical anthem from the war, Julia Ward Howe's "Battle Hym of the Republic," mention a serpent; why did a Civil War military leader come to the conclusion that war "is all hell"; why when Frederick Douglass waxed eloquent about the impact of black men's participation in the Union army did he borrow from the biblical book of Colossians to maintain that "there is no power on the earth or under the earth" that could deny their citizenship; and why did defeated white southern men fashion and then adorn themselves with elaborate horns and claim to be from hell as they terrorized African Americans after the war?[2]

Excellent questions all. And while it is beyond the scope of this work to attempt to answer them (and, in fact, Blum and Matsui have already expertly done so), I cite their work because the material in *War Is All Hell* reinforces one of the core messages that I hope is coming across in this book: Religion has long been, and remains, a powerful force in the political life of the United States, and many social, cultural, and political factors that you and I may be tempted to view as unfolding separately from religion are actually intimately bound up within it.

With that in mind, I won't attempt to address all the instances of demons and the demonic that were invoked during the Civil War. That attempt would take up an entire book, and Blum and Matsui already have written it! Instead, I'd like to address a topic that I believe doesn't get nearly enough attention, particularly as it relates to politics and spiritual warfare in America.

I want to talk about how Abraham Lincoln became, in many people's eyes, a "devil worshipper."

"Was Abraham Lincoln a Spiritualist?"

A surprising amount of ink has been spilled over the question of whether our sixteenth president was a Spiritualist, particularly in the half century following his death. From approximately 1890 to 1920, nine works were published that dealt to one extent or another with this topic. Of these nine, four directly asked the question in their title or offered an answer, as in the case of James Gordon's *Was Abraham Lincoln a Spiritualist?* and James Joseph Fitzgerrell's *Lincoln Was a Spiritualist.*

Even in later eras, the debate continued to receive attention. In 1941, American historian Jay Monaghan wrote an article entitled "Was Abraham Lincoln Really a Spiritualist?" for the *Journal of the Illinois State Historical Society.* (One can almost feel the desire to italicize the "really" coming off the page). Other authors have pecked at the edges of the topic, as in such works as *Free Spirits: Spiritualism, Republicanism, and Radicalism in the Civil War Era* (2016) by Mark A. Lause, a professor of American history, or have offered more direct answers, as did authors Joe Nickell ("Paranormal Lincoln") and Everett Emerson ("Harry Houdini Debunked Claims of Abraham Lincoln's Spiritualism") in the *Skeptical Inquirer*, a magazine published in the late twentieth and early twenty-first century by the Committee for Skeptical Inquiry.

As I suggested in the introduction, I can understand the impulse behind such writings. The desire to neatly package Lincoln into one camp of faith or another (or into the camp of skepticism) is a powerful motivator: He remains one of the most beloved presidents in American history. Yet, believing this possible once more assumes a "light switch" approach: that either Lincoln was a believer or he wasn't, and there is no gray area in between. While I am not a Lincoln scholar, it seems clear to me that the answer is significantly more complicated than that.

Let's consider first his spiritual upbringing. Lincoln's parents were Separate Baptists, a religious movement within the Baptist church that developed in New England during the Great Awakening and spread outward from there. The sect's name was derived from the verse 2 Corinthians 6:17—"Wherefore come out from among them, and be ye separate, saith the Lord" (KJV). Members of this group held emotive and tearful services that differentiated them, or separated them out, from other Baptist movements that held more formal services. The popular revivalist concept of being "born again" was strong in the movement, and the experience of ecstatic religious activities was not uncommon. For instance, the minutes of the Nolynn Association of Separate Baptists in the 1800s record an instance in which:

> A young man, who had been absorbed in prayer, began leaping, dancing and shouting, while to his left a young woman, as though inspired by the example she had witnessed, sprang forward, her hat falling to the ground, her hair tumbling down in graceful braids, her eyes fixed heavenward, her lips vocal with strange, unearthly song, her rapture overflowing until, grasping the hand of the young man, they both began singing at the top of their voices.[3]

The young man described was Thomas Lincoln, Abraham Lincoln's father, and the woman was Nancy Hanks, who would shortly become his stepmother.

I have long had the impression that there is a way in which human behavior follows a modified form of Newton's third law of motion, that is, whenever one person exerts force on another, the second person reacts with equal force. By this, I mean that if someone gently suggests something, the other is likely to either agree or disagree with them gently. If, on the other hand, someone attempts to persuade the other with overwhelming rhetorical force or aggressive argumentation, they're likely to either agree completely or reject everything the person has told them. In the case of the Lincolns and religion, Abraham seems to have done the latter with his parents.

After the younger Lincoln left his childhood home in early adulthood, he went through a period of significant skepticism from the 1830s to the 1850s. During this period, he largely stopped attending church.

According to an 1892 article in the *Chicago Herald*, the Lincoln of this period "was without faith in the Bible or its teachings. . . . [and] exhibited a powerful tendency to aggressive infidelity. . . . It must be accepted as final by every reasonable mind that in Religion Mr. Lincoln was a skeptic."[4]

But what does it mean to be a skeptic? As American historian Christopher Grasso argues in his 2018 book *Skepticism and American Faith: From the Revolution to the Civil War*, the qualities of faith and skepticism ebb and flow in both American life and American individuals. One might go so far as to venture that it is impossible to be either purely skeptical or purely faithful, as all people exist in a place that operates between the two. We are all constantly making choices about untested authority, and while it's possible to fully embrace or reject a religious proposition or figure after drawing reasonable conclusions based on the evidence, that does not mean that we don't at times accept untested claims simply because they appeal to us or to reject sound logical ideas because they offend our deeply held sensibilities.

In a humorous example of this dichotomy (and one that's somewhat reflective of what occurred with Lincoln), Grasso describes in his book's introduction an intellectual debate that occurred between Robert Dale Owen and Origen Bacheler, the former a skeptic and the latter a believer. Theirs was an argument that raged for ten months in 1831 on the pages of the *Free Enquirer*: Owen declared that he had been brought up in a strictly religious household but had shifted from believing due to his readings while Bacheler wrote that he had personally trod the skeptic's path and eventually came to believe that faith was superior. The introduction ends with Grasso quipping, "Owen . . . suggested that it was easy to enjoy life, seek truth, live virtuously, and work for a better world without supernatural props and promises of a blissful hereafter. It was, ultimately, not so easy even for Owen himself, who in later years became a Spiritualist."[5]

Much as it apparently was for Owen, the "relationship of doubting and believing was complicated for Lincoln."[6] On the one hand, he would ardently argue a philosophy known as the "Doctrine of Necessity"—a kind of naturalist predestination that said that events are predetermined and beyond individuals' power to control—with those who would listen. He avidly read works that professed skepticism of traditional Christian positions, such as Thomas Paine's *Age of Reason* (1794–1807), and many contemporaries remembered him as scoffing at Christian tenets and even mocking churchgoers. On the other, he resumed churchgoing with his wife Mary Todd after they married, wrote often on the topic of the Providence and the purpose of God during his presidency (including an unpublished manuscript found after his death entitled "Meditations on the Divine Will"[7]), and clearly knew and made use of the Bible to great effect in many of his speeches. Mary, who had known him through his "skeptical" period as well as his later "faithful" period, later remembered that he was "a religious man always, I think, but was not a technical Christian."[8] What then could he technically be called? I would argue that the word is "complex," much like all of us.

It is within this religious background and context that Lincoln attended at least five Spiritualist séances during his life. According to the accounts of others who attended these same sittings, he was neither unmoved nor consumed by the phenomena that he purportedly witnessed. Some of the statements he made could even be read as expressions of belief.

For instance, at a séance held on February 5, 1863, Lincoln and others sat on a piano in an unsuccessful attempt to prevent it from moving up and down. When told afterward by one of the other sitters that no one would believe what had occurred, Lincoln remarked "You should bring such person here, and when the piano seems to rise, have him slip his foot under the leg and be *convinced* (doubtless) by the weight of *evidence* resting upon his *understanding*."[9] At other sittings, he appeared dubious at best. When the medium at one of these séances needed to leave to tend to her ill father, she was permitted to speak to Lincoln before leaving. Here is how he responded when she told him the reason for her departure.

> Looking at me with a quizzical smile, he said, "But cannot our friends from the upper country tell you whether his illness is likely to prove fatal or not?" I replied that I had already consulted with our friends, and they had assured me that his treatment was wrong, and that my presence was needed to effect a cure. Turning to my friend, he said laughingly, "I didn't catch her, did I?"[10]

Clearly, Abraham Lincoln held complex religious beliefs, beliefs that defied (and defy) easy reduction and categorization. The question of whether he was a Spiritualist or not, cannot capture this complexity.

Conclaves of Darkness

However, if critics were to successfully turn him into a symbol for the causes of the Civil War and the end of slavery they would need to reduce him to something less ambiguous.

The first author to do so was the anonymous "Citizen of Ohio," cited at the end of the previous chapter. The unnamed citizen begins their critique by laying out what exactly they see as being "interior" about the causes of the Civil War. By interior causes, the author means those that are "underlying nature, are influences which operate on the human mind, and which at times upheave society, as internal fires upheave the crusted earth. These influences are indiscriminately called spiritual, supernatural, or INTERIOR."[11]

In the author's mind, it was just such an interior cause that had unfortunately "inoculated the northern mind with its madness." Referencing the reported evidence of floating furniture and spirit rappings, he claims that "investigations have proved, beyond a doubt, a reality, which no imposture can disturb. The acting agents were spiritual. On this point there is no room for disputation. But it is in regard to kind and character that spiritualists have been deceived. They, or rather a majority of them, have drank from a poisoned fountain."[12]

Up to this point, his argument is more or less the same one we have seen anti-Spiritualists make about their opponents. However, the author then takes his assertions one step further, going on to state that he knows "persons who profess to understand the secret conditions of things at Washington."[13] These individuals reportedly claim that Lincoln is a whole-hearted Spiritualist, that he has mediums constantly surrounding him, and the spirits conjured by these mediums are advising Lincoln in all matters, including the war! To the author of *Interior Causes*, Lincoln is a modern-day Saul who has a medium advising him just "as the witch of Endor served the Hebrew king."[14]

This explanation of spiritual delusion is the only one that is reasonable to the author. After all, "slavery," he claims, "as it exists in the United States, instead of being sinful, is a highly proper and humane institution."[15] He further argues that it is only those who have been demonized and Lincoln in his "demented condition"[16] that are unable to see it as good. Instead, he writes, as this demonic influence spreads among people, "the conclaves of darkness . . . rejoiced; for deception had triumphed over truth; they had forced war upon the country, and in its inauguration had secured the vantage ground of having compelled the south to fire the first gun."[17]

And here we get an inkling of something a bit new developing. Prior to this point in time, anti-Spiritualists had claimed that Spiritualists were demonically afflicted, that their messages were emerging from the damned rather than the dead, and that they themselves were poisonous to the health and salvation of the nation. But these claims still presented the Spiritualists themselves as unknowing pawns. Though they were judged to be harming the nation, this result was despite the fact that they were doing what they thought was right.

Now, we see the "conclaves of darkness" painted as shifty, secretly malignant. We read that Lincoln's selection as a candidate was not just "spiritually directed" by demons, but that Spiritualists themselves wanted "to see their policy made permanent in the nation; and they, as a consequence, made the nation's principal rulers."[18] This promise supposedly caused Spiritualists to intentionally deceive others as to their nature and to form secret societies for the purpose of "control[ling] the whole world."[19] While the Citizen seems to balk at accusing Lincoln outright of being involved in this malicious plot, instead simply suggesting he has succumbed to madness, the first suggestion of a shadowy government conspiracy seems to be rearing its ugly head.

The Dark Horse(man of the Apocalypse)

The Ohio citizen's book *Interior Causes* was not an isolated production. The text itself cites several contemporary newspaper articles that made similar claims and suggests that those weren't the only ones making such charges. At the time of its publication, the idea of a Spiritualist conspiracy seemed already to have captured the imagination of more than just this one anonymous author.

The work of the author Fayette Hall around the turn of the century suggests that decades after *Interior Causes*, the conspiracy theory about Lincoln and Spiritualism remained alive and well and was still selling books. Still, Hall's belief in Lincoln's devilish alliance seems genuine; in any case, he attempted diligently to establish it. Hall suggests that it was his research in Spiritualism that brought him to Washington, DC.[20] He was one of the few authors who wrote about Lincoln's alleged

Spiritualism who also had interacted directly with the President. Not only did Hall interview both the mediums who worked with Lincoln, he also interviewed Lincoln himself. After the war, Hall made the following claim in a descriptively and lengthily titled work that was published in 1890—*The Secret and Political History of the War of the Rebellion: The Causes Leading Thereto, and the Effects, Showing How Abraham Lincoln Came to Be President of the United States, Exposing the Secret Working and Conspiring of Those in Power, and the Motive and Purpose of Prolonging the War for Four Years*!—a claim that must seem at significant odds with the Abraham Lincoln that historical memory has given most Americans:

> It is written regardless of fear or favor; it is written, not in a spirit of malice or vindictiveness, but in the cause of truth, justice and vindication. The Lincoln and Republican administration showed no mercy, and spared none, and history will not spare them, but will differ from them in this respect; they falsified, vilified and slandered, while history always adheres strictly to the truth.[21]

From our twenty-first century perspective, which draws on widespread public opinion that Lincoln was one of the best presidents, if not the best president, our country has had, you and I might be tempted to view Hall's writings as an attempt to undermine Lincoln's legacy or merely to enrich himself through libelous claims. Instead, I prefer to view it as a reminder that reasonable people can consider the same people and activities and come to very different conclusions about motivations and results.

Whatever his motivations, Hall's conclusion is simple: Abraham Lincoln had a lust for power, and it was through consorting with Spiritualists that he eventually became the "dark horse" nominee of 1860. Hall goes on to claim the following:

> He consulted them [Spiritualists] continually, and they told him that the spirit of Attila, King of the Huns, was his controlling spirit, that Attila would keep him at the head of the government as long as he lived, that the government was to be changed to suit the time and occasion, and that he was to

> be established for life as Dictator. Abraham Lincoln was fool enough to think that it was to be so, and was conspiring to carry out the instructions of Attila when Wilkes Booth ended his grand scheme.[22]

Quite a claim! Hall then goes on to lay out a case in which he alleged that Lincoln made use of the Republican controlled congress to exercise authority more akin to a dictator than a president, upended the economic system of the nation, and illegally started the Civil War, in addition to a host of other black marks he attributes to Lincoln's record.

Hall revisits these issues a dozen years later, and in a revised edition of *The Secret Political History of the War of the Rebellion*, titled *The Copperhead*.[23] It may be that this title gives us a window into Fayette Hall's motivations: "Copperheads" was a term in use during the Civil War to denote Democrats who were against the war and wished to settle for peace. *The Copperhead* repeats many of the same claims that *Secret History* made. Namely, he reiterates that "spiritualism was one of the chief factors in the management of our national affairs during the reign of Abraham Lincoln" and that the spirits contacted by them "were devilish, for no honorable spirits would require the President to violate his oath and obligations, and perjure himself to obey and carry out their orders by employing the army and the sword."[24]

Throughout both editions, Hall invokes the idea of secret conspiracies working in tandem with Lincoln. These clandestine powers are alluded to throughout both works in near identical language. From *The Copperhead*:

> The better and more honest portion of the republican party [was] in opposition to Abraham Lincoln, and they would gladly have exchanged him for a *better horse* . . . But Lincoln had other resources. He wielded a power and manipulated a machinery such as no ruler of modern times had known. He held the army with its immense power, he held many thousands of civil appointments with all their vast influence, he held the Treasury with its billions of wealth, he held a secret order of armed conspirators ready to do his bidding, and who were sworn to support and sustain him at all hazards, he gagged the press and manipulated the votes of the army to suit his

> purpose. And even after all that the election was to be but a farce. If by any possible chance he failed to secure the vote, they were to hold the power by force, and after his re-establishment the government was to be changed to suit the occasion, and Abraham Lincoln was to be elevated to regal power and a dictatorship for life, as Attila, through the mediums, had assured him was to be his destiny. And at the Inaugural Ball of 1865, a throne with a crown suspended over it was built up of flowers by those in the secret, as symbolical of what Abraham Lincoln was to receive.[25]

It appears that here Hall may have invented the idea of what we today call the "Deep State," a modern term that since the 2016 election has been used by some conservatives to refer to supposed secret conspiratorial elements of the US government. These secret groups are sometimes described in a demonic fashion as well, particularly by far-right groups such as QAnon (which we'll talk about at the end of part 4, in The Modern Takeaway: Satanic Panic Redux). Hall seems to be deploying a similar concept a full century or so before the term "Deep State" comes into use by conservatives and placing Abraham Lincoln at its head. A markedly different view of "Honest Abe" than the one we are taught in history class.

Remembering Lincoln

I don't think it is presumptuous to suggest that Lincoln remains one of the most beloved and respected presidents in the history of the United States. However, in the time in which he lived and for some time after his death, authors such as the Citizen from Ohio, Fayette Hall, and Alfred Gale told another story, one that did not paint Lincoln as the moral compass of the country or a leader working to preserve the union amid violent secession but rather as a figure consumed by a lust for power. In this worldview, secret conspiracies swirled instead around the city of Washington, and the Civil War was largely guided by the hand of the Devil. This is certainly a different vision of Lincoln and the Civil War than the one most of us know.

While it may be that as a country we have largely forgotten this version of Lincoln, with his ties to a demonized spiritual movement, there is another symbol of Spiritualism that would persist in our country's collective memory and experience, one that would become an emblem of the supposed dangers of communicating with the dead. Still to this day, many parents fear that their children might use it to conjure demons. Because out of all the trappings of Spiritualism, there is none that is more demonized than the one that has followed us into the modern day: the Ouija board.

CHAPTER TEN

The New Black Magic

IN 1868, THE AMERICAN writer and journalist Kate Field published a short book entitled *Planchette's Diary*. Merely a French word for a *small plank or board* prior to the days of Spiritualism, in *Diary* "Planchette" referred to "a little board of varnished wood, fashioned in the shape of a heart, seven inches long and five inches wide, that formed a sort of table by means of two pentagraph wheels at the broad end of the heart, and a lead-pencil inserted in a socket, one inch and a-quarter from the point of the heart."[1]

Although in the book Planchette is an object and not a person, the friend who reportedly introduces Field to the board refers to Planchette as a "lady." Field reveals that when hands are placed upon Planchette, "she" writes wildly about things that could not be known by the controller, sometimes while swearing like a sailor, to the shock of the audience. The book is structured as a kind of dialogue between Field and Planchette in which Field is credited not as author but as editor.

Field was not alone in her experience of experimenting with a planchette: Around the turn of the century, hundreds, if not thousands, of individuals engaged in similar experimentation. On March 28, 1886, the *New York Daily Tribune* published an article entitled "The New 'Planchette,'" in which an unnamed man describes to the reporter the necessities for using the then-new divining tool:

> The first requisite is the operating board. It may be rectangular, about 18 × 20 inches. It is inscribed like this: The 'yes' and the 'no' are to start and stop the conversation. The 'good-evening' and 'good-night' are for courtesy. Now a little table three or four inches high is prepared with four legs. Any one can make the whole apparatus in fifteen minutes with a jack-knife and a marking brush. You take the board in your lap, another person sitting down with you. You each grasp the little table with the thumb and forefinger at each corner next to you.

The man then proceeds to discuss how the new planchette (the "little table" mentioned above) is moved across the larger board beneath it to indicate messages from the spirits. A much more efficient method of communication than the pencil-based Planchette described in Field's work.

It was not until 1890, however, that Elijah Bond, a lawyer from Maryland, would submit the patent for the version of this new tool that we recognize today: the "Ouija board." Shortly thereafter, sales of the new device exploded, and by the end of the 1920s millions of people were using it.

As one might expect, the invention of the Ouija board created a problem for anti-Spiritualists. Before the advent of the Board, mediums were required to contact the spirits. While it doesn't appear that there were any significant shortages of individuals who were able to fill the role, that requirement still meant that the spread of the demonic influence was stymied by limited access to these supposedly ghostly communications. After all, most Spiritualists did not perform for free, so one would either need to host a sitting or purchase a ticket to one of the popular shows to be exposed to these messages.

Now, however, an advertisement in *The Brooklyn Daily Times* promised that the board "surpasses in its results second sight, mind reading, or clairvoyance" and that it would produce an "intelligent answer to any question." While the $1.50 price was a not-insignificant sum to charge for such a device (~$50 in today's market), consider that many people in the twenty-first century pay this much or more for popular board games which offer very little in the way of mysterious answers from beyond the grave!

The result at that time: Millions of prospective Witches of Endor were now working their black magic in homes across America.

The Truth About the Ouija Board

While there are several authors who, before Spiritualism's decline in the 1930s, off-handedly discussed the dangers of the Ouija board (or sometimes dedicated an entire chapter to it) in their writing, there is only one that I know of who devoted an entire book to the device during that time: J. Godfrey Raupert.

Raupert had been born in Northern Germany in 1859, and as a young man attended the University of Leipzig. At 19, a growing interest in journalism sent him to London where he could be nearer to the British Library. There, he attended an Anglican church and was eventually persuaded to take orders in 1887. Sometime later, he developed an interest in Spiritualism and joined the Society for Psychical Research in the United Kingdom; this caused him to have opportunity to attend several séances.

Raupert's son Gregory later reported that at many of these séances Godfrey received requests for prayers from individuals whom he earnestly believed had passed on. Due to this, "he was led to believe in the extreme likelihood of a Purgatory."[2] Interestingly, this led Godfrey Raupert to convert to Roman Catholicism, a transition that then caused him to reevaluate his contacts with what he'd once believed were the dead but that he came to see as disguised contacts with demons. He subsequently became a critic of Spiritualism and spent the remainder of his life lecturing and writing on the subject, producing several volumes about the topic that argued that the entities people encountered in séances were really "Fallen Spirits or Demons cleverly impersonating the Dead."[3]

In his 1919 book *The New Black Magic and the Truth About the Ouija-Board*, J. Godfrey Raupert lays down what he perceives as the new threat that the Ouija board brings to the table (pun-intended). Yet, as much as the Ouija board itself was then new, the threat that it presented was rather old. Despite the presence of the divining tool's name in the book's title, Raupert's book actually contains only one chapter that directly addresses the use of the Ouija board; the remainder is a synthesis that suggests that this new invention is just one more manifestation of the perils of Spiritualism. For instance, Raupert's first mention of the Ouija board is in a quoted statement by an unnamed doctor in a psychiatric asylum who claimed that the item "had brought about a state of dementia" in patients. In the very next paragraph, Raupert writes of his own experience:

> In all the cases which have come under my observation, the automatic process had proved a destructive one, the victim remaining subject to a recurrence of the invasion on the slightest provocation, and incessantly battling with the

> inclination to write. Where this impulse is systematically yielded to, as in the case of public automatic or inspirational mediumship, the invading spirit ultimately paralyzes the normal thinking powers, dominates the will and the sensory organism, until the mental and moral powers of the subject decay and he becomes an imbecile.[4]

Here we see all the standard accusations of anti-Spiritualist fare: the subjugation of the will, the gradual physical and mental decay, and moral degeneracy.

It is in his ninth chapter that Raupert develops some interesting concepts. He begins with his claim that there are two camps of people who are interested in the phenomenon of the Ouija board. The first is motivated by curiosity and anticipates that there is some kind of natural explanation for the phenomenon that is lodged within the unconscious mind. The second camp, which Raupert states is populated by more advanced and probing investigators, maintain that there must be some kind of intelligence behind the productions of the Board.

Both camps are correct, Raupert argues. Regarding the position of the first, he notes that the mind is indeed much more complex than previously believed and "a very great part of its operations is what is termed subconscious, lying below the threshold of the ordinary conscious working mind."[5] Raupert further suggests that the subconscious functions as a kind of storehouse for all of the experiences that anyone has ever had over the course of their life. These memories lie beneath the surface of the conscious recollection, just waiting to be plucked from obscurity for inspection. He writes, "There is, strictly speaking, nothing, from our childhood upwards, no impression received, no word heard or uttered, no picture looked at, no occurrence or incident, no feeling or emotion, of which a record is not preserved in the secret recesses of the subconscious mind, however unable the normal working mind may be to recall them."[6] As a result, according to Raupert, the mind is able to make correlations that might otherwise seem impossible, revealing information via the Board that only appears to emerge from a supernatural source.

But this explanation, in Raupert's view, does not preclude the additional presence of supernatural intervention. He argues that the second camp is also correct, in that accessing the unconscious mind requires the increasing passivity that Spiritualists extol and anti-Spiritualists demonize. Once an appropriate degree of passivity is reached, Raupert argues, "it is possible for an external intelligence or spirit to invade the mind and to gain access to the contents of this well-furnished subconscious storehouse."[7]

Just as with the practice of the seemingly more overtly supernatural Spiritualism, he says, practice with the Board leads to the decay of the mind and body. Once more, this is due to neurological stress caused by the interaction with the demons:

> Persons habitually and systematically using the ouija or planchette board, or similar automatic devices for obtaining spirit messages, experience, after a time, a peculiar condition of lassitude and exhaustion—in many instances accompanied by severe pain at the top of the spine and gradually spreading over the entire brain. This state of prostration is due to the now well-established fact that, in order to obtain the movements of the board, vital or nerve energy is withdrawn from the organism of the experimenter, often out of all proportion to the physical health and constitution.[8]

Here we see that we have again reached the same terrible end. Psychiatric institutionalization and death are the inevitable results of both "old" Spiritualist practices and the "new" practice of the Ouija board.

The End of Spiritualism

Raupert's book *The New Black Magic* was published in 1919, and Spiritualism's popularity peaked in the 1920s. But after the roaring '20s, interest in speaking with the dead began to wane. This decline was due to a variety of different factors including efforts by such famous figures as Harry Houdini to debunk the phenomenon, a general proliferation of other new forms of entertainment (such as film), and a significant extension of the average lifespan (due to factors like medical advances, public health programs and regulations, and improved living standards), which somewhat diminished the urgency of the need for such communication.

While Spiritualism itself would go into decline, however, the demonic brush with which anti-Spiritualists painted it and related tools would not. There is a high likelihood that you have seen a film that features the Ouija board conjuring demonic entities. *The Uninvited* (1944); *13 Ghosts* (1960); *The Exorcist* (1973); *Amityville 3-D* (1983); and *The Witchboard* and *Ouija* films are just a few examples. You might also be familiar with the terrifying notion that people who hold séances or use talking boards of various kinds risk their lives and souls through discourse with demons. Even some objects that most of us wouldn't immediately recognize as a talking board are almost immediately branded demonic, as in the case of the viral Charlie Charlie Challenge of 2015, in which individuals (usually teenagers) played a divination game using two pencils and a piece of paper to communicate with a supposed spirit named Charlie.

While we as a nation might have collectively forgotten their source, these old ideas about speaking with spirits, and the demonic nature of such "spirits," have stuck with us long after the Spiritualists and the anti-Spiritualists who once advanced them passed away. And a scant few decades after Spiritualism's decline, they would come roaring back into the public imagination, carrying the same types of religious and political narratives with them.

The Modern Takeaway

Gender and Conspiracy

There remain in the modern public American imagination very visible and identifiable elements of our country's anti-Spiritualist legacy. The Witch of Endor still rears her head on Christian websites that purport to discuss the dangers of modern day "occultism," a nebulous term that can be used to designate anything from paganism to Pokémon. And although Spiritualism has already had its heyday, the New Age, influenced by ideas in Spiritualism and the groups that emerged alongside of it, would again terrify conservative Christian pundits in the United States starting in the 1960s, an experience that (as we shall see) continues to this day. The Ouija board continues to be an evergreen boogeyman of the United States, with rebellious teenage operators of the board perennially attempting the practice at sleepovers and horror films consistently showing us the grisly results of this mistaken bravado.

While all of this is fascinating, it is important that we pay attention not just to these historical developments but also to the issues that percolated underneath the critiques that anti-Spiritualists levied. The fact is that many of the issues they raised remain the subject of conservative Christian dialogue to this day. In particular, two related issues remain near daily points of discussion by these groups: (1) gender and women's roles and (2) new ideas of demonic conspiracies.

Let's start with the ideas of gender roles that are at the heart of the anti-Spiritualist critique of the Free Love movement and suffragism. Now, we're about to launch into some touchy subjects here, so it will be useful to be clear about what we mean by this terminology. When I use the term *gender role* in this context, I'm not referring to a particular genome configuration or to the anatomical arrangement of a person's reproductive organs. Those traits are all effectively invisible: none of us can see people's DNA and it would be gauche (and would make for a very awkward social interaction) to casually request to see someone's genitals as a way to determine their gender.

Instead, we look for visible markers to clue us in to how another person may be identified. For instance, long hair, flowing garments, and a willingness to cry are all factors that have at times been read as indicators of a person's gender (though what gender is presumed to be expressed by these three traits has also varied across different cultures). People then use these identifying characteristics to place others into different groups that come with culturally developed ideas of shared behavior. Those culturally developed ideas of behavior are what I mean by gender roles.

Let's move to a familiar, concrete example. Let's imagine you're walking down the street. You see on the sidewalk across from you someone wearing a crop top who appears to be gossiping with their friends. They have full hips and breasts, wear lipstick, and walk with a gentle sway to their stride. Due to a variety of different historical and cultural factors, people in the United States historically (though, no longer entirely today, thanks largely to the advocacy of nonbinary, transgender, and gender-diverse individuals and support networks) have recognized two gender categories: male and female. If you were asked to put the individual I just described into one of these two groups, which one would you guess they most likely belonged to?

The likelihood is that you said *female* for a variety of reasons. First, there are some traits, such as fully developed breasts or hips, that you probably have been taught to physically associate with being a woman; that is, with being female. Second, there might be indications that the person *wants* to be identified as a woman: wearing lipstick and crop tops are behaviors that are, in the United States, most commonly aligned with the category *woman* and not *man*. Finally, there is the language I chose, by which you might realize I was attempting to predispose you to choose the category *woman* in the first place; while individuals who fit into both categories might talk animatedly with their friends, many individuals who identify as male would be offended if someone suggested they were "gossiping." In fact, the term *gossip* originally had a specifically gendered meaning in the Middle Ages: It referred to a group of women who gathered around a pregnant woman to aid in her birth.

The point of this lengthy explanation is that there are a variety of different ways by which people can craft and perform gender roles (both individually and as a group), and there is actually quite a bit of power that comes with being able to "critique" and "correct" other people's performances of gender. For instance, think about a time in your life when your gender role was questioned: when you were told you weren't behaving correctly as a boy or a girl, or as a man or a woman. Perhaps you were informed that something you did (or didn't do) meant that you weren't "man enough," or maybe you were acting unlike other girls in a way that labeled you a "tomboy." You probably had an extreme reaction to the message you received: either pride (if you didn't feel the need to conform to the role someone was trying to place on you) or shame (which led to a perceived need to correct your behavior).

In fact, our understanding of gender roles is often so deeply ingrained that these definitions of gender can feel "natural" to us or even "God-given." However, once we accept this idea of gender as being God-prescribed, then those who "fail" to perform their supposedly God-given gender role are often interpreted as demonic. As we saw in these chapters, anti-Spiritualists took sharp aim at women who wanted to escape from abusive relationships and have their own political voice. When we look at this criticism through the lens of power dynamics, the reason becomes clear: These critics wanted women to remain powerless in their relationships and politics. In their eyes, women "belonged" in the home and not the political arena, women were "supposed" to be submissive to their husbands. That was God's design. In their eyes, any other behavior had to be induced by demons.

But this conclusion is not just some outdated way of thinking that's since been left behind in the past. At this present moment in the United States, the reinforcement of traditional gender roles is just as important to conservative Christians as it was in the time of the anti-Spiritualists. In fact, an enormous industry has sprung up in conservative Christianity around the business of telling people how to be "real men" or "real women." Religious leaders like controversial evangelical pastor Mark Driscoll have attracted hundreds of thousands of followers on social media platforms like X and YouTube, where they post messages designed to instruct their listeners on how to be "real" men and women. This teaching includes how their followers should behave in their marriages (including their sexual relationships), as parents, and even as voters. (Driscoll opined on October 31, 2024, on X: "I am planting my flag on this: There is no argument that can be made for a Christian to support a Harris/Walz administration.")

Camps and groups proliferate that also profess to teach men and women how they are "meant" to behave as "Christian men" and

"Christian women" such as "Man Camp" or the "School of Biblical Womanhood."[1] Spiritual-political figures toe the same line: Paula White, the current leader of the White House Faith Office, stated in a video posted by the right-wing media network *Real America's Voice* that "God has an order. . . . The head of my household is my husband, Jonathan Cain. Period. . . . It's not hard to submit."[2] It's hard to miss the hint of irony here: A woman who it consistently in the spotlight and wields substantial political power claiming that she has "submitted" to her husband.

Not surprisingly, a whole host of demons have been cited as an explanation for why people might act outside of these God-given roles. We'll be discussing these entities, including Moloch and the Jezebel Spirit, in the fourth section of the book. Since we're already discussing gender roles, though, it's worth noting here that, since modern day conservative Christians often also interpret the Bible as only advocating heterosexuality and a two-gender schema for the world, they often claim that demonic intercession has influenced the theology of those groups that support individuals who identify as LGBTQ+. Given all we've learned, it's hard to shake the feeling that much of this kind of demonic thinking about gender, including nineteenth-century ideas about how women were "supposed" to behave, started with the anti-Spiritualist belief that support of women's rights and the pursuit of women's ability to free themselves from destructive marriages was the result of demonic deception.

While the origins of many controversies about gender in the current political landscape likely have their seeds in the anti-Spiritualist movement, the authors of these claims also created the architecture that allowed other new ideas of demonic conspiracy to develop. The anti-Spiritualists understood demons to be covert actors, creatures that could infiltrate séance circles and partially possess mediums. Once this demonic influence had affected a critical mass of voters, they could use these individuals to make sweeping political changes (such as pushing for abolition) or install individuals that anti-Spiritualists saw as illicit political figures (as Fayette Hall saw in Lincoln).

To make clear what this shift looked like, let us consider the difference between the European idea of witches (another demonic conspiracy) and Spiritualists as seen by their opponents. While European witches were understood by their accusers to be *deliberately* choosing their path to damnation, in the eyes of the anti-Spiritualists, Spiritualists could *accidentally* tread the same path. Witches reportedly made love to the Devil in the form of a giant, flying, black goat (pretty hard to mistake that for anything else but intentional engagement with the demonic!). Yet Spiritualists might simply want to hear from a spouse or child who had died an early death. And perhaps the most damaging difference of all in terms of long-term effects on US politics: Witches only wreaked local havoc, whereas Spiritualists were understood to have spread a diabolical political agenda that would plunge the country into its fiercest conflict ever, pitting brother against brother until American soil ran red with American blood.

In this understanding of the interaction between the spiritual and physical worlds, curiosity is not a positive quality but a sin. One by which covert demons can lead the sinner down a dangerous path without them ever knowing that anything is wrong. The demons might disguise themselves as the person's deceased parent or child, a new progressive political idea, or a popular board game.

The only protection a person has in the face of these threats is to cleave tightly to what authoritative teachers tell them the Bible is saying. They must do what the teachers tell them, believe as these leaders believe, and interpret the Bible as they interpret it. If one strays from outside of these protective boundaries, their very soul would come under threat from demonic agendas. And those demons were not only coming after people's individual soul; they were coming after the souls of our country and the world at large. These political demons, critics argued, were electing their own candidates into the White House and plunging the world into chaos.

Reading all this, you might get an eerie sense that this environment felt much like the one we live in today. If so, you'd be right.

And it would only get worse.

Intermission

The Shape of Things to Come

AT THIS POINT in our examination of how the spiritual and the political came together in the United States, we have established the two primary building blocks that would lay the foundation for ideas of the demonic that are currently popular in the United States: (1) the American desire to see the Apocalypse around every corner (part 2) and (2) the anti-Spiritualist paradigm that developed in the nineteenth century (part 3). In our final two parts (particularly the last), we'll discover how the looming possibility of the Antichrist and the Apocalypse once again become a significant part of imagining the demonic. Here again, the idea that people could accidentally, frequently, and copiously invite demons into themselves without knowing it becomes an increasingly complex and influential factor in American politics and religion.

Before we get into the nitty-gritty of how that occurred, though, there are two general theological developments in the United States that are important for us to cover. Before I describe them, I want to acknowledge that from the 1950s to today, the marketplace of ideas in this country has become increasingly saturated and the origins of ideas and the influences upon them more difficult to untangle. Consider, for example, how many more books were published in the twentieth century than in the nineteenth (and in the twenty-first than in the twentieth), particularly as small presses (alternatives to large commercial publishers) and self-publishing have become established and then taken off. Add to that the impact that social media and video platforms like YouTube have had upon the dissemination of information, and you begin to get an idea of how many sources any one person might have access to. Given the scope of available information, it simply isn't possible to cover the following subjects at length in a work as short as this one. With that in mind, I've attempted here to balance accuracy and concision as much as possible, two standards that I recognize can at times be at odds with one another.

Dispensationalism

The first major development related to apocalyptic thought in the twentieth-century United States that we're going to look at is the spread of a theoretical framework known as dispensationalism. Developed in the early nineteenth century by John Nelson Darby, a Nonconformist Christian reverend, dispensationalism was a popular interpretation of the biblical end times that wove Revelation together with readings from the books of Daniel and Isaiah. Though the concept of dispensationalism was established in the 1800s, it did not gain wide acceptance in the United States until after the publication of the Scofield Study Bible in 1909. While it is a complex theological position that cannot be explored fully here, I want to point out a few aspects of dispensationalism that distinguish it significantly from other ideas about the Apocalypse that have been taught in the history of Christianity.

First, dispensationalism teaches that there is a point in the apocalyptic timeline called "the rapture." The rapture is an unidentified point in the future in which "the Church" (a somewhat nebulous term that often refers to true Christian believers) will be swept up bodily into the heavens. Some dispensationalists believe that this event will either save those who already believe in Christ from the "tribulation," a time in which the Antichrist and his allies will take over the world and wreak the havoc believed to be foretold in Revelation; others believe that the faithful will be forced to experience some of this tribulation as well and will only be raptured sometime during the tribulation period. According to some interpretations of prophecy, those who remain behind will have an opportunity to repent before they are condemned to Hell for eternity.

Second, dispensationalists believe that the time of the tribulation represents something of a valley in the timeline of history. That is, if we think of history as having high points and low points—times of humanity's greatest triumphs and greatest adversities—tribulation would be the absolute lowest point. Thus, while the exact time and date of the rapture is not specified in the Bible, dispensationalists looking to identify its beginning often look for signs that we are heading toward the lowest point in human history.[1] In this understanding, the rapture will not occur until the world has reached this lowest point. The development of this aspect of dispensationalism likely had something to do with the growth of rapture theology after the Civil War. For many Americans at that time, it was no longer possible to believe in America as the millennial land of saints now that it had nearly been divided in two. If you've heard some variation of the phrase "things have to get worse before they get better," then you've encountered a dispensationalist idea.

Third, dispensationalism is peculiarly beloved by Americans. While we as modern Americans have lived with it for long enough to generally accept it to be a long-held theological position, in truth this way of understanding the biblical text is quite young and until recently was largely unknown outside of the English-speaking world. Yet despite this newness, dispensationalism has exerted a considerable influence over evangelical theology from its formulation into the present day.

Demonic Gateways

As we saw in part 2, anti-Spiritualists came to see Spiritualist practices as gateways through which demons could enter the human body without the person knowing it. In this way, a person's participation in séances, mediumship, and automatic writing (just to name a few Spiritualist rituals) invited demonic possession and demonic manipulation.

As Spiritualism began to wane as a practice, however, conservative Christian authors began to warn about other gateways that demons could use to invade the human body. While in the contemporary world there are a bewildering array of entry points that demons are imagined to be able to use to manipulate people, at that time such newly imagined gateways tended to revolve around three main issues: alternative religious practices, sexual impurity, and compulsive behaviors.

In some ways, a focus on alternative religious practices may be seen as a natural outgrowth of what came before. Just as the original anti-Spiritualists focused on Spiritualism being supposedly demonic, the new anti-Spiritualists of the late twentieth century would concentrate their ire on Spiritualism's intellectual child: the New Age Movement. Concurrently, as that movement was on the rise, Americans (and often, the same Americans who were engaged with New Age teachings) increasingly were developing interest in other world religions such as Hinduism, Buddhism, and Taoism.

Many conservative Christians felt threatened not just by these religions but also by groups that are also Christian but that they considered too different from their own denominational practices to be "really" Christian (e.g., Mormonism, Jehovah's Witnesses, Christian Scientists, etc.). Many Americans also developed a new interest in old magical practice through the New Age movement, through new religious movements like Wicca and Neopaganism (a reinterpretation of ancient pagan traditions and practices). That interest led conservative Christians of the twentieth and twenty-first centuries to brand most practices that looked magical in nature from the outside with the vague and menacing term "the occult."

Separately, sexual impurity became a kind of umbrella term used to identify a variety of different sex roles or practices that conservative Christians considered threatening to traditional understandings of sex and gender roles. These included many that one might expect: adultery, incest, and homosexuality, for instance. However, this area of concern has at times also extended to ideas about how men and women are supposed to behave. One example of this is the idea of the "Jezebel Spirit," a term used, with increasing frequency and acceptance in conservative Christian communities in the United States, to describe women who fail to behave in a sexually traditional manner. The use of pornography and even the way people fantasize sexually or perform sex in marriage are also areas that can fall under this category of sexual impurity.

Finally, those who believe that demons can gain access to humans through gateways also see compulsive behaviors as possible points of entry. In this area of critique, we tend to see notions of addiction (such as drugs and alcohol) taking center stage, but some authors include caffeine and nicotine, or various eating disorders, within this grouping as well.

Two Parts of One Whole

As you'll see in the next two parts of this book, the following forces are far more connected than were the apocalyptic thinking of the Revolutionary War and the anti-Spiritualist influence of the nineteenth century. I have divided the two parts that follow not because they are entirely independent movements, but because it will be easier to understand their impact by looking at them separately. In truth, however, the Satanic Panic of the 1980s and '90s (part 4) and the rise of the NAR (part 5) are both far more connected to one another, and to the election of Donald Trump, than not.

Part IV

The New American Apocalypse

The Twentieth Century

CHAPTER ELEVEN

Merrill Unger

The First Horseman of the New American Apocalypse

AS SPIRITUALISM BEGAN to wane as a movement, it became increasingly difficult for conservative Christians to reinforce belief in the demonic. While anti-Spiritualist sentiment was still booming among some conservative Christian groups, manifesting ghosts, séances, and political pronouncements from Spiritualists were no longer around for anti-Spiritualists to brand as demonic. With no seemingly supernatural evidence left to point to, it became harder for those who believed in demons to galvanize those who did not: at best in a post-Spiritualist America, believing in demons seemed archaic and useless; at worst, it looked ridiculous and foolish.

How then did belief in demons ultimately defeat the historical gravity that threatened to drag it down? The answer is complex. But while ultimately there were many figures that contributed to this diabolical resurrection, four in particular had an outsized effect upon how Americans would perceive demonic influence in the mid-twentieth century.

By combining the anti-Spiritualist and apocalyptic trends that had already unfolded within American thought, these four Christian authors of the mid-twentieth century—in some cases, dependent on each other's work; in others, thinking independently—forged a new way that people could think about demons: as subtle personal and political tempters who were preparing the world for the End of Days. In a few short decades, their influence would help to reenergize belief in demons as the United States once more entered a politically divisive time. The first of these figures—or, the horsemen of the new American Apocalypse, as I like to call them, since they were all to varying degrees developing an idea of America's and Americans' role in the Apocalypse—was a Bible scholar and theologian named Merrill Unger.

Merrill Unger

A Life in Interesting Times

Imagine you were born in the early 1900s, like Unger (1909–1980). In just a few short decades, you would have seen the fate of the world spin out from a state of relative peace and prosperity into what must have seemed like a living hell on earth. From 1914 to 1918, the First World War engulfed Europe. While the Civil War may have been the most destructive war fought on American soil—with a total of roughly three quarters of a million dead—World War I, which unfolded overseas, dwarfed that number. Conservative estimates suggest that fifteen million soldiers and civilians lost their lives during what was at that time called the "Great War."

While that war did not make it to American shores, the economic effects of it certainly did. As often happens when conflict occurs, the war swelled American pockets, increasing the purchasing power of wealthy and middle-class Americans alike. Much of this wealth was funneled into risky financial market investments, and in 1929, a stock market collapse triggered first, a national economic downturn, then a worldwide one that we now know as the "Great Depression." This period of severe economic stagnation would last approximately a decade.

Around the globe, the economic toll wrought a terrible human cost, and this in turn led to the rise of social unrest and extremist political movements. The clearest example of this is the rise of Adolph Hitler and the Nazi party in Germany. Offering the German people a vision of relief from their hardships, Hitler combined economic promises with conspiratorial thinking in his political takeover, one that ultimately led to World War II.

This time, the death toll was roughly four times what it had been in the first. The revelation, as the war was ending, of the existence of death camps made comprehending what had just occurred even more difficult, and people found themselves asking difficult questions about human nature that no one seemed well prepared to answer.[1]

The modern West needed a framework that would help people to understand the horrors that seemed to have struck time and time again. None of this brutality seemed consistent with what people wanted to believe was true about being human. If humankind could perpetrate such atrocities, that meant people would need to rethink what it meant to be human. It would mean seeing the kind of brutality that had occurred as a thing inherent in human nature and thus likely to happen again. In the face of this conundrum, a young theologian named Merrill

Unger offered an alternative: Perhaps all this violence and unrest wasn't humankind's fault, at least, not entirely; perhaps the cause was demons.

Caught Between Two Worlds

Merrill Unger was brilliant. Born in 1909 in Maryland, he grew up and studied at Johns Hopkins University, where he earned his BA and PhD, in addition to working with one of the premiere biblical archaeologists of the day, William Albright. Afterward, Unger went to Dallas Theological Seminary where he earned master of theology and doctor of theology degrees.

This educational background meant that Unger had his feet in two worlds. On the one hand, Johns Hopkins was a research-oriented university, one of the first in the United States. And while it would be incorrect to suggest that Johns Hopkins is a perpetually liberal place, its focus on medicine and the physical sciences would seem an odd choice for the conservative Unger.

On the other hand, Dallas Theological Seminary was the hub of dispensationalist theology and an important point of diffusion of ideas to fundamentalist preachers and movements throughout the United States. Many of its most famous alumni have been, and remain, both widely influential and profoundly conservative. Yet, this does not necessarily mean that they are all predisposed to the idea of the literal demonic, as Unger was.

This unique blend of training positioned him perfectly for the work that was to come. Since belief in demons was viewed as an intellectually backward position, demon-believing Christians needed a champion to help them spread their message, and Unger was the ideal candidate. After all, if someone with three advanced degrees believed in demons, surely it must be a defensible position!

Unger seems to have combined his learning at both institutions to synthesize his conclusions about demons. True to the teachings at Dallas Theological Seminary, Unger was a devoted dispensationalist and fundamentalist. His writings suggest that he cleaved to biblical literalism, the idea that Scripture was divinely inspired, as well as to the notion that the end times were close at hand.

True also to the influence of Johns Hopkins, Unger took an evidence-based approach in his writings. His doctoral dissertation at Dallas Theological Seminary was entitled "Biblical Demonology", and it became the foundation for what would arguably become his most influential book: *Biblical Demonology: A Study of Spiritual Forces at Work*

Today (1952). In this book, Unger addresses the origin, nature, and practices of demons via arguments that continue to shape the thinking of Christians in the present day. In it, Unger unpacks Greek and Hebrew etymology; makes complex, biblical historical arguments; and offers a comparative history of ideas that seems worthy of his Johns Hopkins training. While I disagree with many of the foundational assumptions that Unger makes, his arguments are well-researched, and his academic chops are on full display.

An Academic for Evangelicals

Unger's book isn't intended for all readers: The target audience is clearly an educated person who knows their way around the Bible. Unger crafts detailed arguments, in which he often quotes multiple historical sources in several languages, which he claims necessitate belief in the demonic. These arguments often assumed agreement with fundamentalist logic and dispensationalist ideas, positions that were appealing to evangelicals of the day.

For instance, in his first chapter, Unger goes to great lengths to try to prove the uniqueness and superiority of biblical demonology. This is done to address two problems faced by fundamentalists. The first, as we noted in chapter 1, is that there really are no demons in the Hebrew Bible, at least, not like we know and understand them in the New Testament. Yet, this is a problem: Why would God "keep" information from the Israelites and only reveal it in the New Testament? He wouldn't, fundamentalists reason, so some of the weird monsters and antagonistic gods in the Hebrew Bible must necessarily be demons.

The second problem is that many of these weird monsters and antagonistic gods were also in narratives that developed in nations that bordered ancient Israel, and some of those narratives appeared to be older than the Israelite ones. Since the mid-twentieth century, biblical scholars have been pointing out that profound similarities existed between the mythologies of the ancient Israelites and those of their neighboring cultures. This similarity was best explained by the idea that groups of people who live close together tend to exchange and build their stories together, often resulting in a shared tradition. Since the mythologies of these cultures also featured such gods and monsters, the idea that God had uniquely told the Israelites about what Unger would think of as "demons" (rather than these entities being a shared cultural legacy among these nations) seemed increasingly suspect.

Unger rejects this conclusion on fundamentalist grounds, claiming that any similarities between traditions should be chalked up to "the purity and accuracy of the Genesis traditions, reproduced as they are in the Scriptures by divine inspiration."[2] That is to say, God gave the Israelites information about demons, and their neighbors were just commandeering bits and pieces of it.

Using this reasoning, Unger feels comfortable concluding that "biblical demonology, then, as it exists in its elemental though essential form in the earlier chapters of Genesis, is the ultimate source and basis of all demonology—ethnic, later biblical, Jewish and Christian."[3] A bold claim: Unger is asserting no differences in interpretations of biblical passages nor changes in thought occurred from the days of the pre-biblical Israelites to those of the early Christians!

In addition to his focus on divine biblical revelation about demons, Unger also writes about humankind as living in the end of days. This dispensationalist view of the world is necessarily pessimistic and also woven into ideas of the demonic. For example, Unger writes about the "translation of the Church of Jesus Christ to heaven" (the rapture), citing the same Bible passages that dispensationalists usually lean on. Once the Church is gone, Unger writes:

> there will be nothing to hold back the full manifestation of diabolic power, which will then burst upon a Christ-rejecting world with shocking violence and unbridled fury. The dammed-up tides of iniquity and evil supernaturalism, so long held in check by God's restraining Spirit, will deluge the earth, as the floods held back by some gigantic dike are let loose to inundate a whole countryside, when the dam is suddenly demolished.[4]

In Unger's thinking, the rapture necessarily leads to an important conclusion about demons. After the rapture, they will overrun the earth.

An Anti-Spiritualist for a New Generation

Unger's arguments rely substantially on anti-Spiritualist ideas. For instance, he devotes an entire chapter to the idea of necromancy and biblical demonology, addressing the Witch of Endor and her relationship to Spiritualism.[5]

However, Unger offers some modifications to anti-Spiritualist ideas as well, updating them to reflect the historical context of the mid-twentieth century, effectively making anti-Spiritualist ideas relevant to the present day. Like the anti-Spiritualists who lived before him, Unger links mental illness and the demonic together. But whereas in the nineteenth and early twentieth centuries mediumship was most often seen as the link between the two, Unger imagines diabolical influence to have been far more pervasive. He argues that the "career of the drunkard, the criminal, the libertine, the harlot, the dope fiend, the demented, the gambler, and the suicide" were all indicators of a deeper demonic reality that he claimed was an ongoing influence on human psychology.[6] For Unger, suicide especially seems to have a demonic cause, since he says "self-destruction seems far better explained, at least in the majority of cases, by demonic influence or possession, than by insanity, which is often urged as an excuse for the act."[7]

Although Unger is writing before the advent of the New Age movement, he already displays in his work a concern over alternative religious practices. In particular, he focuses a good deal of attention on narratives of demonic possession with which missionaries to China, Korea, the Sudan, and other areas of the globe were returning home. He blames these possessions on animism, superstition, and paganism; that is, on the native religious practices found in those lands.[8]

Unger also adopts the anti-Spiritualist idea that demons were manipulators of politics in the United States, but he also expands upon that, beginning to suggest a more global, organized demonic conspiracy than did those authors who came before him. He claims that the "world rulers of this darkness" cited in Ephesians 6:12 are demonic beings who are active in politics, and he warns that there is little protection to be had from them. Even good rulers, Unger says, can be easily manipulated "like pawns on the international chess board, moved to and fro by the *real* rulers of this darkness."[9] Wicked dictators on the other hand, "offer the ideal medium for the untrammeled operation of these evil ruling spirits."[10] Unger further argues that history has been nothing more than the march of rulers manipulated by demonic hands; from the Pharaohs to Nero to Hitler, human politics is simply demons tugging the strings.[11]

Whereas anti-Spiritualists strictly focused on politics from the 1850s, Unger, however, updates his argument for the world of the 1950s. He condemns "the frightful destruction brought upon Europe by Adolf Hitler, [and] the awful persecution of Christians on the part of Communism in its swift progress around the world."[12] Indeed, he seems to reserve a special anger for communism:

> Under Communism, satellites in Europe and Asia are undergoing a more fearful process of demonization than under Hitler; this, unless averted by divine grace, must inevitably lead to a third world war, more frightful and terrible than its predecessors. Never before have demon forces, as though let loose from the abyss (compare Revelation 9), so blatantly published their lies as truth, paraded their slavery as freedom, pronounced wrong as right, been so ambitious of world conquests, so cunning in their deception, or so malevolent in their lawlessness and rebellion against God as they are today in the program and propaganda of Russian communism.[13]

Whereas anti-Spiritualists primarily imagined the spread of the demonic across the United States, Unger sees the whole world as a demonic playground. Unsurprisingly, this kind of reimagining has political consequences. Let's consider a couple of them.

First, a person reading the anti-Spiritualist authors might be inclined to think that the only recourse to removing demonic forces from politics is political action. That is, people must be informed that certain individuals in politics are influenced by demons (and told who those people are), after which they must vote, and their votes must turn the tides. Unger, on the other hand, seems to put very little faith in the idea of politically correcting such issues. In Unger's mind, the presence of the demonic in politics is simply an expected facet of the end of days, which are swiftly approaching. The solution is not voting; it is praying. In his mind, demonic political forces operating within rulers can be overcome only by "God's restraining Spirit and the prevailing prayers of believers."[14] When these believers put on the "full armor of God," Unger claimed, they are able to combat the demonic political forces operant in the world. Or as he put it in his own words: "For if our real foes are spiritual—'we wrestle not against flesh and blood'

(Eph. 6:12)—our effective weapons are also spiritual; 'for the weapons of our warfare are not carnal, but mighty to the pulling down of strongholds' (II Cor. 10:4)."[15]

A second consequence of this reimagining is that, unlike the anti-Spiritualists, Unger does not see the demonic as resting primarily within individual political figures; rather, he sees it in political movements. As we saw earlier, several anti-Spiritualist authors claimed that Abraham Lincoln had been demonically influenced, but in that line of thinking, the problem was necessarily over once Lincoln was dead.

Unger's shift to communism as a demonically inflected political and ideological system marks a distinct change. Since the specter of communism can remain after its individual leaders have perished, in making this pivot, Unger creates a never-ending font of demons to which conservative Christians can always point.

The Necessity of Demons

Through his scholarship, Unger offered legitimacy to all those who wanted to believe in demons. At a time when such beliefs appeared backward and medieval, Unger's intellectual pedigree provided the clout that proponents of demons needed to validate their beliefs in the eyes of those who might be on the fence. His writings established demons as a necessary part of the world order.

Unger's work, however, wasn't directed at just anyone. His book had been adapted from his Doctor of Theology dissertation, which meant that it was directed at an audience of his peers (other holders of ThDs). As a result, many of his arguments required the listener have at least a passing familiarity with a few dead languages and a substantial knowledge of the Bible, not to mention the ability to grasp fairly complex sentence structures and sophisticated vocabulary choices.

What was needed, if his teachings were to catch on, was someone who could read what Unger was writing, see the value in it, and then translate and offer it to audiences that might not otherwise be able to understand its usefulness. Someone needed to move Unger's work from a niche group of scholars to a wider pastoral or even broadly Christian audience.

That someone was author Michael Harper.

CHAPTER TWELVE

Michael Harper

The Second Horseman of the New American Apocalypse

Merrill Unger's work had two noticeable problems. The first, as we've already seen, is that his use of ancient languages, word choice, and historical focus would be a stumbling block for many who might be inclined to his arguments. Although educated pastors and priests might be able to consume his work, the run-of-the-mill-man-on-the-street was left out.

Second, despite ascribing quite a bit of power to prayer, Unger gives very little advice on the subject. That is, he does not offer a blueprint for how such prayer should be practiced or thought of by Christians of his day. While it is clear that he thought prayers had the power to dispel demonic influence, Unger provided surprisingly little practical instruction on how this might be accomplished.

Spiritual Warfare in the Footsteps of Unger

It would be another two decades before our second horseman would remedy this problem. And surprisingly, despite the influence he would have on American theological thinking, this horseman would not live in the United States at all.

Born in London, England in 1931, Michael Harper attended Emmanuel College at Cambridge as a young man. One day, while attending religious services at King's College Chapel, he had an intense religious experience that precipitated his desire to become ordinated in the Church of England, which he went on to do in 1955. In 1962, while reading the book of Ephesians, he experienced another profound religious moment in which he saw a vision of the Church deeply divided. This occurrence eventually led him to become a leader in charismatic Anglican circles—that is, those participants in the renewal movement within the church who feel they continue to be blessed by the gifts of the

Spirit—and eventually to write *Spiritual Warfare* (1970), a work that would prove massively influential, first within the British charismatic movement and later among American charismatic Christians.

While the idea that Christians had been fighting against demons was nothing new, Harper's work put a new spin on this old idea. According to him, God no longer tested only the extraordinarily holy—*a la* Job. Instead, Harper proposed, every common work-a-day Christian today is constantly bedeviled.

With this teaching, *Spiritual Warfare* became one of the genesis points of what we know today as the contemporary spiritual warfare movement in evangelical and charismatic Christianity, a movement that has since its inception continued to posit that for various reasons, every Christian must be on guard for Satan's ever-present temptations and consciously make war against the demonic in their midst. But Harper did not arrive at his conclusions entirely alone; it is impossible to miss how much he depends upon Unger for his ideas. Harper's citation of *Biblical Demonology* is frequent and copious (making up more than a third of his citations), and he praises the work as being "the most illuminating on the subject [of demons]."[1]

It is perhaps not surprising then that Harper appears to be as ardent an anti-Spiritualist as Unger. Even before he begins to lay out his arguments in earnest, Harper tells his audience in his introduction that "there are a number of references in this book to what is generally called today 'spiritualism'. This word has been used rather than 'spiritism', which more correctly describes it, since it is the one in more common use."[2] That is, Harper seems here to be identifying Spiritualism, the movement we have read about so far, with spiritism, what he perceives as the practice of speaking with the dead more broadly outside this historical frame. This is likely meant to reinforce for the audience that the practice of speaking with demons is found at all times and all places, not just mid-nineteenth to twentieth-century America and Europe. Given this preamble, it is not surprising to find in his pages an extensive discussion of necromancy and the Witch of Endor, as well as to encounter such strongly worded statements as "the Bible condemns all forms of spiritualism. . . . To consult mediums and make contact with the dead is to break faith with God. . . . Both spiritualism and adultery are punishable by death."[3]

Harper also takes aim at the new Gateways that he sees beginning to emerge. In a chapter entitled "The Devil's Pentecost," he offers the following lament:

> Together with this throwing off of restraints [for Harper, the rise of "homosexuality and lesbianism," promiscuous sex, pagan worship, etc.] is the alarming rise throughout the Western world of drug taking, which together with alcoholism is contributing more and more to the rise in crime, road accidents, suicide, mental illness, promiscuity and abortion. The rise in figures does not tell the whole story of misery and depravity which is resulting from the present climate of permissiveness, which is really another form of rebellion against God.[4]

Much like Unger, Harper sees social ills as an example of demons acting in the world.

In several areas of this same chapter, Harper calls out *Soka Gakkai*—a Japanese sect of Buddhism that was rising in popularity in Great Britain at the time—by claiming that it "mocks every basic Christian belief."[5] On the pages that follow, he also targets the emergence of witches, the incorporation of the first Satanic Church in the world, and the practice of alternative medicine. Again, much like Unger, Harper sees a demonic threat in the religious views of non-Christian groups.

Harper is not a Dispensationalist. Like Unger, however, he is convinced that the end of time is swiftly approaching. In his introduction, he warns that the need for spiritual warfare "will increase as the end of the age draws nearer, and Christ's return becomes imminent."[6] Certainly, "as we draw nearer to Christ's return there is no indication of a lessening of this power."[7] While Harper is not anticipating a rapture, he is clearly thinking that the time left on earth is short.

Expanding the Demonic

Although Harper is clearly influenced by and agrees with Unger, he also expands much of what Unger was doing in his work. Unlike Unger, who gave no practical advice on the subject, Harper offers numerous examples of ways in which the Devil's power can be defeated, a kind of strategic guide for the fight against the Devil. He relates paradigmatic cases of spiritual warfare, which serve as models for personal emulation. He discusses how to achieve personal purity (answer: by desiring the Glory of God above all things); creates extensive lists of biblical passages to be used as "weapons;" and over the course of an entire chapter interprets the "armor of God" passage from Ephesians 6, breaking it down in terms of behaviors that protect believers against the demonic. Harper even includes, in an Appendix, translations of several exorcisms from various traditions: More weapons for the reader's personal war against the demonic.

True to his idea of the greater presence of demons in the life of Christians, Harper suggests the need for these methods of protection is significantly greater than previously believed, expanding the range of influence that demons can command over an individual person's life. While Unger already condemned criminal behaviors, sexual promiscuity and suicide as demonic, Harper tacks on offenses like chain-smoking, hatred, lying, "sadism, indecent exposure, a violent temper, blaspheming and swearing, covetousness that leads to exorbitant spending, and so on." He goes on to say that not "all such bondages are the work of evil spirits. But we should be open to the possibility."[8] Harper appears to hedge his ideas here: best not to see demons around every corner, he seems to say, just around most of them.

Most problematic, Harper uses the language of warfare—that is, flesh-and-blood modern military terms—in his discussions, a first use of such terms for this purpose from what I am able to tell.[9] He discusses ideas of what to do when demons launch "frontal assaults" versus "sieges" or "blockades,"[10] from communal resistance to casting out the demons responsible. He describes demonic possession as "an invasion and occupation" and warns of the "protracted battle" that may occur as a result.[11] Likewise, some areas of ongoing struggle in people's lives constitute "strongly held enemy territory" in the eyes of Harper, who states that when someone faces a compulsion that is demonically suggested, it is because demons have erected a "bridgehead" within them.[12] While Harper did not intend his militaristic metaphors to be taken literally, this language of warfare that he pioneered had the potential to lead to violence, and as we will see in future chapters, eventually would do exactly that.

Warnings, Unheeded

At the same time, Harper is perhaps the most careful about his own work of all the Horsemen and seemingly aware of the effect that it could have. He frequently cautions his audience that the demonic is one explanation among many. In his eyes, while the phenomenon of demonic warfare is very real, one should not leap to the conclusion that demons are behind every stray thought or problem.

There is a certain irony in Harper's words of caution. It is almost as if he saw *exactly what would happen from people reading his book and tried to prevent it.* He warns especially against three practices that should be avoided: people "specializing" in the expulsion of the demonic, the use of "deliverance centers" that purport to cast out demons, and the habit of unnecessarily seeking out the demonic.[13] Yet, each of these three phenomena would only *escalate* as a result of people reading Harper's work.

At the very end of his book, Harper muses about the tactics that demons might use to destroy the good that his book seeks to put into the world. Two tactics seem to anticipate the twenty-first century in the United States to a startling degree:

> (2) Get the book adopted as the textbook of the "super-supernaturalists", and get them to see Devils: everywhere and in every person.
>
> (3) Get people to take the subject too seriously. This might well be his [the Devil's, but the literal context is C.S. Lewis's fictitious demon "Screwtape" from Lewis's 1942 book *The Screwtape Letters*] trump card. Let their joy and serenity be taken away. Fill them with fears. Rob them of a sense of humour. Get them to think all the time of evil, rather than "whatever is true; whatever is honourable, whatever is just, whatever is pure, whatever is lovely, whatever is gracious".[14]

It is a shame that Harper's warnings went unheeded. He would probably be horrified by the way spiritual warfare has consumed many people's lives and caused them to see demons around every corner. His cautions appear to have been intended to instill a serious concern, but not outright obsession. Yet we seem at present to live in an America that suffers from all of the troubles Harper predicted. For many believers in spiritual warfare, joy and serenity have fled, evil is a constant consideration, and "humour" is rarely found.

And yet, Unger and Harper wrote to what were, at first, relatively small audiences. These original audiences cannot account for the explosion of ideas regarding spiritual warfare in the following decades. Given that, one must ask: How did this fear get inside the everyday American?

CHAPTER THIRTEEN

Fertilizing Fear Through Film

AT THIS POINT, it's necessary to briefly shift topics. You have seen the first two of our four horsemen lay the groundwork for understanding the demonic in America in a different way. But one of the catalysts for making it possible for Americans to believe in this new way—or for some Americans, even at all!—may be surprising. That catalyst is film.

It might seem strange to consider that film has played such an important role in our understanding of our religious experience. After all, we might say to ourselves, film is clearly fiction while we wholeheartedly believe our religious experiences are reality. Surely, we wouldn't mistake one for the other.

But the truth is, film has been central to the American religious experience ever since it became widely accessible, and it shapes thinking more than we often realize. Consider this personal example: Can you think of the parting of the Red Sea without imagining Charlton Heston as Moses doing it? Now consider two examples of film's broader influence: What are we to make of the success of *The Passion of the Christ* (2004), which was due in large part to the fact that churches advertised the film from the pulpit and even attended the film as a religious community? And would the multiplatform success of *The Chosen* series (2017-) have been possible without the $100 million in production funding that was raised by those who wanted to see the events of the Gospels depicted in a particular way?[1] "Seeing is believing," after all, and film gives us a means to see what we can only otherwise imagine.

Specifically, in the movie theaters of the late '60s and early '70s, America saw demons. Of particular note from this time are three films that have been dubbed the "unholy trinity" by religious scholar Joseph P. Laycock and film scholar Eric Harrelson: *Rosemary's Baby* (1968), *The Exorcist* (1973) and *The Omen* (1976).[2] If you haven't seen these 50-year-old films, be warned: Spoilers lie ahead.

Rosemary's Baby

Let's begin with director Roman Polanski's film. *Rosemary's Baby* tells the tale of the eponymous Rosemary Woodhouse and her husband-actor Guy Woodhouse. At the outset of the film, the two are looking for a new apartment in Manhattan and decide upon an old and stately building called "The Bramford." The couple quickly comes in contact with Minnie and Roman Castevet, their elderly neighbors.

Although Guy is initially reluctant to strike up a relationship with the Castevets, he soon warms to them considerably. Around the same time a stroke of "good luck" occurs: Guy is cast in the lead role of an important play after the former lead is struck blind.

In part due to this success, Guy and Rosemary decide to conceive a baby. On the night that they plan to do so, Minnie delivers a special dessert that Rosemary complains tastes "chalky." The dessert, it turns out, was laced with some substance, and Rosemary passes out. In her stupor, she dreams of being raped by a demonic force.

Over the course of Rosemary's pregnancy, it becomes apparent that something supernatural is going on in the Bramford. By gradually connecting clues, Rosemary is able to uncover the fact that the Bramford has long been a hideaway for a coven of witches who worship Satan. As Rosemary comes closer and closer to term, evidence of the coven's influence and social reach becomes more and more apparent. Seemingly everywhere Rosemary turns, events conspire to put her within the grasp of the witches.

When she finally gives birth, Rosemary is told that the baby has died. She suspects otherwise as her breast milk is being pumped and collected and she periodically hears the cries of an infant through the thin walls of the Bramford. The climax of the film occurs when Rosemary discovers a hidden door in her closet that leads to the Castevets' apartment. Inside, members of the witches' coven, which seemingly now is international in its reach, gather around a bassinet over which hangs an upside down cross. Roman reveals to Rosemary that her child is the son of the Devil, the future Antichrist.

The Takeaways from *Rosemary's Baby*

Of course, all of this is too wild to be believed, right? Unfortunately, not really. First, let's consider the frame of the narrative itself. At its core, *Rosemary's Baby* is telling us a story about the purported birth of the Antichrist and the existence of witches in the world. Regarding the first, we've already seen that some Americans up to this point have accepted that the Antichrist can exist in their own time. As for the witches, perceiving them as a real modern presence was not just an act of unsubstantiated belief. From the '50s through the '70s, witches had appeared more frequently in the news: From the rise of Wicca to the radical feminist group of the 1960s Women's International Terrorist Conspiracy from Hell (WITCH), witches were becoming a more present phenomenon for the people living at that time.

Moreover, the idea that such groups would work together to cooperate in an international conspiracy had already been promoted as nonfiction in the evangelical Christian community. One example is a 1972 book entitled *The Satan-Seller* written by the author Michael Warnke, in which Warnke claims that before he converted to Christianity, he was the high priest of a satanic cult that used witchcraft and demons to strike down its enemies. Warnke further insinuates that satanic cults in the modern day are guided by an international secret society called the Illuminati, an idea that calls to mind the international coven in *Rosemary's Baby*. The Illuminati was a secret society founded in Bavaria in 1776 and banned by the Bavarian government less than a decade later. While there is no evidence to support their continued historical existence after this point, they are a popular group for conspiracy theorists to invoke as the name of a shadowy organization that rules the world. By linking the cult he leads to the Illuminati, Warnke depicts the satanic threat he introduces to his audience as omnipresent and enormously powerful.

Around this same time, a public speaker named John Todd was also igniting the evangelical speaking circuit. Todd made claims similar to Warnke's: A vast satanic conspiracy (again, the Illuminati) existed that was poised to take over the world. Todd claimed that he was aware of this satanic cabal's plans because he was a former witch—born and trained in a family of witches—who had progressed to the rank of "Grand Druid High Priest" before converting to Christianity. A year after *Rosemary's Baby* came out, Todd claimed that the satanic takeover had already begun.[3] Todd's claims were magnified, in part, due to their acceptance and depiction by Jack T. Chick, the creator of brief evangelical Christian comic books that were used as an evangelistic tool and distributed en masse. According to the Chick Publications' website, over one *billion* of these comics have been sold.[4]

In the end, both Warnke and Todd proved to be hucksters. An exposé in 1992 by *Cornerstone Magazine*, a Christian publication, outed Warnke's narrative as a fantastic yarn spun by a gifted storyteller.[5] He currently maintains a ministry that still describes his experience as factual.[6] Likewise, Todd was gradually outed by the increasingly outlandish claims that he made and inconsistencies in his stories.[7] He was also arrested for and found guilty of rape, imprisoned, and after being released, was institutionalized before dying in 2007.

The Exorcist

All of this was nothing compared to the impact that would be made by *The Exorcist*. While *Rosemary's Baby* gave us a popular picture of an end times scenario, the Antichrist can be born to only so many people. Conversely, *The Exorcist* paints demonic possession as a common event. The plot of the film revolves around a young girl's illness, one that gradually turns out to be supernatural rather than medical. As the original movie poster proclaims, "Something almost beyond comprehension is happening to a girl on this street, in this house . . . and a man has been sent for as a last resort." There are no distinguishing features described in this statement: It could be any girl, any house, and any man.

This sense that possession could happen to anyone, at any time, in any place is the foundation of *The Exorcist*'s social impact. Although the possessed girl, Regan, is part of an upper middle-class family and her mother is a film actress, there is little in the plot itself to distinguish Regan from any other little girl or her mother from any other mother.

The film frames Regan's possession as what appears initially to be a medical phenomenon. Regan suffers from symptoms that include restlessness and hallucinations, her mother takes her to a doctor, and the doctor evaluates the symptoms and gives a diagnosis. After this diagnosis and subsequent ones prove incorrect, and additional symptoms present themselves, Regan returns to the doctors who evaluate her once more, and either argue that their original diagnosis is correct or offer a new one. These developments are not unlike plot points found in a lot of medical dramas that we might watch on contemporary television today.

The difference is that Regan's medical malady is demonic. Since the doctors are not willing to accept this, they suggest somewhat tongue in cheek that Regan should pursue an exorcism, at which point we never see them again. The exorcism is performed, is successful, and Regan is cured.

The Takeaway from *The Exorcist*

The fact that the film couches Regan's possession as a medical phenomenon is important. That's because research on medical dramas indicates that viewers can have their perception of medical conditions influenced, be encouraged to self-diagnose, and experience increased fear about medical procedures they view.[8] This effect is powerful enough that it even extends to the practice of medicine: Medical dramas can also inform doctors' and nurses' self-perceptions, both positively and negatively, and can be used to educate them.

Looking at *The Exorcist* through this lens of understanding, we can then see that its audience is not just watching a film that begins in the medical field and ends in the supernatural. They are also watching a film that offers a diagnosis and a treatment that can be pursued when standard medical diagnoses fail. It should not be surprising then to learn that in the years after the film was released, members of the general public began to request exorcisms and the idea of the demonic became increasingly tied to issues of mental health.

For a conservative Christian audience, belief in filmic depictions of demons causing mental illness or physical strain was an even smaller step. After all, both Unger and Harper had already connected the demonic to mental illness, and anti-Spiritualists before them to neurological health. As we will see in subsequent chapters, our other two horsemen of the new American Apocalypse would go on to make contributions to this dynamic as well: Billy Graham by building up the mystique of *The Exorcist* (mainly by claiming it is "repulsive, disgusting, pornographic, and obscene" and saying that he refused "to expose myself to this type of thing"[9]), and the Hammonds by deepening the claims of connection between the medical and the demonic.

Finally, a scant two years after the film's release, an ex-Jesuit priest, Malachi Martin, would publish a book entitled *Hostage to the Devil* (1975). Whereas *The Exorcist* is a work of fiction, *Hostage* claims on the book's cover to be the nonfiction account of "the possession and exorcism of five contemporary Americans." Martin paints a lurid picture of an America that is filled with demonic presences that entered the country through the gateways of emerging transgenderism and homosexuality. Drawing directly from the fictional example of *The Exorcist*, he depicts the purportedly true accounts of the exorcisms of five individuals whose narratives seem too rich, detailed, and politically loaded to be anything other than fictional creations.[10] The work would propel him to fame as an expert on the topics of demonic possession and exorcism, landing him in a category with other media figures who spoke on the topic, including Ed and Lorraine Warren, the self-described "demonologists" who investigated several alleged hauntings and demonic possessions and were later depicted in films such as the *Amityville Horror* (1979) and *The Conjuring* universe.[11] While there is significant reason to doubt both Martin's and the Warrens' accounts of demons,[12] both sets of authors continue to be perceived by many as offering genuine proof of the demonic in the modern United States.

The Exorcist and the authors that followed in its footsteps opened something of a Pandora's box for the United States. By suggesting that demons might be responsible for mental health conditions and that their involvement might be signaled by physical ailments, a nagging doubt about the origins of disease began in the American mind. This doubt would later be exacerbated by works such as Frank and Ida Mae Hammond's *Pigs in the Parlor* (1974), which we will discuss in chapter 15.

The Omen

Our final film, released in 1976, features the appearance of the Antichrist once more, this time in a more substantive role. In *The Omen*, Robert Thorn is an American diplomat living in Rome. His wife Katherine gives birth, but Robert is told by a priest working at the hospital that the child died. The hospital chaplain persuades Robert to adopt a baby that was recently born in the hospital; he does not tell his wife of the switch.

The couple raises the child, Damien, as their own until he reaches the age of five, around the time that they return to London. At that point, mysterious things suddenly begin to happen around Damien, from the benign—animals panicking at his presence—to the profoundly disturbing—Damien's nanny hanging herself at his fifth birthday party. In the midst of these odd occurrences a priest warns Robert that Damien is not what he seems.

This leads Robert on a quest to discover Damien's origins. Eventually in Rome he uncovers the fact that Damien's biological mother is a jackal and that his own child was murdered to pave the way for Damien's adoption. He calls Katherine to warn her, and Damien's new demonic nanny throws Katherine from a window. Upon his return to London, Robert confirms Damien's diabolical heritage through the presence of a birthmark that looks like three conjoined sixes. As he attempts to kill Damien, Robert is killed by the police.

The last scene of the film depicts the president of the United States and the first lady attending the Thorn's funeral. Standing beside them is Damien, who turns to the camera and gives the audience a knowing smile.

The Takeaway from *The Omen*

The Omen is an inherently political film. While it certainly follows the spiritual thread of Robert Thorn discovering that his child is the Antichrist, this is set against the presumed necessity of the Antichrist being involved in politics. The Thorns' biological child is killed so that Damien can be adopted into a political household. Likewise, the implication at the end of the film that the US president and first lady have adopted Damien suggests that this was all part of the Devil's plan from the get-go. Damien is now perfectly positioned to exert political power as many, particularly dispensationalist and evangelical Christians, believe the Antichrist will.

The film's audiences had no doubt been primed for such a message by the phenomenal success of *The Late Great Planet Earth*, written by the evangelical writer and apocalyptic theologian Hal Lindsey and published in 1970. Lindsey's work was invested in the idea of a political Antichrist who would appear after the rapture. Referring to this being as the "Future Fuehrer," he claims that the Antichrist, whom he also thinks of as the Beast in Revelation, will emerge at a time of international lawlessness.[13] According to Lindsey, this being will likely be relatively unknown by the public until such time as he recovers from a seemingly fatal wound. At this point, he will be propelled into political power, and a ten-nation confederacy with seven leaders will bend knee to him.[14] This development will precipitate him becoming the "absolute dictator of the whole world."[15] Throughout his book, Lindsey both described prophetic events that were seemingly already fulfilled and sought to link current events up with the Apocalypse, cementing the idea for the audience that the end times was nearly upon them. By the time *The Omen* was released, *Late Great Planet Earth* had sold over a million copies;[16] two years after, the film by the same name would be released.

The world was primed for the Antichrist and the rapture.

Seeing Is Believing

By this point, *Rosemary's Baby* had helped to establish the idea of shadowy cults in the world. *The Exorcist* had connected the medical with the demonic and paved the way for others who will make claims about the reality of spectacular demonic activity and exorcisms. *The Omen* had grounded the Antichrist and the end of the world in a political context. While on their own, each film might not have had much impact, together and with what seemed like corroborating evidence in popular "nonfiction" literature of the time they painted a vivid picture of a world that was teetering on the edge of disaster. Witches once more prowled the night, shadowy conspiracies and cults threatened the world, possession became a common phenomenon rather than a rare instance, and the Antichrist seemed ready to pop up at any moment.

Now, Americans needed hope. They needed to feel empowered. While Harper's *Spiritual Warfare* had built upon Unger's work and started to lay the practical foundations for combating the demonic, it was up to our last two horsemen of the new American Apocalypse to prepare the average American for war and give them their marching orders.

CHAPTER FOURTEEN

Billy Graham

The Third Horseman of the New American Apocalypse

DURING THE SAME span of time that the world was consuming Unger's and Harper's works and the films we've discussed were laying fertile ground for belief in demons, the Antichrist, and the end of days; one of the most influential evangelists in American history was already busy at work.

Billy Graham had been born on a dairy farm near Charlotte, North Carolina. According to his autobiography, Graham grew up living a simple country life: one full of family, hard work, and faith.[1] After leaving Charlotte, he went to several schools including Bob Jones College (a private conservative evangelical Christian institution he attended for a short time), Florida Bible Institute (where he earned a Bachelor of Theology), and Wheaton College (where he got a Bachelor of Arts in Anthropology). Through it all, he showed a remarkable ability to communicate with just about anyone he encountered.

Graham held his first "Crusade" in 1947 in Grand Rapids, Michigan. These religious revival meetings began in the United States but quickly began to sweep the globe from England to India. While it can be difficult to pin down exactly how many people Graham reached with his message, the author Thomas G. Long, in his anthology *The Legacy of Billy Graham: Critical Reflections on America's Greatest Evangelist*, estimated that over the course of his life time Graham reached approximately 210 million people in 185 countries through the various media in which he communicated.[2] Graham wrote over thirty books in his lifetime, several of which became major best sellers.

In these books and sermons, Graham disseminated ideas that emerged from both Harper's and Unger's work, though it is difficult, given the verbal nature of his presentations, to tell whether he acquired them directly or from another source using Harper and Unger. By using a simple and effective speech style, Graham was able to convince his audience of the diabolical nature of political movements, the constant presence of Satan in their life, and the necessity of spiritual warfare. Not only that, but this style also helped him to convince his audience that they needed to act, personally, in order to combat the Devil's actions in the world. In this way, Graham gave a larger platform to these ideas that would far exceed the readership of both Unger's *Biblical Demonology* and Harper's *Spiritual Warfare.*

Turn or Burn

Although his body of work is vast and covers much ground, there are some commonalities that are consistent throughout Graham's preaching. First, Graham often pointed hyperbolically to problems that he saw as a great evil of the day. From looming Third World Wars to the threat of communism to the AIDS epidemic, Graham was consistently painting a bleak picture of reality for his listeners. In his description of it, the world was always on the brink of collapse.

While Graham liked to paint the world in dire straits, however, he also knew that these proclamations would not motivate his audience to action. The next phase of his sermon then would often collapse the larger problem down into the realm of the personal, as a matter of the individual human heart. The problem isn't the world, Graham essentially told his audience, the problem is you! You have fallen short and failed God, either by giving in to sin or by masquerading as righteous. All of this is your fault.

While it did not appear in all of his sermons, the threat of Hell was ever present for Graham. Not simply an abstract idea but a real place where those who rejected Christ would go. As Graham wrote, "No one can read the Bible even casually without realizing that there is a day of reckoning and judgment coming. No one can read the Bible without recognizing that there is a hell."[3] Given Graham's position, the message is clear: Eternal separation from God will result from the mistakes you have made.

At this point, he would move into the third part of his sermon, which promised that there was a solution. If you will turn to God and ask for his forgiveness, this will all be remedied. God can fundamentally change who you are, and in so doing, you can fundamentally change what the world is. You can fix this. Not only will you free yourself from the maw of Hell, but you can save the world from the same fate!

For this to happen, all the listeners had to do was join Graham on stage and publicly declare their readiness to serve God and desire Christ. The formula couldn't be simpler. And as Long explains, "nearly three million people over the last sixty years have walked forward at the end of Graham's sermons" as a result.[4]

"Satan's Religion"

Of course, in this line of thinking, the fact that a person fell away from God wasn't entirely their fault. In Graham's cosmology, Satan was an ever-present threat, a master of temptation who was active in a person's daily life. Whenever someone felt the sting of temptation, that feeling was caused by the literal Devil who lorded over a literal hell and was singling the individual out to draw them into sin.

Frequently, this battle with Satan was sexual in nature. While Graham did not believe that sex itself was inherently sinful, he did argue that it must be performed within the bounds of marriage. As the Christian ethicist Karen Lebacqz writes, Graham felt that sex was "powerful. It is one of the ways that Satan works to tempt us, and its power must be harnessed appropriately."[5] As Graham once wrote,

> The Bible teaches that Satan is the author of sin. Sin is the reason we have afflictions. The demons that serve him are busy writing pornographic literature and producing sexual materials that pollute the mind. He has infiltrated our education system, teaching hedonistic and permissive philosophy. The culture is bombarded by a sexual tempest.
>
> Table talk these days centers not only on sexual perversion but every sinful thought and deed. It is true that society has become so obsessed with sex that it seeps from all the pores of our national life. Sex revolution, no! But sex pollution? Yes!![6]

Graham often focused on the individual's battle with the Devil. But he was no stranger to linking Satan with political movements as well. In his writings and sermons, he at times painted politically oriented movements such as feminism and civil rights with a diabolical brush. For instance, Graham once claimed that what he saw as the feminist tendency to reject traditional women's roles was a "Satanic deception of modern times."[7] Likewise, in a 1958 sermon near his hometown, Graham proclaimed: "We see the forces of evil stirring up racial tensions all over America. . . . It seems as if the whole world is a pot and the devil has a big stick stirring everybody up. Why, he has even got the church stirred up."[8]

Yet, this charge of satanic influence pales in comparison with Graham's associations between the Devil and communism. The August 1954 issue of *American Mercury*, features a short article by Graham entitled "Satan's Religion," in which he claimed that the battle between communism and Christianity "is a battle to the death—either Communism must die, or Christianity must die, because it is actually a battle between Christ and anti-Christ."[9] According to Graham, Satan's orchestration of this deception dated back to the Garden of Eden: Communism was just the latest iteration of a religion that worships Satan. Unfortunately, Graham said, there is a "large segment of society" that has chosen to believe this false religion, and "the Devil is their god; Marx, their prophet; Lenin, their saint; and Malenkov [a leader in Soviet politics and the Communist Party in the mid-twentieth century] their high priest."[10]

Like his sermons, Graham's writing on communism neatly packages what he sees as the global problem, the human problem, and the solution:

> Our experts agree that bombs and bullets are powerless to cope with the threatening menace of Bolshevism. There is only one antidote for the poisonous venom of Sovietism, and that is the truth of the gospel of Christ. And that truth must be demonstrated to a hungry, fearful, perplexed, confused world. Too long we have preached and not practiced. Too long we have theorized and not demonstrated. The world must not only hear that Jesus lives, but they must see Him living in us. The fanatical loyalty as witnessed in the lives of those who live in countries behind the Iron Curtain should inspire us to a new, deeper loyalty to Christ. The choice is clear-cut—it is either revolution and chaos, or Christ and righteousness.[11]

In this passage, the global problem depicted is the might of communism, the human problem is that Christians preach but do not practice faithful Christianity, and the solution is to be reborn in a "new deeper loyalty to Christ."

However, Graham does not stop there. Next, he lays out a clear five-point plan to stop the spread of communism in the United States, a five-point plan that, it's important to note, continues to be echoed by contemporary conservative Christian commenters speaking about the subject of communism today. First, Graham claims, we must solve the problem of communism through "old-fashioned Americanism."[12] Here, Graham invokes the American Exceptionalist view that the United States is the greatest country that has ever been, and that it rose to this position through ideals "gathered around the dignity of the individual, a faith in God, an adherence to the Bible, and a respect for human life."[13] By simply adhering to the good old-fashioned values that built the country, he says, we can jumpstart the salvation of the United States.

Yet, this is not enough. In the next point, Graham explicitly calls out conservative and evangelical Christianity as an essential element in the defeat of communism. He defines this Christianity as "a personal faith in a personal God, a belief in the Bible as the rule of faith and practice, and an experience of the regenerating grace of God, which transforms character."[14] From there, the third through fifth elements seem to grow more diluted: all three are more or less extensions of the second. Graham encourages his audience to pray since communism will not be able to "penetrate the barrier of a praying nation."[15] He also suggests that the United States needs a "spiritual revival" since it will purge "cities and towns of evil wickedness."[16] People in the United States must also have personal experiences that draw them to Christ, because "the greatest and most effective weapon against Communism today is to be born again Christian."[17] Here, Graham is following the key tactics of his sermons: The world is broken, and the only way that it can be fixed is for you to join the battle for its soul.

Anti-Spiritualism and Spiritual Warfare

Of course, Graham's focus on a personal Devil was not just effective in converting listeners, but also conducive to the idea of spiritual warfare. To show a representative example of his ideas on this subject, I want to look at one sermon that he delivered in Phoenix, Arizona, aptly titled "Spiritual Warfare" (1974),[18] since it clearly shows the impact anti-Spiritualist ideas had on Graham.

As usual, Graham begins by laying out the horrors of the modern world. In his recounting, a "mother of six" is stabbed twenty times by "warlocks" in the back of her car. A devil worshipper kills a "twenty-two-year-old social worker" who had the misfortune to pick him up in her car. A retired woman is attacked by a young woman who claims to reporters that this crime is "her sacrifice to the Devil."

Graham has made a careful selection of anecdotes here. Each includes a kind of "damsel in distress" scenario that would appeal to his conservative Christian audience: a traditional mother, a gentle heart caring for others, and a helpless old woman.[19] In each of these cases, the Devil enters their lives in the form of his worshippers: first a coven much like that seen in *Rosemary's Baby* and then two solo devil worshippers.

Graham goes on to contextualize these killings. He claims, "the whole Bible is the story of a conflict between the forces of God and the forces of the Devil." Interestingly enough, he next encourages his audience to turn to Deuteronomy 18:10–11, which contains, among other things, an injunction against necromancy. He then follows this verse with an explanation of Saul and the Witch of Endor.

Turning back to the United States, he suggests that Americans waffle between two poles. On the one hand, he claims, many people "deny the existence of the Devil"; on the other, many have an unnatural fascination with him, in part "because of the success of *The Exorcist,*" which has led to new films "being made on the subject of the Devil and evil right now." In this way, he articulates for his audience the same problem that Michael Harper did for his readers in *Spiritual Warfare*: Some people give the Devil too much credit while others don't give him any!

Graham goes on to say that there is a "great intensification and acceleration of evil in the world at this moment because the Devil knows his time is short." This purported intensification includes "thousands" of witches living and practicing in Great Britain and Germany, and a growing interest among Americans in the "occult." Graham further suggests that covens are springing up in universities (presumably in the United States) when he cites an anonymous professor who claims that "there were dozens of covens on their campus."

But once more, there is hope. Graham reminds his audience that the Devil works in individuals, and if you're able to deny the Devil his due, then he weakens. If enough people can deny him, then his power will fade. To aid people in this goal, Graham strays from his usual, concise message structure and proceeds to give a crash course on the Devil and how to perform exorcisms to his audience, a crash course that ultimately takes up an astounding third of his sermon. The remainder of the sermon is then taken up with the task of articulating Harper's idea of the armor of God described in Ephesians 6:10–18, armor which both men claim protect people during the course of spiritual warfare.

Demons for the Masses

In his 1952 book, Unger offered an excellent intellectual defense of the existence of demons but one that is far too erudite for the standard reader. In 1970, Harper condensed some of this material and translated it onto a personal battlefield with the demonic. The films and the "nonfiction" work that parroted or supported these ideas then created a sense of the necessity of action: demons and devils are most certainly alive in this world and working their evil will! Next to these large steps, it might seem that Graham simply regurgitated and amplified other people's ideas. If that were true, it would still be enough for his work to have had an impact. Graham bringing Unger's and Harper's ideas to the pulpit would have increased their consumption exponentially as millions of people swayed under his hypnotic delivery.

However, Graham did more than this: He also changed the playing field. By that I mean that Unger and Harper painted a picture of a world that needed to be endured; one in which the Devil and his minions swept through an unbelieving populace and a person could, at best, only protect themselves. Graham did something different: He connected the global to the personal. By changing yourself, you can change the world. You can take the fight to the Devil himself. The cosmic battle can be won.

At this key moment, what believers in demons needed most was a "how-to" manual, a playbook that would allow them to confront the demonic head-on. A guide that would allow anyone to combat the forces of the Devil and be a warrior for God. Graham never provided such a work, an absence that can likely be explained by Graham's focus on evangelism as well as the focus of that evangelism: the teaching that conversion, not exorcism, was the best means to defeat the Devil.

This was not enough for some. It was time for the last of the horsemen of the new American Apocalypse to arm the common man. It was time for Frank and Ida Mae Hammond.

CHAPTER FIFTEEN

Frank (and Ida Mae) Hammond

The Fourth Horseman of the New American Apocalypse

FRANK AND IDA Mae Hammond may well be described as a phenomenon of religious influence, albeit a phenomenon that many mainstream Christian and secular believers likely have never heard of. The two ministered for thirty years in the last half of the twentieth century through a ministry that focused much on casting out demons, and during that time Frank wrote more than two dozen books (a handful coauthored by his wife Ida Mae), many of which were converted into audio recordings for wider audience distribution. Their landmark work, *Pigs in the Parlor: The Practical Guide to Deliverance* (1973), has sold over a million copies to date; my copy of the book is from an astounding *sixtieth* printing. While the book is credited to both Frank and Ida Mae, and while Ida Mae was an essential element of their shared ministry, there appears to be only one chapter in *Pigs in the Parlor* that we can trace to her, whereas personal pronoun use in the rest of the text suggests the vast majority was written by Frank, which is why I've identified him as our primary horseman.

There is likely a twofold reason why the Hammonds' work has proved so influential. First, the Hammonds provide a clear, concise, and, best of all, systematic approach to expelling demons. Whereas authors such as Unger and Harper tended to talk about demons as a phenomenon, the Hammonds offer a guide to identifying them, ministering to the afflicted, and ultimately casting out these offending spirits. Second, as the charismatic movement in the United States swelled from the 1960s forward, the Hammonds' publication met a growing demand for "deliverance ministry," the charismatic term for the practice of exorcism. (We'll discuss the charismatic movement and its effects in greater detail in chapter 17.)

Frank Hammond was an ordained Baptist minister, but one who was clearly influenced by charismatic strains of Christianity. That is to say, while Hammond was part of a conservative Christian denomination, he also slowly came to the belief that people could be "baptized in the Holy Spirit," a process by which recipients are understood to be filled with the Holy Spirit who awakens within them certain spiritual gifts. These spiritual gifts could be things like speaking in tongues, prophetic abilities, spiritual healing, or the capacity to work miracles.

But if a person was to be filled with the Holy Spirit, one other thing needed to happen first.

They needed to clear out the demons.

Pigs in the Parlor

The name of the Hammonds' book might seem odd at first, but there is a logic to it; it's a reference to the idea in the Hebrew Bible that there are both clean and unclean animals. The Hammonds take this idea another step, drawing a connection between the idea of an "unclean animal," such as a pig, and an "unclean spirit." "What would you do if a herd of filthy pigs came into your parlor and began to make themselves at home?" the Hammonds ask their readers, "Would you invite such a thing? Would you pay no attention to them in the hope they would soon leave of their own accord?"[1]

In the Hammonds understanding of the world the questions they pose are not idle ones. In their minds, demonic incursions are constant and unrelenting, and the human body is a house that is perpetually under assault. If demons are allowed to enter, then they will take up residence and hedge out the Holy Spirit. The Hammonds claim that this is a problem that affects everyone from all walks of life, even children and unborn fetuses.[2]

The promised solution to these incursions is to drive out the demons. To this end, the Hammonds lay out a seven-step process for determining the need for what they call "deliverance" (their term for a kind of Protestant exorcism) and then seven more steps that a person can take to accomplish this feat. These instructions are followed by seven final steps for maintaining one's delivered state, which are needed since the demons that have been expelled from one's body will attempt to find a way back in again.

The guide is eminently practical. For instance, the Hammonds cover expected topics like public and private deliverance but also drill down even further, noting that in the composition of a deliverance team, a secretary should be appointed and stating what the person should record. Signs and symptoms of different types of demons are discussed, to aid in their identification, and the names of different demons are helpfully set off in the text with italics (e.g., *spirit of rebellion*, *demon of anger*, *bitterness spirits*) so that they can easily be located by readers at a later time. Methods of deliverance are discussed including the dos, don'ts, and how-tos, and advice is given on how to deliver both oneself and those who do not wish to be delivered. There's even a discussion about whether the role of a deliverance minister might be right for the reader.

A Poisonous Worldview

It is possible that for some people, the Hammonds' techniques actually worked, though not necessarily because they were teaching people to wield the supernatural power of the Holy Spirit. In fact, much of what the Hammonds proposed readers do mimicked advice that was already being given by psychologists.

Consider the following example. The Hammonds suggested that common symptoms of demons dwelling within a person include "emotional problems" such as feelings of anger, resentment, and rejection; "mental problems" and "sex problems," which they more or less describe as unwanted, excessive, or pathological sexual states; and "addictions" such as alcoholism, smoking, and drugs. Once demons have been identified as the problem, sufferers are told to be honest about their problem, express humility about their state, desire to change, and seek forgiveness for their failings. The individual's deliverance team is encouraged to ask the sufferer questions that get to the root issues of what allowed demons to get into the person in the first place, and to blame the demons and not themselves for the undesirable behavior.

The Hammonds further contend that demons with different functions tend to multiply a person's problems by dwelling together within that individual. For instance, a demon of rejection and a demon of anger might compound a person's problem by making the human they possess furious at small slights, which separates them from others and deepens their sense of rejection, which only leads to greater anger, and so on. This claim seems to mimic modern day ideas about emotional feedback loops and comorbidity, or the idea that multiple coexisting health conditions can interact and intensify one another.

All of this seems a lot like a therapy session. Just as the Hammonds advised members of deliverance teams to do, therapists help their patients seek out problems in their lives, the root causes of those problems, and then to set about resolving these problems through honest discussions about the issues. They advise patients to replace self-blame with self-compassion. They seek to isolate comorbid psychological features and find a path for resolution.

Given these similarities, a person might find themselves wondering: Why not accept the Hammonds' approach, then, instead of going to a professional psychologist? The answer is, in part, one of limitations. Once again, it's likely that the Hammonds regularly achieved results with people's small-scale problems, possibly even with a few large and complex ones. The chances, however, that someone would find a long-term resolution for crippling addictions, suicidal depressive states, and other major psychological disturbances by working with what amounts to untrained, amateur talk-therapists seems slim. Yet the Hammonds are clearly advocating for the use of their technique in such situations. Ida Mae's most identifiable contribution to the work is an entire chapter that deals with delivering those who are afflicted with schizophrenia, arguably one of the most devastating mental illnesses one can suffer from. Furthermore, after the work of the deliverance ministry is over, the Hammonds' approach requires very little additional responsibility:

> What we are after through deliverance is to cast out the demons and their influence in order to replace them with Jesus and the fruit of the Spirit . . . to gain permanent benefit from deliverance, the 'house' must be filled and kept filled [with the Spirit]. Otherwise the evil spirits will return and may return to greater force than before.[3]

That is to say, once the Hammonds' technique has "healed" a person, it's up to them to maintain their healed status. This is an unreasonable stance to take when attempting to help people who are suffering from mental illness, as such individuals often fluctuate in mental health, a natural occurrence, which, if not dealt with professionally and compassionately, might lead them to blame themselves (and possibly, their community to blame them) for failing to keep their house "filled" with the Holy Spirit.

Also concerning is the Hammonds' claim that the supposed benefits of their deliverance ministry applied not just to the psychological but also to the medical realm. They assert that "many diseases and physical afflictions are due to spirits of infirmity" and that there is a "close relationship between deliverance and healing."[4] Frank Hammond even claims that he was "casting a *demon of cancer* out of a woman" at one point in his ministry.[5]

Frank Hammond also claims that his parents both died of heart trouble as did his aunts and uncles. He says that his doctors had warned him about heart issues, and he had apparently suffered two heart attacks by the time his book was written. However, Hammond states that he "cast out the *demon of heart attack*. That was five years ago, and I have never had another pain in my chest and no longer expect to have one."[6] Now, admittedly, Hammond lived another three decades, dying at the relatively ripe age of 83, and I've not been able to find his cause of death anywhere. Still, given his confidence in the ability to heal cardiac issues through exorcism, if I were a betting man, my guess would be heart attack.

Politics and Personhood

Perhaps the most problematic aspect of the Hammonds' ministry is that they were some of the earliest popular proponents of the idea of territorial spirits. We'll delve a lot deeper into this issue in part 5, but it will suffice for now to note that the Hammonds believed that the same kinds of demons that bedeviled individual people also had powerful siblings who ruled over political territories.

This is a small but significant shift from our other horsemen's views of demonic politics. Although Unger talks about demons deceiving nations, he discusses them as an amorphous vast presence or as part of a vast Satanic system described as a whole rather than with individual, specific moving parts.[7] Likewise, Harper's focus on demonic politics is minimal, though he does describe the influence of Satan among the nations in a somewhat similar fashion to Unger. And while territorial demons might be a feature tucked away in some of Graham's work, in his book *Angels* (1995) he treats politics and demons much as Unger and Harper do.[8]

In contrast, the Hammonds state plainly that "the angel that visited Daniel reported that he had encountered and fought with the 'prince of Persia,' meaning the ruling demon potentate over that nation. We see this as evidence that Satan has assigned a powerful demon ruler over every nation of the world, and, in turn, over every city and community."[9] In other words, not only do people have their own individual demons, but every community in the world has a resident ruler who organizes his underlings.

The Hammonds go on to give an example of a community that had a demon of jealousy ruling over it. This demon is described in a vision (presumably given to Frank) as a "large, octopus-like creature hovering over the community. . . . Its tentacles reached down and were entwining and crushing every facet of community life."[10] This demon, which Frank identifies as "Jealousy," was in this case not a unique demon assigned to one person but rather a larger scale version of the many demons of jealousy that inhabit individual people. In this way, they show that the spirits that can dwell in people are the same spirits that control cities and countries.

And that means they can be fought in the same way. That is to say, these demons' methods and names can be ferreted out and used against them, prayer can be used bind them, and eventually they can be expelled from the political body just like they can the human one.

These ideas put forth by the Hammonds remain with us. By this I mean that contemporary religious and political movements (such as the NAR, which we will discuss in part 5) that believe demons are influencing the political fabric of America in the present day are continuing to use the Hammonds' ideas as a blueprint for dealing with political demons.

Wrestling with the Powers

At the end of their discussion of political demons, the Hammonds proclaim:

> Hope for our communities and nation does not lie in social and governmental programs. Neither does it lie in education

> or science. Our problems are basically spiritual, God has given us spiritual weapons and resources for victory. The church has the answer. It must take the offensive against the ranks of demonic powers while there is yet time. How is this done? By wrestling with these powers in spiritual warfare. Vocalize your position in Christ and your authority over these demon forces just as you would in personal warfare. Praise God, Christians everywhere are learning these techniques of spiritual battle. A revival is being loosed![11]

These words seem somewhat prescient. As interest in the demonic was poised to explode in the United States, Frank and Ida Mae found an unexpectedly large audience eager to devour works like theirs, works that were in short supply. *Pigs in the Parlor* quickly became one of the most influential deliverance manuals, and Frank and Ida Mae some of the most trusted practitioners of deliverance ministry.

As the '80s dawned, a new breed of political-spiritual warrior would take the Hammonds up on this charge. Such individuals would see demonic cults attacking the most vulnerable and poisoning the nation through vice and excess. Armed with this knowledge, they would propel a man to the presidency who shared their beliefs and who would go on to make good on promises to combat the forces of evil.

The man I'm referring to is, of course, Ronald Reagan. And in the 1980s, he ran for the office of the presidency using a unique campaign slogan that was especially appealing to conservative Christians: Let's Make America Great Again.

CHAPTER SIXTEEN

The Satanic Panic

FROM THE MIDDLE of the twentieth century to the end of the '80s, a unique stew of spiritual-political messaging had been quietly brewing beneath the surface of the United States. The messages of the four horsemen and other theologically conservative spiritual teachers had slowly mixed with contemporary fictional media, creating a mélange of popular American demonology that now had many conservative Christians looking over their shoulders for the demons in their midst. Inserting themselves into a mix of true believers, con artists of every stripe contributed to the promotion of these ideas, with many claiming to be ex-witches, Satanists, or experts on the topics of these same groups. The idea of demons and the cults that worshipped them at first trickled into the American mind and then flooded it. Of course, as often happens in a deluge, a dam eventually burst. The ideas that the dam had held back are the ones noted above. The flood that engulfed America came to be known as the "Satanic Panic."

As we'll see in this chapter, the Satanic Panic was an idea that would grip the American mind for over a decade. From 1980 to 1994, it would be widely believed that shadowy Satanic cults were abusing children at daycares and luring teens into their deviant ways with rock music and roleplaying games. Seemingly all parts of American society participated in this shared delusion, from psychologists and law enforcement officials to political figures and stay-at-home moms.

The effect of the Panic (intentional or not) was the creation of a sociopolitical environment that was conducive to conservative Christian values. Accessing abortion services and sending children to daycare were two practices that came to be associated with demons, a taboo that increasingly drove women away from two services that allowed them to choose a path other than traditional motherhood. The sitting US president overtly associated communism with the Devil. Pornography and drugs became outlets through which the Devil recruited people.

And it was a single book that started the flood.

Michelle Remembers

In many ways the United States today is still trying to process the Satanic Panic. As immersed as our country is today in the ideas of spiritual warfare and of cults ruling the United States from behind the scenes, many people feel that only a very small minority of Americans hold such beliefs. In one class in which I taught about this very subject, a student once commented, "Sure, but isn't that just crazies on the internet?" The idea that there once existed in our country an idea of a Satanic conspiracy that was so vast and well-believed that psychologists, law enforcement, talk show hosts, and political figures all rallied behind it is difficult to grasp. But that is exactly what happened.

The first tip off that something was profoundly wrong was the public reception of the book, *Michelle Remembers*. Written by the Canadian psychiatrist Lawrence Pazder, the book allegedly details the recovered memories of his patient, anonymized with the name "Michelle Smith." (The patient's name was actually Michelle Proby, that is, until she later married Pazder following the book's release. Let the ethical implications of that biographical fact sink in for a minute). During the course of her therapy with Pazder, Michelle is alleged to have uncovered memories of her ritual abuse at the hands of a secret Satanic organization. In many ways, this account reads as the opposite of the aforementioned Michael Warnke's *The Satan-Seller* (see "The Takeaways from *Rosemary's Baby*" in chapter 13). Whereas Warnke claimed to have dealt drugs and summoned demons as the leader of a Satanic Cult, Michelle was the victim of just such a group, which Pazder identified as "the Church of Satan."[1]

If the presence of a secret, underground cult was the only fabulous narrative that the book claimed as fact, it would perhaps be understandable that people believed the story. However, the work also purports that a possessed woman (whose head twisting, tongue wagging actions appear to be taken straight out of *The Exorcist*) accosted Michelle, that Michelle was subsequently imprisoned within a "demonic idol," and that she was drenched in the blood of babies during a Satanic ritual. At the apex of the book, the Devil—the literal, embodied Devil—appears, wraps his tail around Michelle's neck, and drags her around while spouting poorly rhymed prophecy.

Besides presenting all of this as fact, the book clearly attempts to paint Michelle as some kind of holy figure. Before the readers' eyes, she is given a unique window into the Devil's plan for the End of Days, meets with Jesus and Mary, and receives advice from the archangel Michael. It is as if yet another of the Saints' Lives from the Middle Ages, chock full of miracles and demonic manifestations, has come to life under the influence of Pazder's pen.

And people believed it. The book became a bestseller, and Pazder was propelled into the media spotlight as the one and only expert in what was perceived to be a new category of criminal abuse: satanic ritual abuse (SRA). As Megan Goodwin writes in *Abusing Religion: Literary Persecution, Sex Scandals, and American Minority Religions*:

> Through the publication of *Michelle Remembers* and the dissemination of his expertise through seminars, workshops, and distributed materials, Pazder molded Michelle Smith's memories into a repeatable narrative of ritual abuse, informing investigations and prosecutions of satanic ritual abuse, and later codified and institutionalized in the revised third edition of the American Psychiatric Association's Diagnostic and Statistical Manual of Mental Disorders (DSM-III-R).[2]

Once more, demons had bled into the field of psychology, this time, officially.

What could have compelled people to accept such a fantastic narrative? First, as we've discussed, people had been primed by conservative Christian theology (from the four horsemen and others) to accept the supposed reality of demons. They had also been exposed to films that offered a visual confirmation of this idea of demons, and the growing phenomenon of tell-alls branded as nonfiction and written by fictitious ex-warlocks, ex-Satanists, ex-witches, etc., seemingly supported the idea as well. Meanwhile, some indisputable real-life facts connected with the imagined narratives. For one, a disaffected showman named Anton LaVey had recently incorporated an atheistic organization called the "Church of Satan." Although its members did not literally believe in or worship a real-life Satan and the church rather was established as a symbol of rebellion against religious and other authority, many people found its name alarming and made assumptions about its followers.

Around this same time, widespread interest in the New Age movement and its related practices and philosophies had created more witches, so-called Satanists, and Spiritualists than one could shake an oaken wand at.

All of these were critical factors in people's acceptance of the idea of a Satanic conspiracy. However, I would suggest that the real reason that people accepted these far-fetched stories (and also the reason people generally accept such narratives) is simple: They wanted to believe it. In the book *Michelle Remembers*, conservative Christians found (perhaps, unconsciously; perhaps, not) not only a validation in their apocalyptic and demonic beliefs, but also a way to skew the political narrative in their favor once more.

Demonic Daycare

In the wake of Pazder's book, copycats began emerging by the dozens. By 1994, *over twelve thousand accusations* of SRA were under or had been under investigation by the United States government, spanning over a hundred trials. Of all of these, the most influential set of accusations by far occurred in the so-called McMartin Preschool Trial, which remains at the time of this writing the longest and most expensive trial in US criminal history.

The accusations began in 1983 with a mother named Judy Johnson who accused an employee of McMartin Preschool in Manhattan Beach, California of sexually assaulting her son. As the accusation was investigated, other children were gradually enfolded into the investigators' interview process. As these other children were interviewed, they told additional stories of abuse, and accusations of cannibalism, infant sacrifice, and orgiastic practices were slowly added to a growing list of felony child abuse charges (fifty-two in all).[3]

The problem we encounter here is the same problem that may have plagued Pazder's work: In the first half of the twentieth century, memory had been generally viewed as a kind of infallible picture that was stored away somewhere in the brain. Pazder himself promoted the idea that hypnosis and questioning could bring out those memories accurately without influencing them.

Unfortunately, that's not actually how memory works. Instead, researchers have discovered that our memories are more or less constructed (and reconstructed) every time that we are asked to recall them. One particular factor worth noting in the context of the McMartin Preschool case is that methods of questioning can significantly impact this process of remembering, especially in impressionable populations like grade school aged children. Memory can also be coerced if someone wants a person to answer in a certain way badly enough.

Which explains why when Pazder became involved in the case, the accusations took a demonic turn. Pazder was convinced that an international satanic conspiracy was at the heart of the McMartin accusations, and he met with parents and therapists involved in the trial in 1984 to discuss the conspiracy.[4] Smith likewise met with the supposed victims in the case.[5] And their discussions were influential: "law enforcement officials, social workers, forensic investigators, parents, and prosecutors were so convinced by Pazder and Smith's account that they compelled young children to adopt Smith's story as their own."[6] The accusations were salacious enough that they quickly spread through tabloids and talk shows.

To understand how this outcome might ultimately prove advantageous to conservative Christians, we need to take a step back to think about the progression of women's rights and feminism. We've already encountered in earlier chapters what is referred to as "first-wave feminism": many of our Spiritualists were suffragettes pursuing the right to vote. Later, in the 1960s, a second wave of feminism began, a movement that turned its attention to matters of the home: reproductive rights, domestic matters, and workplace inequality.

By the 1970s, that movement clearly understood what was needed for the equality it sought for women to be achieved. As Linda Charlton, reporting for *The New York Times*, said of a feminist march on Fifth Avenue: "Demands for free abortion on request, a system of 24-hour day-care centers for the children of working mothers and equality of educational and employment opportunity are the three central issues."[7]

The reason these three issues rose to the top is that access to these supports allowed women the freedom to choose "traditional" domestic motherhood, an occupation, or a combination of the two without unnecessary sacrifice. That is to say, someone could choose whether to be pregnant or not (abortion), choose whether to work or not (childcare), and choose their occupation freely (education).

The problem was that such access flew in the face of conservative Christian gender roles. From the perspective of many such groups, a woman's place was in the home. Then and now, conservative Christians saw, and continue to see, sharp divisions in labor distribution between what they recognize as only two genders. In this paradigm, men are protectors and workers while women are nurturers and child-rearers. The idea that women and men might switch places (or that women would be able to feasibly become mothers outside of marriage) was intrinsically threatening to those who held these beliefs.

By the '80s, this fear had, in part, contributed to a surprising and previously unforeseen partnership: Conservative Roman Catholics and conservative Protestant Christians had become relatively lockstep on the urgent issues of abortion and birth control. While this collaboration may seemingly "make sense" from our present viewpoint, it would have been inconceivable even two decades before it happened: while the Roman Catholic Church had always been relatively opposed to abortion and birth control, most mainline Protestant Churches had supported Roe v. Wade in 1973, and saw no reason to join Roman Catholics in their protests.[8] Yet, a decade later, conservative Protestants and Roman Catholics became unlikely bed fellows.

All of this might explain why fetuses and aborted babies factor so significantly in SRA narratives, as a moral element that some authors may have chosen unconsciously. In *Michelle Remembers*, one of the most grotesque scenes includes one of the Satanists using a fetus in a ritual involving Michelle.[9] *Satan's Underground*, another famous work from the Satanic Panic period we'll discuss shortly, includes the claim that Satan favors the sacrifice of "infants—sometimes taken directly from a pregnant young mother."[10] SRA narratives also invoked the idea that individuals were forced to have abortions or that aborted babies were used in ritual abuse. The overall effect was that abortion would become associated with Satanic practices in the public mind.

At the same time, the SRA narratives induced widespread fear of the "dangers" of childcare, a beneficial outcome for those who sought traditional household gender roles. This was a natural response. After all, as more and more accusations began to mount and spread in popular media, how was one able to tell if they had found a "good" daycare or one that was overrun by Satanists? Better to simply stay home with one's children than risk them being scarred for life by SRA or worse.

The Evils of Communism

The Satanic Panic has an eerie correlation with the presidency of Ronald Reagan. At the time of his election, the Panic was just beginning its rise, and by the end, it had started a long, slow process of collapse. While Reagan did not have the same kind of close relationship with the evangelicals of his time that President Trump has had with QAnon and conservative evangelical groups of our day (relationships that we will discuss in part 5), he *was* similarly propelled into the White House on a wave of evangelical support by signaling that he shared the same values that they did.

Despite these shared values, though, Ronald Reagan does not appear to have held many substantive beliefs in the demonic. Rather, he seems to have been very good at mirroring conservative Christian concerns while not also parroting their exact language. It is unclear whether behind the scenes he believed in the same spiritual concepts they did, but he did give one speech that seems to suggest he at least had a general notion of the Devil being active in the world.

"There is sin and evil in the world, and we're enjoined by Scripture and the Lord Jesus to oppose it with all our might," Reagan declared to the National Association of Evangelicals in 1983. In his so-called Evil Empire speech, Reagan took aim at communism, the same demonic boogeyman that had been popular with Unger and Graham, by declaring that the Soviet Union was the aforementioned Evil Empire and that the struggle in which the United States was engaged was a "struggle between right and wrong, good and evil." In this struggle against evil, Reagan saw great promise in the United States, noting that "there's a great spiritual awakening in America, a renewal of the traditional values that have been the bedrock of America's goodness and greatness." If the Evangelicals in the room were initially unsure whether he was talking to them, he later drove that alignment home with his claim that the people who embody such goodness "disapprove of adultery, teenage sex, pornography, abortion, and hard drugs." He then reminded his listeners of the words of the former Communist spy Whittaker Chambers: "Marxism-Leninism is actually the second oldest faith, first proclaimed in the Garden of Eden with the words of temptation, 'Ye shall be as gods.'"[11]

Even at a time when public pronouncements lacked many of the inflammatory characteristics that are so common today, a sitting US president was still willing to claim that communism had been created by the Devil.

Pornographic Pandemonium

This proclamation is not the only important takeaway from the Evil Empire speech. Reagan's laundry list of "adultery, teenage sex, pornography, abortion, and hard drugs" was not just a nod to the evangelical faithful; it was also a list of demonic gateways that had exposed America to its present hardships. Unsurprisingly, this list was already near and dear to the hearts of conservative Christians who represented the base of his support.

One such conservative Christian was Edwin Meese, who was the attorney general for the Reagan Administration from 1985 to 1988 until he was forced to resign due to a financial scandal. Before that scandal, Meese personally took on two prongs of the aforementioned laundry list: drugs and pornography. With regard to drugs, he chaired the National Drug Policy Board, which coordinated Nancy Reagan's memorable "Just Say No" anti-drug campaign that every child of the '80s grew up with.

With respect to pornography, Meese became instrumental in establishing the Attorney General's Commission on Pornography (1986), a federal investigation that Ronald Reagan ordered and that became nicknamed the Meese Report. The Meese Report found connections between pornography and a host of social ills that included organized crime and sexual violence. According to the report, pornography was a virtual horror show that threatened the United States.

Unfortunately, the Meese Report wasn't conducted terribly well. Both lay organizations and scientific groups raised concerns about the commission's handling of evidence regarding pornography. Reflecting back on it decades later, the American journalist Tim Alberta, wrote in Politico:

> When it landed, the 1,960-page Meese Report surprised exactly no one: It concluded that pornography was a threat to society

> and recommended harsher enforcement of obscenity laws. In a particularly memorable passage, the report said the link between porn consumption and violence "requires assumptions not found exclusively in the experimental evidence," yet concluded, "We see no reason, however, not to make these assumptions . . . that are plainly justified by our own common sense."[12]

Of course, "common sense" is a horrible scientific justification for any conclusion.

In light of all the factors we've examined, it is perhaps not surprising that the final "great" work of the Panic, Lauren Stratford's *Satan's Underground: The Extraordinary Story of One Woman's Escape* (1988), reads as something of a love letter to Edwin Meese. Stratford was actually the pen name of Laurel Rose Willson, who, in keeping with figures like Warnke, Todd, and others, had created an elaborate narrative of ritual abuse at the hands of Satanists that she said led to her experiencing miracles and eventually converting to Christianity—although her claims about her abuse were later discredited.

Like Mike Warnke and Michelle Smith, Stratford drew from film and other media to create a convincing (for the time) picture of a Satanic cult that was abusing people. Like Warnke, she also claimed that drugs were an essential part of her descent into the Satanic underground; like Smith, she claimed horrendous abuse at the hands of the cult.

What was different about Stratford's claims was the way in which she extensively integrated pornography into them. In Stratford's fantasy world, pornography and Satanism were inextricably connected. The two are clearly portrayed as inseparable when she states in the book's opening that her account is not *just* for the benefit of those "who need to be informed of the realities of pornography and satanism."[13] From this foreword that links the two phenomena, Stratford goes on to describe being regularly drugged and forced to take pornographic pictures "with animals, with other women, and with children."[14] Shackled by drugs, abusive keepers, and death threats, Stratford eventually is brought to "Victor," the leader of an organized crime ring to become a prostitute. She claims that while she was at Victor's ranch the clients who came to her were "men with money, prestige, position, and power. They knew how to use it, and they knew how to hide behind it."[15]

Drugs, pornography, alcohol, and a host of other vices flowed at Victor's ranch; until finally the ultimate drug, Satanism, made an appearance. According to Stratford, "Victor would never be bored again, for Satan knows no limits in his diabolical schemes."[16] Since Victor had chosen Stratford to be "his girl," she was pulled into Satanic worship as well. She claims to have witnessed people selling their souls (and the souls of their unborn babies) to Satan, to have seen demons being summoned, to have participated in satanic orgies, and to have been trapped in a barrel with dead babies.

In the eyes of Stratford's audience, the connection was clear: Pornography and drugs lead to Satanism. It was as if Stratford had read the Meese Report and woven a diabolical narrative around its core themes. It was as if to say that the only thing that Meese left out of his report was the Devil.

Talk Show Satanism

By this time, the Satanic Panic was big business. Truckloads of books by authors whose stories supported it had been sold, accusations upon accusations had been levied, and news programs had churned out lurid stories that fed into the fear it spread. Now, it was time for the talk show circuit.

The first such program to make a splash was Geraldo Rivera's "Devil Worship: Exposing Satan's Underground," which aired in 1988. In this ostensibly "investigative" report, Rivera alleges that Satanism is "flourishing" in America. The first part of the program includes quotes from actual members of the Church of Satan taken out of context, footage from rock concerts, videotaped scenes of deliverance ministers expelling demons, and wild claims by law enforcement officials about cult activity, all set against an ominous musical soundtrack. The effect is to link these matters together in the mind of the audience, uniting all of these disparate elements into one massive, connected, amorphous threat.

The remaining hour and a half follows the same pattern. Rivera groups an unlikely cast of guests together, from real and benign "Satanists"—like Michael Aquino of the Temple of Set, a successor organization to Anton LaVey's Church of Satan, and Zeena Schreck, LaVey's daughter—with con artists such as Stratford herself, who makes an appearance in which she talks about sacrificing the hearts of infants to the Devil. Along the way, Ozzy Osbourne is called in to defend heavy metal music and deny its "obvious" connections to Satanism; an earlier interview between Geraldo and Charles Manson is aired; and various historical "facts" about Satanism are offered to the audience.

The special was immensely popular. According to an October 27, 1988 article in the *Los Angeles Times* that followed the show's release "'Devil Worship: Exposing Satan's Underground' won its two-hour time period Tuesday night with a 21.9 rating and a 33 share of audience—meaning it was seen in about 19.8 million homes, one-third of the number that were watching TV between 8 and 10 p.m."[17] These were the highest ratings for a documentary at that point in time.[18]

Two years earlier, in late 1986, what would become one of the highest rated talk shows in American history, *The Oprah Winfrey Show*, had just begun its eventual twenty-five-season run. Records of the show are hard to come by (as are the episodes themselves), but there appear to be several episodes spread across '88 and '89 that dealt with Satanic Panic material. In one episode, both Michelle Smith and Lauren Stratford related their tales to the audience. According to the journalist Dan Shewan writing for *Pacific Standard* in 2015, "both women's experiences were presented by Winfrey as incontrovertible fact, and not once did she question the authenticity of any claim in either book."[19]

The Sally Jessy Raphael Show, another popular talk show that began a long-term run starting in the early '80s, also hosted Satanic Panic accusers. Erika Ingram, one of a pair of sisters who accused their father of SRA, came on the show to describe her experiences, one of which included "a ritual abortion. 'The baby was still alive when they took it out,' she said, 'and they put it on top of me and then they cut it up.'"[20]

These talk show hosts knew a key element of their business: Fear is a powerful motive for media consumption. People around the nation waited with bated breath to hear about the cults that had infested their communities. And less than a decade later, it would turn out to be nothing more than a fantasy.

A Fantasy Goes Underground

Perhaps somewhat fittingly, on Halloween of 1994, Daniel Goleman, then a science journalist at *The New York Times*, published an article entitled, "Proof Lacking for Ritual Abuse by Satanists." In the opening of the article, Goleman states:

> Tales of satanic ritual abuse, with well-organized cults sacrificing animals and babies and engaging in sexual perversion and cannibalism, is the stuff of tabloid television. Now the first empirical study of its actual prevalence, based on information from district attorneys, social service workers, police officials and psychotherapists, suggests that these tales are usually just that—figments of imagination.[21]

By that point, the National Center on Child Abuse and Neglect had researched more than twelve thousand accusations of SRA and found "not one that investigators had been able to substantiate."[22]

Despite all the supposed first person accounts of engagement with Satanic rituals and witchcraft, the claims of a Satanic conspiracy, the supposed recovery of repressed memories of abuse, the accusations and in-depth investigations of incidents of SRA, presidential concerns about the struggle between good and evil, government investigations into pornography, and lurid accounts delivered by questionable guests on episodes of beloved talk shows, in the end the fantastical accounts of underground, international, shadowy Satanic cults had ultimately proved to be just that: a fantasy.

The Modern Takeaway

Satanic Panic Redux

GOLEMAN'S ARTICLE DID not just debunk the SRA claims from the period of the Satanic Panic. It proved to be somewhat prophetic as well. Toward the end of the piece, Goleman notes "There are, of course, people who will be unswayed by this new study because of their belief that abusive satanic groups do exist but are successful at eluding detection."[1]

And that is exactly what happened. While the Satanic Panic ended for the vast majority of Americans, a substantial number of people remained unconvinced by the evidence. Some of these became convinced that the more overt manifestations of the Satanic Panic were over, but clung fast to the idea that drugs, pornography, and communism remained windows by which people could fall into demonic possession and Satanism.

Still others continued to nurse the full Satanic Panic in secret. For these individuals, both popular culture and discredited psychologists would become ever-present sources of ideas for how such groups could hide in plain sight, while conspiratorial media would launch the trend of "alternative facts." Together, these would continue to feed the ongoing Satanic Panic until it transformed into something altogether more dangerous: the far-right conspiracy theory and movement QAnon.

Drugs, Pornography, and Communism

The idea that drugs, pornography, and communism are gateways for the demonic to enter a person is just as strong today in the minds of many conservative Christians as it was in the '80s. One need look no farther than YouTube to see the impact such ideas continue to have. On that platform, search terms such as "spiritual warfare and addiction" will turn up countless videos purporting to offer prayers to help people break addictions to drugs and pornography permanently, explanations of how both temptations function as gateways to demonic influence, and advice from exorcists and deliverance ministers on the same subject.

Searches for "spiritual warfare and communism" turn up a significant number of videos as well. A surprising number of these are simply newly posted examples of popular speakers from the '70s and '80s such as the Pentecostal pastor and Bible teacher Derek Prince, whose work inspired the Hammonds, and Billy Graham.

For those less technologically savvy or inclined, books, of course, still continue to be published on the subject. For instance, Paul Kengor, professor of political science at Grove City College and editor of the conservative magazine *The American Spectator*, in 2020 published a book entitled *The Devil and Karl Marx: Communism's Long March of Death, Deception, and Infiltration*. This work purports to explore the "diabolical side of Karl Marx" and provide "a chilling retrospective on an evil that should have never been let out of its pit."[2]

"How could the Father of Lies not be involved?" the last sentence on Kengor's book jacket asks. Within the text itself, Kengor seems to play both sides, on the one hand hedging via milquetoast statements like "For the record, I will state upfront that I have not encountered nor do I present evidence of Karl Marx, say, conducting séances or engaging in black Masses or Satanic rituals, even as other writers on Marx have speculated on that stark possibility" and "Well, I certainly have no proof that Karl Marx was a Satanist, nor can I can confirm whether he was possessed. I would not dare hazard such a charge."[3]

On the other hand, the book has been remarkably popular with conservative Christians, a group to which he was no doubt attempting to appeal when he chose as the grounding biblical quote for his work a line commonly referenced in arguments about spiritual warfare: "For we are not contending against flesh and blood, but against the principalities, against the powers, against the world rulers of this present darkness, against the spiritual hosts of wickedness in the heavenly places" (Ephesians 6:12 RSV).

Following the Satanic Panic, the supposed connection between demons and addictions to pornography and drugs also works its way into a variety of different published works. While books with titles such as *Breaking the Spirit of Addiction* (2011) or *Demons, Drugs and Deliverance* (2018) broadcast the connection their authors see between evil spirits and forms of addiction in relatively clear language, just as many other writers play their cards close to the vest. For instance, *Setting Captives Free* (2020) punts this point to the subtitle "How to Break the Chains of Demonic Influence" and includes scenes in which the author

Jake Kail relates his accounts of delivering groups of men from spirits of lust and pornography and answers the question, "Can there be a demonic influence in alcoholism, drug abuse, and other addictions?" with "Yes, absolutely."[4] Still other modern volumes continue where the Hammonds left off, as in the work of Southern Baptist minister Don Dickerman, which includes such illuminating titles as *Keep the Pigs Out: How to Slam the Door Shut on Satan and His Demons and Keep Your Spiritual House Clean* (2010) and *People, Pigs, and Principalities: The Reality and Power of the Supernatural in Your Life* (2014).

QAnon

The Return of the Satanic Panic

While pornography, drugs, and communism are mainstream elements of the Satanic Panic that continue to be linked with demons in our time, the more outrageous claims of the Panic also continue to exert an influence on some far-right conservatives as well. That includes sensationalistic claims of SRA.

As many readers may recall, in 2016, amid the Clinton-Trump election face-off, a viral rumor began to circulate online that linked the emails of John Podesta, the chair of Hillary Clinton's presidential campaign, to Comet Ping Pong, a pizzeria in Washington, DC. In this fictitious accounting, a basement existed inside of Comet Ping Pong that housed a child sex trafficking ring that was owned and operated by Hillary Clinton: an idea that seemed to mirror the long-ago debunked claim that tunnels existed beneath the McMartin Preschool and SRA was carried out in them. In December of 2016, a couple of months after the so-called PizzaGate rumor began, a gunman who took it upon himself to "investigate" the claim entered the restaurant and fired three shots into the floor and a door, only to find that Comet Ping Pong had no basement.

That should have been the end of it. But in 2017, a new figure arrived to organize the former PizzaGate believers: a poster on the online message board 4chan who identified as Q. Q claimed that he had "Q Clearance," a real-life security designation in the Department of Energy. Ostensibly, Q was posting in order to inform "patriots" with "crumbs" of information about a gradually unfolding plan made by then-President Trump to remove from their government positions members of what he called the "Deep State": a shadowy network of individuals—often tarred with a Satanic or demonic brush—working from within the government to undermine Trump and to control the United States.[5]

Eventually, this idea of the Deep State expanded to include the notion that there existed organizations of child-molesting and devouring Democrats who were worshipping Satan and colluding with demons. Followers of Q's conspiracy theories, often called "Anons" for "Anonymous," posted purported "evidence" on various websites, including quotations from some of the con artists we've discussed, clips from programs like *The Oprah Winfrey Show*, and analysis of other media content that they claimed exposed the secret goings-on of various elements of the so-called Deep State.

In other words, the Satanic Panic that had once been driven underground was back out in the open air.

It is interesting to me that news programs that air stories about QAnon often exclude from the discussion the parts of the following that have to do with Satan and demons. It may be that this omission is partly due to ideas we have about the intellectual legitimacy of demons; if the general population dismisses these dangerous groups because we feel that they are ridiculous, then news programs are perhaps correct to make such exclusions.

However, I fear this omission may be partially designed to mask how clearly aligned the movement is with conservative Christian thought, something that might cost them audience members. Consider, for example, the following excerpt from Q's opening salvo of posts: "Open your eyes . . . Many in our govt worship Satan."[6] While this claim in and of itself could be understood as a metaphor, a kind of over the top suggestion of just how "evil" the government is, Q also frequently invokes spiritual warfare ideas or demonic ideas, such as in *ten* tweets in which he quotes "Put on the full armor of God so that you can take your stand against the devil's schemes. For our struggle is not against flesh and blood, but against the rulers, against the authorities, against the powers of this dark world and against the spiritual forces of evil in the heavenly realms"[7] (Ephesians 6:11–12, NIV) as well as additional invocations to his followers to "put on the armor of God."[8]

In reading all this, you might be inclined to see all of these wild claims as outlandish. You would not be wrong.

And as outlandish as all this might seem? You ain't seen nothing yet.

Part V

Rise of the New Apostolic Reformation

The New Millennium

CHAPTER SEVENTEEN

Out with the Old and In with the New Apostolic Reformation

OF ALL THE groups I write about in this book, the NAR (remember my visit to "The Courage Tour" in Chapter 1?), is one of the most challenging. That is because it is nebulous in structure and nature: not a denomination but a movement. While very few churches or individuals will openly identify themselves as being part of the NAR, many websites offer advice on how to detect the movement's impact in one's congregation. One such resource, "How to Spot an NAR Church,"[1] can be found on the website of Holly Pivec, coauthor of several books critical of the movement, including *Counterfeit Kingdom: The Dangers of New Revelation, New Prophets, and New Age Practices in the Church* (2022).

The movement is powerfully influential. Individuals involved in it today have, through their rhetoric and significant financial resources, helped propel Donald J. Trump to victory in two elections. It is also pernicious. The NAR believes in a "dominionist" theology, that is, the idea that Christians are mandated to ascend to positions of power and turn the government toward biblical understandings of law and society, and while dominionist theologies are not unique to the NAR, the NAR is unique in that it seems poised to realize its goal in the United States.

As a result, the NAR is a challenging movement to nail down. For that reason, rather than worry about exactly which groups explicitly or implicitly identify themselves as NAR churches or movements, I'm instead going to focus in this chapter on the NAR as a kind of intellectual configuration. Specifically, this part of the book will focus on writers and groups that have an idea of spiritual warfare that operates on multiple levels (we'll talk about those levels in the next chapter), at least one of which must have a political dimension. That is to say, "NAR" in this section is a placeholder for groups or authors who believe that what they see as biblical demons are influencing the sociopolitical environment of the United States.

But before we talk about the power the NAR movement wields today or about its rather unique view of the demonic, let's talk a little bit about how it began.

Pentecostalism and the Latter Rain[2]

Like many social movements and Christian organizations, the NAR movement did not emerge in a vacuum. First and foremost, the movement is theologically influenced by Pentecostal Christianity, a branch of Protestantism that emphasizes the direct experience of God through the Holy Spirit. The name *Pentecostal* comes from Pentecost, an event in Acts in which the Holy Spirit is said to have descended upon the apostles. This descent precipitated an experience among the people present that is commonly referred to as "speaking in tongues," and further signs and wonders were promised "in the last days" (Acts 2:14).

Pentecostals generally accept the idea that the so-called last days have arrived and that signs and wonders are appearing again, and that those who are "baptized in the Spirit" are able to perform such wonders. In this sense, Pentecostals can be also classed as what are often called "charismatic Christians"—the word *charismata* in Greek refers to gifts of grace or spiritual gifts. Pentecostalism is a large and diverse Christian movement that began in 1906 with the Azusa Street Revival, a series of revival meetings that took place in Los Angeles in the early 1900s. By the late 1940s, a movement had arisen within Pentecostalism that would later have a big influence on the NAR. That group was the Latter Rain.

The theological concept of latter rain is rooted in a motif found largely in the Hebrew Bible, as in the following examples of Joel 2:23 and 2:28–29:

> *Be glad then, you children of Zion,*
> *And rejoice in the Lord your God;*
> *For He has given you the former rain faithfully,*
> *And He will cause the rain to come down for you—*
> *The former rain,*
> *And the latter rain in the first month.*

> *"And it shall come to pass afterward*
> *That I will pour out My Spirit on all flesh;*
> *Your sons and your daughters shall prophesy,*
> *Your old men shall dream dreams,*
> *Your young men shall see visions.*
> *And also on My menservants and on My maidservants*
> *I will pour out My Spirit in those days."*

These verses speak of two periods of rainfall in the land of Israel, "the former rain" and the "latter rain," which were crucial to agricultural cycles. For Latter Rain believers, these two periods became analogous to two historical periods during which God did and would "pour out" his holiness on the faithful: first, the outpouring of the Holy Spirit during the days of the early church, as at Pentecost, and a later period that would precede Christ's return, which they believed had already begun.

The group believed that this "pouring out" of holiness would result in truly spectacular spiritual gifts. A clear example of these spectacular, final gifts is discussed in the book *The Feast of Tabernacles*, in which Canadian theologian George H. Warnock describes a Latter Rain doctrine known as the "Manifest Sons of God." In this work, Warnock claims that the latter rain period will see a "manifestation of the sons of God and the glorious display of God's power and glory."[3] He suggests that those "sons of God," or "Overcomers," will be gifted powers like the ones held by Jesus himself. They will be able to evade capture by authorities by disappearing or being "caught away in the Spirit like Philip the evangelist."[4] Opponents will find their blades "blunted as truly as if they had charged an armored tank" and bullets will "glance off his brow, as it would from a heavy plate of steel." Prison doors will unlock, poison will have no effect, and even "the most powerful atom or hydrogen bomb ever invented shall be perfectly harmless" to such people.[5] In essence, the manifested sons of God are superheroes capable of many otherwise impossible acts.

The Latter Rain movement also taught that there are five distinct ministry roles that exist within the church, as identified in Ephesians 4:11: "the apostles, the prophets, the evangelists, the pastors and teachers." Even today, it remains common in NAR circles for church leaders to identify themselves as *apostles* and *prophets* rather than as pastors. Since the Latter Rain movement tended to emphasize the autonomy of churches, this often meant that self-described "apostles" and "prophets" experienced little to no supervision over how they ministered to those under their care.

The Charismatic Renewal, Deliverance, and the Shepherding Movement

A decade after the emergence of Latter Rain, a new charismatic movement began to take shape. In 1960, "approximately seventy members of St. Mark's Episcopal Church in the Los Angeles suburb of Van Nuys . . . suddenly started speaking in tongues and engaging in other kinds of ecstatic worship after experiencing baptism in the Holy Spirit."[6] At this point in time, Pentecostals had been having such experiences for over half a century. However, the occurrence at St. Mark's signaled a socioeconomic shift. The Azusa Street Revival of the early twentieth century had been led by William Seymour, a black preacher, and as Seymour's words spread, they had largely stayed within lower socioeconomic black and white communities. Pentecostalism had been, essentially, the religion of "America's downtrodden urban ghettos and forgotten rural outposts."[7] St. Mark's, by contrast, was a predominantly white parish composed of upper-class congregants.

After Van Nuys, speaking in tongues and baptism in the Holy Spirit began to spread geographically and then denominationally. By the late '60s, this new, middle-class charismatic wave had infiltrated almost every mainline Protestant denomination as well as Roman Catholicism. The Charismatic Renewal had begun.

Now, you might be thinking "Gee, this sounds like something I read in that chapter on the Hammonds." It is. The Charismatic Renewal is the reason that the Hammonds (Baptists) believed in a Pentecostal idea (Baptism in the Holy Spirit) that fell outside the purview of Baptist theology. The Hammonds' book *Pigs in the Parlor* would go on to influence the Charismatic Renewal that occurred in Roman Catholicism.

And the one who influenced the Hammonds was a British-born Bible teacher named Derek Prince. Prince and another individual in the Charismatic Renewal, a Bible teacher from Texas named Don Basham, were, for a time, the two key figures at the heart of a movement within charismatic Christianity that became known as "deliverance ministry." As its name implies, deliverance was the act of casting out of demons or of freeing individuals from demonic influence. Both Prince and Basham were part of the rapid spread within the Charismatic Renewal, and their ministries were largely concerned with the demonic.

Both men also became part of the so-called Fort Lauderdale Five, a group of Charismatic Revivalist teachers who together formed an organization named Christian Growth Ministries. This group was largely responsible for what became known as the "Shepherding Movement," which taught that Christians should be "shepherded" (sometimes called "covenanting" or "discipling" as well) by a more spiritually mature believer who guided them in their decisions.

The Shepherding Movement emerged from a feeling among these leaders that the Charismatic Renewal was starting to lose its grounding; that is to say, it was beginning to follow in the footsteps of other churches and become too "worldly." As a result, the Five became "a kind of infallible leadership caste. They claimed that they had been especially empowered by the Holy Spirit to define strict lines of authority for charismatic prayer groups across the country."[8] Under them, individual spiritual elders or "shepherds" were positioned to care for communities, communities that "were required to submit themselves, totally and unflinchingly" to such leadership.[9] As you might guess, accounts of abuse suffered at the hands of such shepherds are varied and myriad.[10]

Adding to these teachings was the Shepherding Movement's focus on demons. Given that Prince and Basham, whose ministries both dealt with the demonic, were the forefront of the Shepherding movement, this is not surprising. People saw demons around every corner, and deliverance ministries were a common feature within the movement. In some cases, deliverance ministries in Shepherding communities even appear to have been used as a punishment or corrective measure: as Michael Cuneo writes, "If someone stepped out of line or appeared insufficiently cooperative, insufficiently submissive, there was better than a decent chance that he or she (especially she) would be diagnosed as demonized and subjected to remedial deliverance."[11]

Eventually, this basic structure of Shepherding communities appears to have been used, writ large, to construct NAR social networks. Meaning, the idea of a group of networked churches led by apostles has roots in the Shepherding Movement. The NAR also seems to value the shepherding concept of covering, the idea that believers must submit themselves to a rigid hierarchy of oversight, as a method of preventing damage to the movement through the use of social control.[12]

Manifest Sons displaying supernatural abilities like teleportation and immunity from bomb blasts, a pouring out of holiness aligning with ancient rainfall patterns, and dominating modern apostles and prophets who use the threat of demons to suppress or control their followers: It's a dubious family tree for a movement to be sure. And these are just the origins of the NAR that we have time to cover!

For now, let's move on to what might *seem* like a less explosive element of this movement's pedigree. In 1982, at Fuller Theological Seminary, two men, John Wimber and C. Peter Wagner, cotaught a course entitled "Signs, Wonders, and Church Growth." Before we talk about that course, it is necessary to say a few things about its instructors, since Wimber's charismatic practices would eventually cause Wagner to become one of the foremost thinkers and organizers within the NAR.

Even before the course, the two men had much in common. First, both began their religious careers in denominational Christianity before incorporating charismatic worship. Wimber started out a Quaker. Wagner was initially a Congregationalist Minister, who describes himself as having been enraged when "Pentecostal faith healers would come to town and put up their tents."[13]

After experiencing charismatic worship while at a fellowship group in the late 1970s, however, Wimber left his Quaker denomination, where charismatic expressions of faith were not widely accepted, to pastor a congregation that under his guidance eventually became a Vineyard Christian Fellowship denomination. He soon took over as head of the then-young charismatic "Vineyard Movement," which would go on to expand exponentially under his leadership. It now encompasses thousands of churches that claim to be "doin' the stuff" that Jesus did in the Gospels.[14] By the 1970s, Wagner too had witnessed the explosive growth of Pentecostal churches and had experienced miraculous healing of an infected cyst at a Pentecostal healing service.

Both men could also be classed as "evangelicals." As used here, the term *evangelical* doesn't indicate a specific denomination, even though some denominations include the word in their names. Rather, it points to a broad approach to Christianity that scholars typically associate with four characteristics: a focus on personal conversion (that is, the idea of being "born again" or "coming to Jesus"), a belief in the Bible as being highly authoritative and inspired by God, the centrality of Christ's crucifixion (crucicentrism), and an active expression of faith through evangelism (proselytizing) and social activism that aligns with their ideals.

This intersection of evangelical and charismatic beliefs was relatively new. Wagner would later go on to describe this combination of beliefs as the "Third Wave" or the "Third Wave of the Holy Spirit." This term denoted the idea that the Holy Spirit has moved in three major periods or waves in modern church history. Wagner taught that the Pentecostalism of the early 1900s and the Charismatic Renewal of the 1960s and '70s were the first two waves. The Third Wave was primarily influential among evangelicals and emphasized the active presence of the Holy Spirit. Following in the footsteps of Wagner's ideas, the NAR is itself part of this "Third Wave" movement.

Both Wimber and Wagner were also affiliated, to one degree or another, with Fuller Theological Seminary, located in Pasadena, California. And this is, in fact, where they met in the 1970s. For Wagner, this association with Fuller was more formal: He was professor of church growth at the institution, and in 1974, Wimber took one of his classes. Wimber's own subsequent professional association with Fuller was by invitation.

By 1982, Wimber, as leader of the Vineyard Movement, was in full charismatic swing, and Wagner was beginning to list in the same direction. At this time, Wagner invited Wimber to teach "a new course in Fuller Seminary, MC510, first called 'Signs, Wonders, and Church Growth,' later renamed 'The Miraculous and Church Growth.'"[15] Notably, the course included demonstrations of the so-called signs and wonders. This was the term Wimber used to describe supernatural manifestations of the Holy Spirit, such as healings, miracles, prophecy, and deliverance from demons. That is, Wagner felt that he was seeing supernatural feats occur in front of his very eyes in the classroom! Wagner later wrote about this class experience, "night after night I saw words of knowledge verified on the spot, sick people instantly healed, evil spirits cast out, and many other manifestations of supernatural ministry."[16] The term *signs and wonders* quickly became a signature phrase of Wimber's ministry within the Vineyard Movement and throughout the world.

Word of the course spread across the nation, and, as one might expect given the topic matter and hands-on experience with it, it became deeply controversial. Within four years, pressures surrounding this controversy forced Fuller Theological Seminary to withdraw the course. But the impact on C. Peter Wagner was not so easily removed.

In his work *Churchquake!: How the New Apostolic Reformation Is Shaking up Church as We Know It*, Wagner notes this significant shift in his attention.

> The decade of the 1970s focused on the technical side of church growth. I organized courses and wrote books about such things as the vital signs of healthy churches, church pathology, institutional factors, contextual factors, church planting, the ministry of the Body through spiritual gifts and pastoral leadership. During the 1980s, my focus shifted to the spiritual side of church growth, teaching courses and writing books about power evangelism, divine healing, demonic deliverance and the like. More recently, prayer and spiritual warfare have headed my research agenda, including some new areas such as strategic-level spiritual warfare, spiritual mapping, identificational repentance and prayer evangelism.[17]

A lot of those terms might be opaque to you at this time, don't worry, we'll get into them in the next chapter. For now, what's important to know is that Wagner is ultimately saying that before his experience with Wimber, he was focused on the *human* factors of church growth. After his experience with Wimber, he was focused on the *supernatural* factors of church growth.

A New Kind of Evangelism

If I had to choose a trait that I most associated with the NAR as it was conceived by C. Peter Wagner and those around him, it would be this front-and-center emphasis on the idea that supernatural factors impact church growth. And as you might have guessed from the terms used in the quotation above—"strategic-level spiritual warfare," "spiritual mapping," "demonic deliverance"—the chief supernatural factor that Wagner and other members of the movement are concerned with is demons.

In fact, one of the primary ways that Wagner began to think about evangelism was that it could be impeded by demonic forces. In his 1988 book *The Third Wave of the Holy Spirit*, Wagner wrote in a chapter titled "Victory over Evil Spirits" that Satan had assigned demonic forces to rule over specific geographic areas or cultural groupings. These territorial forces then blinded the people who fell under them to the truth of the Gospel and impeded attempts to evangelize them. As Wagner puts it, "if these ruling spirits can be identified and if their power can be broken through spiritual warfare on a high level, the preaching of the gospel of salvation will presumably have freer access to the hearts of those who are lost."[18] Thus, if demonic forces are bound and expelled, conversion would be rapid and plentiful. Today, this idea, that demons attach themselves to certain places and can be cast out through spiritual warfare, is known as *spiritual mapping*.

Although the idea of spiritual mapping and its attendant practices did not originate with Wagner,[19] he and other authors that we'll discuss in the next chapter were integral in spreading the practice around the United States. One way to get a sense of this relationship is to note that while the NAR movement incorporates a number of distinctive teachings that we've already discussed, from the return of signs and wonders to the idea of the fivefold ministry to an emphasis on being led by modern day prophets and apostles, none of these teachings are exclusive to the NAR, and their presence alone doesn't necessarily mean that an individual or group is associated with the movement. On the other hand, spiritual mapping is much more clearly related to the NAR; as a result, whenever I see its language or practices start to swirl around an author or group, there are very few instances in which I don't then associate them as part of the larger intellectual movement of the NAR, regardless of whether they identify as such or not.

With that established, let's return to an idea that I introduced at the beginning of the chapter. Originally, I said that I was, in this section, using the NAR as a placeholder term for people who operate in an intellectual world in which biblical demons are influencing the sociopolitical environment of the United States. Generally speaking, we can conceive of these ideas as falling under the rubric of spiritual mapping. It is the ideas behind spiritual mapping that would go on to make the NAR and affiliated groups both incredibly powerful and incredibly dangerous. From a political perspective, both groups and individuals can be swayed by these ideas to vote in a particular way or support specific political causes, all with the operating assumption that they are participating in a struggle against "evil" and "the demonic."

As we shall see, this doesn't preclude the use of violence as groups and individuals fall under the spell of spiritual mapping, believing that they are putting "boots on the ground" to fight against the demons that are unmaking their country.

CHAPTER EIGHTEEN

Spiritual Mapping

As I've suggested, the NAR and adjacent movements (and the considerable number of people who belong to them or who follow these movements' teachings, whether they realize that's what they're doing or not) see demons in a new way: not just as impacting individual human beings but also as holding sway over distinct geographical and cultural areas. This way of looking at the world imagines a kind of hierarchy of demons that can be fought by individuals often referred to, by those who believe in spiritual warfare and deliverance ministry, as "prayer warriors" or "intercessors".

The problem with this theological framework is that it can quickly devolve into paranoia and conspiracy. In such a demonology (or system of thinking about demons), diabolical influence becomes omnipresent and those impacted by the movement become hyperfocused on battling these beings. As scholar of American religion Sean McCloud points out in *American Possessions: Fighting Demons in the Contemporary United States*, such all-consuming ideas "play *the* crucial role in the Third Wave imaginary."[1] Without demons, the Third Wave—the charismatic movement of which C. Peter Wagner saw both himself and the NAR as a part—would lose its moorings. That's because demons are an essential component of the theological imaginings of the group; as we shall see, removing them would cause the theology of the group and its raison d'être to collapse. This is why spiritual mapping, which we touched upon in the previous chapter, is one of the NAR movement's most important concepts. While it is difficult to quantify how many people are involved in this movement, C. Peter Wagner suggested "considerably more than 100 million" adherents worldwide in 1996.[2] While this number is likely inflated, the actual number has no doubt grown from Wagner's writings in the past three decades—it is clearly operant throughout the United States and the world at large, mostly being spread via hierarchical church/apostle relationships known as "apostolic networks."

In this chapter, I'm going to be laying out for you the core ideas of spiritual mapping. I do this for three reasons. First, the words that are used for these practices vary, so it's useful to know what to look for in order to identify people performing or discussing the practices. Second, spiritual mapping is something of a cornerstone for the other politically dangerous ideas that we'll discuss in this section. If one doesn't understand the connective tissue between them, it can be easy to dismiss these ideas as being either unconnected to demons or unrelated to one another. Finally, you're presumably reading this book because you're interested in the idea of demons. Let's give you what you came for.

In my description of spiritual mapping, I'm going to be condensing a wide variety of sources and information together to give you a bird's eye view of the practice. I'll also be using some descriptions and terms that will help facilitate understanding of spiritual mapping but are not native to the NAR movement itself. Since the movement can be very diverse in its views (owing to its highly individualistic and nondenominational approach), some who identify as belonging to NAR and associated groups might reject these ideas about spiritual mapping as only partly true. That's all right: while there's no way to create a picture that everyone in the movement will agree on, our aim is to arrive at one that is descriptive enough to be useful in understanding what these practices look like and how they influence the movement's political views.

To start, it's important to know that practitioners of spiritual warfare tend to use the term to designate any spiritual combat against demons. However, individuals who are practicing spiritual mapping tend to differentiate between three different "levels" of spiritual warfare: ground-level spiritual warfare, occult-level spiritual warfare, and strategic-level spiritual warfare. These levels get progressively broader in scope from one level to the next: from demons accosting individuals at the first level, to combating intellectual and religious competition at the second, to addressing political and cultural groups in the third. These three terms were largely pioneered by C. Peter Wagner in his 1992 work *Warfare Prayer: What the Bible Says About Spiritual Warfare*,[3] though George Otis, Jr., a missionary and founder of the Sentinel Group, was another significant thinker in the field as well whose work we'll discuss later in this chapter.

The First Level

Ground-Level Spiritual Warfare

We'll start off with an analogy: demonic influence as fishing. To those who (knowingly or unwittingly) hold NAR beliefs, demons do not inhabit the air or the earth as suggested by our early Christian authors in chapter 2 nor the electromagnetic spectrum as our first anti-Spiritualists thought in chapter 7. Instead, they inhabit a separate world entirely, known as the Spirit Realm, the Invisible World, or the Heavenlies. This world, as the second term would suggest, is not one that people can normally see, but it does overlap with our own world. In effect, demons can "see into" our world, but we cannot typically "see into" theirs.

We can think of this arrangement like a river. When someone looks down into it, they might see fish moving around underneath the water from their higher vantage point on a dock or the riverbank. Conversely, it might be challenging for the fish to see a person from their position in the water. In this scenario, the person standing on the dock or riverbank is a demon and the fish are human beings.

Let's say the person on the shore (the demon) wants to catch (influence) the fish in the river (us). They have a few options. First, they could bodily wade into the water and grab hold of a fish. Reaching for terminology we've already used in this book, you or I might call this "possession," but C. Peter Wagner didn't like that word. In a *Fresh Air* interview on NPR in 2011, Wagner stated on behalf of those in the NAR movement:

> We don't like to use the word possessed because that means they don't have any power of their own. We like to use the word afflicted or, technical term, demonized. But there are people who—yes, who are—who are directly affected by demons, not only in politics, but also in the arts, in the media and religion in the Christian church.[4]

As we see, he states clearly that the NAR prefers to say people are influenced, not possessed, by demons—likely an idea inherited from the Charismatic Renewal and authors like Derek Prince who preferred to use terms like "having a demon." People in the movement also refer to this spreading of demonic influence as demonization. The implication of this idea is that people remain in technical control of their actions (and thus, are at fault for them).

Once again, we can think about direct demonization in terms of fishing. Picture a demon on the shore. They attach a nice juicy worm to the hook or an enticing looking lure, then throw it into the water to see what they can catch. NAR thinking imagines demonic temptations as being found all over the place, from educational initiatives to drugs to sexual licentiousness. These are the proverbial worms and lures that the demons are using in order to compel obedience. Once the "fish" bites down, they can be yanked around the stream with minimal hassle and encouraged by the hook snared in their mouth to do the demon's bidding.

Like our previous authors, NAR adherents believe that a person can fight back through the process of spiritual warfare. Efforts by the fisherman (demon) to catch individual fish (people) constitute what the NAR would refer to as "ground-level spiritual warfare."[5] That is, it is a spiritual attack upon a single person, and it can likely be resolved by that person or a small group of people practicing deliverance ministry.

The Second Level

Occult-Level Spiritual Warfare

For the vast majority of Christians, the idea of demonic influence ends there: with the lure and enticement of individuals. However, in NAR thinking, demons have additional options available to them that help them to influence or control groups of people.

At this second level of our fishing metaphor, demons might choose to chum the water a bit. Instead of casting out individual hooks, the demon might draw numerous fish into a single area by offering lots of goodies for them to eat. The fish get enticed to one spot and signal to other fish through their actions that there are good things to eat there. This attracts more fish. With so many fish around, multiple demons are able to fish the same area effectively since there are more fish overall and each individual fish becomes easier to catch.

This is what the NAR refers to as "occult-level spiritual warfare."[6] The term *occult* here can be confusing. On a technical level, it is a Latin word that means *hidden* and was originally used to describe groups that had secrets they were keeping from non-members. However, since some of these secrets were magical ideas about the world and these ideas were distinctive to those outside the groups, the term *occult* eventually took on a wishy-washy meaning that basically amounts to "anything that's magic."

When those with an NAR mindset use the term, it becomes even broader. From religious practices that differ from conservative evangelical Christianity, such as Tibetan Buddhism and Jehovah's Witnesses, to just reading one's horoscope in the local paper, such individuals generally use the term *occult* to mean anyone or anything whose beliefs are in competition with theirs. That might mean groups that practice magic (e.g., branches of Wicca), but just as often it simply signals people who don't agree with the NAR or aren't conservative evangelical Christians.

For instance, consider C. Peter Wagner's description of the occult in *Warfare Prayer*. He begins his description by saying that, "It seems evident that we see a kind of demonic power at work through shamans, New Age channelers, occult practitioners, witches and warlocks, satanist priests, fortune tellers, and the like."[7] Some of these individuals could easily fall within the notion of "magic as occult" discussed above (shamans, New Age channelers, witches, etc.) while others (fortune tellers) seem farther afield. Yet, he then goes on to include in a later grouping "Freemasonry . . . [and] Eastern religions."[8] That is, now the definition has expanded to include a largely Christian inflected organization (Freemasonry) and religions that began to compete with Christianity in the '60s like Hinduism and Buddhism. Wagner then refers readers to NAR prophet, author, and leader Cindy Jacobs's *Deliver Us from Evil*, whose cover depicts a praying family and a list of supposed occult influences that include "Pokémon" and "Harry Potter."

While adherents to an NAR worldview wouldn't use this term, I tend to think of what they call "occult-level spiritual warfare" as "propaganda-level spiritual warfare." That's because by designating a phenomenon (e.g., Pokémon) or religious movement (e.g., Wagner calls out Mormonism as a "false cult" in his discussion of occult ideas in *Warfare Prayer*)[9] as "occult," the NAR is declaring that any competing religious belief or phenomena with a significant following is a demonic influence. This evocation of spiritual warfare is meant to isolate that competition and designate it as demonic so people will avoid it, particularly where elements of it already exist within the fold. By calling these competing religious beliefs or phenomena demonic, the NAR also ensures that people won't leave their pews for another religion and won't devote time to problematic fads when in this viewpoint they should be evangelizing instead. Not only that, but believers alerted to the dangers of this "occult" influence might also make a more concerted effort to convert friends and family, out of an abundance of concern for their well-being. After all, no one wants to bend their knee to demons, right?

A clear example of occult-level spiritual warfare being waged can be found in Cindy Jacobs's aforementioned 2001 book *Deliver Us from Evil*. In her first chapter, Jacobs describes being shocked to discover that "occult" material like "Pokémon and *Harry Potter*" is readily available in her local bookstores.[10] She claims that shows like *Buffy: The Vampire Slayer*, *Charmed*, and *Sabrina: The Teenage Witch* "aim their demonic themes at the teen and Generation X markets" and that such "media has helped push the occult" before blithely attempting to connect this supposed phenomenon to school shootings including the one in 1999 at Columbine High School in Colorado.[11]

From this early chapter, Jacobs continues to sow fear and panic. It turns out that Satan is everywhere! Jacob warns: from the tabletop roleplaying game Dungeons and Dragons to the collectible card game Magic: The Gathering to a wide range of video games, children's entertainment offers seemingly endless windows through which demons can reach in and grab hold of your offspring (remember the Satanic Panic from part 4?). Careful, your neighbor might be a witch who is involved in a "plot" to indoctrinate your children into witchcraft because "Satan is sly and knows there is a tremendous revival coming."[12] And don't even think of reading your horoscope: doing so may seem benign, but Jacobs alleges "Satan has worked so hard for so long at gaining mainstream acceptance of horoscopes."[13]

As the author John Weaver points out in his 2016 book *The New Apostolic Reformation: History of a Modern Charismatic Movement*, occult-level spiritual warfare can have "huge negative consequences."[14] The problem is that this belief designates rival religious groups as demonic; the only cure for which is conversion. Furthermore, the physical objects (e.g., ceremonial masks) and practices (e.g., the use of sweat lodges) that are derived from such groups are seen as demonically infused and as requiring destruction. Particularly in developing nations where NAR groups exert significant authority, Weaver warns that this way of thinking:

> has the potential to exacerbate ethnic and religious tensions. . . . The wanton destruction of other cultures' treasured religious artifacts, while interpreted by the NAR as an act of spiritual enrichment and

> evangelization, is often seen by these cultures as a form of imperialism, one with devastating consequences to their own cultural stability. In regions where there is great religious diversity these practices may be especially dangerous to implement.[15]

Put another way, occult-level spiritual warfare encourages members to suppress other religious groups and potentially destroy important cultural artifacts. Culturally, these practices are questionable in that they ask groups to permanently sacrifice their heritage. Religiously, they seek to create a uniform idea of what Christianity is, a kind of "my way or the highway" approach to belief.

The Third Level

Strategic-Level Spiritual Warfare

The final option left to the demon (fisherman) determined to impact humans (beyond trying to catch one fish at a time and chumming) is to poison the water. This means at a spiritual level that, since the spirit world and the natural world overlap, demons can spread their negative influence over many humans at once, as if through a cloud of toxins. By setting up shop in a particular area or over a particular group of people (a "stronghold" in NAR parlance[16]), demons can exert a kind of widespread demonization (the spreading of demonic influence). People in the stronghold fall under the demons' power, either by unintentionally or intentionally submitting themselves, and begin to act on behalf of the demons that control them. Often, these so-called territorial spirits are depicted as powerful entities,[17] demon lords that must be dealt with through special practices like "prayer walks"[18] (either praying on site in a particular location or walking through specific troubled areas while in prayer). The NAR teaches that by putting boots on the ground and banishing these demonic oppressors, Christians can make it possible for people in particular places to hear the good news of the Gospels and to fully enjoy God's blessings.

By dealing with these spirits in this way, the NAR claims to be engaging in what they call "strategic-level" spiritual warfare.[19] This is the major leagues of spiritual warfare. In *Wrestling with Dark Angels: Toward a Deeper Understanding of the Supernatural Forces in Spiritual Warfare*, C. Peter Wagner opines that confronting territorial spirits "should not be undertaken casually. If you do not know what you are doing, and few who I am aware of have the necessary expertise, Satan will eat you for breakfast."[20] He then goes on to describe two anecdotal accounts of people who ventured unprepared into such warfare: reportedly one pastor died and the other suffered a stroke.

Apart from such threats, there is plenty about this practice that may be found to be alarming. First, let's return to the example of Cindy Jacobs. In addition to writing numerous books, Jacobs also cofounded the ministry Generals International with her husband, Mike Jacobs. Generals International advertises itself as "a global training & equipping organization that mobilizes the body of Christ in prayer, intercession, and prophetic ministry."[21] Obviously, terms like *generals*, *training*, *equipping*, and *mobilizing* are all military terms, much as we saw in Michael Harper's *Spiritual Warfare*. Here, the idea seems to be that the organization is equipping every person to be a general in their own front of spiritual warfare.

Unlike Michael Harper, however, in Jacobs's case this terminology extends past the mere idea of war and into that of literal war. In some of the posts to the Generals International website, Jacobs has encouraged her "army" to engage in prayer that is meant to impact *actual* war. For example, in one communication with her followers on October 24, 2023, Jacobs's greeting reads "Dear Prayer Warriors."[22] She goes on to discuss the then-emergent crisis in the Gaza area, claiming that there are "dark clouds coming against the nation [Israel]," then quickly pivots to the idea that there is a "threat of attacks by terrorists on our own soil."[23] She goes on to claim:

> I had already felt a strong warning that sleeper cells were already spread across America and were going to "hatch", and had been sharing it as a prophetic warning. At first, like many, I pictured this being a loose group of extremists who had been radicalized. I no longer feel that way. I now believe there is a connected group here in the United States that is very much like the group that planned the 9/11 attacks.[24]

Jacobs then instructs her followers as to how they should pray so that the influences behind these sleeper cells (presumably, demonic influences, given that she is calling for her generals of spiritual warfare to intercede and signs off with the peculiar phrase, "Warring in the heavens!"[25]) are cut off at the source. Prayer is being depicted here as a method of warding off a real-life coordinated physical, terrorist attack on the United States, a depiction that also legitimizes the idea that there ever was such an attack being planned (to my knowledge, there was not).

The language the NAR uses in public communications to discuss strategic-level warfare also often contains a fair number of what you or I may think of as demonic "dog whistles." A dog whistle, in this context, refers to the use of a coded word or message that carries a specific meaning to a group of people, but may be seen as benign or neutral to others. Thus, when NAR communications address the public, it's not apparent that the authors are discussing demons unless one is already in the know.

Consider again Jacobs's website. If you stumbled upon it, you might not immediately realize that it was the product of individuals who are obsessed with demons. A search of the site using Google advanced search revealed no results with the terms *demon*, *demons*, *principalities*, or *evil spirit*. The only term that appeared to come close was a being that Jacobs termed "the robbing spirit," which she claimed steals prosperity. Yet even this phrasing allows some degree of deniability: those unfamiliar with naming conventions like those found in *Pigs in the Parlor* might simply understand this as a metaphor and not as a specifically named demon.[26] As a result, this language could conceivably draw people in who might not—at first—agree with the idea behind the movement.

The Twilight Labyrinth

But why are all of these levels of spiritual warfare necessary? That's a complex question, but after studying the issue I've arrived at what I believe are a couple of likely answers.

The first is that the NAR consistently strikes me, in my readings and in my conversations with adherents, as being experientially focused. As you might imagine, it takes quite a bit of stretching to make the text of the Bible conform to these ideas of spiritual warfare. However, if a person can have a visceral experience of the demonic—for example, feeling something that they associate as being overwhelmingly evil or being the subject of a deliverance ministry and sensing something leave their body or perceiving themselves to be healed afterward—then they might be inclined to assume that their experience of truth must conform with another source of truth in their life, the Bible.

And these individuals do report having these experiences—and they give them great credence. Often times, NAR thinkers will report that demons are present or impacting the world around them, citing their own sensations and feelings rather than on any objective criteria that could theoretically be used to verify such influence. For instance, in *Warfare Prayer*, C. Peter Wagner writes often about people sensing the presence of demonic powers or those powers being broken or sensing that God wants a particular outcome to a situation or action undertaken.[27]

It makes sense then, that, since a large part of human experience is grounded in group dynamics and political concerns, any form of occult- and strategic-level spiritual warfare and spiritual warfare principles would have to include these dimensions. This experiential focus might also explain why demons occupy such a large intellectual space in the NAR movement: When your beliefs are threatened by the culture you live in, it is easy to imagine that there is an evil force behind the rejection of what you hold true and dear.

Consider the following. There is a framework that has developed within Methodist theology that is called the "Wesleyan Quadrilateral." This framework offers a way to understand the pursuit of God's truth by emphasizing four essential sources: the Bible (the primary source), tradition, experience, and reason. You may imagine it like a car navigating the road of life, with each of these sources functioning as one wheel that is guiding the journey. Although all four wheels are necessary to make the car go, the vehicle always lists slightly toward the "Bible" wheel, reflecting its key importance.

By contrast, the NAR tends to favor the experiential. NAR literature is replete with language centered on feelings and personal encounters. The first time I read C. Peter Wagner's idea of spiritual mapping, in fact, I was a bit shocked at how little biblical support he offered. At one point, Wagner assures his readers that he wouldn't make a recommendation that he wasn't "personally convinced" was biblical.[28] He then offers as evidence for his theory only Ezekiel 4:1–3 (a passage where Ezekiel lays symbolic siege to Jerusalem on behalf of God) and a few archaeological examples from a book written in the '50s.[29] Returning to the metaphor above, if the Wesleyan Quadrilateral is a car with four equal-sized (if arguably imbalanced) wheels, the NAR interpretive mode is instead essentially a Big Wheel: a vehicle with one enormous experiential wheel in the front and two small wheels of Bible and reason in the back. (The NAR more or less abandons the wheel of tradition and inadvertently devalues the Bible and the importance of reason as well.)

This leads into my second theory about why the NAR sees all these levels of spiritual warfare as necessary, which is that it's because they believe spiritual darkness is deeply embedded in the world and it can only be dismantled by Christians who experientially confront and engage it. Let's examine this idea more closely.

In 1997, George Otis Jr., founder and president of the Christian research and media organization The Sentinel Group, published a book entitled *The Twilight Labyrinth*. Plastered across the front cover was a single question: "Why does spiritual darkness linger where it does?" Consider for a moment how this query is phrased: The question presumes that the person asking has already concluded that spiritual darkness exists in certain places. And how did Otis come to this conclusion? You guessed it: personal experience.

The first chapter consists of forty-five pages depicting Otis's extensive travel experiences across the world, during which he encounters what he believes to be the "spiritual darkness" of the above question. Flitting from Tibet, to the American southwest, to India, to Haiti, Otis offers up accounts, both his own and others', that he believes confirms the lingering demonic presences that the book will cover. There is no reference to a specific established Christian theological framework that I can detect (other than "different religions = demons"), and in the forty-five pages there is only a single citation of the Bible.

What follows next in the book is a kind of creative imagining of the central importance of demons, which Dutch theologian and scholar René Holvast identifies as the systematic work "at the heart of Spiritual Mapping."[30] Otis portrays the spirit world as what he calls the Twilight Labyrinth: a winding maze filled with dead-ends and disorienting turns capable of ensnaring those who venture into it. Despite its dangers, Otis claims that it is necessary that we understand the spirit world. His reason for this is that he sees a cause-and-effect relationship between the spirit world and natural world. When things happen in the spirit world, they are reflected in the natural. In his imagination, the former "enfolds" the latter.[31]

And this is where Otis's imagination truly takes wing as he draws from a bewildering array of sources, from Anglican theologian Edwin Abbott's *Flatland* (1884) to theoretical physicist Michio Kaku's *Hyperspace* (1994), to argue that dimensions beyond ours are neither impossible nor unsupported by principles of science. He then ventures into a somewhat amateurish exercise in comparative mythology, claiming that widespread fascination with dragons and serpents suggests that every culture has had some experience with the Devil.

Otis appears then to suggest that the Bible contains some errors of omission and sets about filling them. For instance, when Genesis states that God "walks" in the Garden of Eden, Otis interprets this as evidence that Eden was built on top of a dimensional gateway that facilitated God's presence there.[32] When God tells Adam to name all the animals, Otis concludes that God must have gifted Adam with a perfect memory and heightened cognitive ability since "the mere act of naming the creatures must have required him to remember millions, perhaps billions, of appellations so as not to duplicate them."[33] From these interpretations, Otis constructs an idea of Adam as a kind of superhuman figure who is gifted with such psychic abilities as remote viewing, psychokinesis, teleportation, and communication with animals. (This idea may be beholden to the idea of the Manifest Sons of God discussed in the last chapter, who evinced supernatural powers like teleportation and skin that turns aside weapons.)

Otis then shifts to the idea that humankind was created by God to acquire supernatural wisdom. But then, that damn snake came in and ruined the whole thing. Realizing humankind's potential, Lucifer tempted Eve with the promise that she could become more like God, nearly effortlessly. And Eve listened. Humanity had fallen.

After this, Otis plays cleverly with the paleontological and archaeological record. He suggests that what was left of the garden after the fall, what he calls "Eden's fading glow," remained capable of sustaining abundant life, including "fifty-foot crocodiles," enormous trees, and men and women who were able to live for a thousand years.[34] Guided by demons and surrounded by abundance, humankind subsequently engaged in violence and unbridled sexuality. Eventually, God used the Flood to wipe the slate clean again.

In Otis's understanding, the human population after the Flood was reduced to a single family (i.e., Noah's, the man with the ark), a culling that resulted in all of humanity becoming centered in a specific population area. Since demons have no interest in being anywhere but around humans, they swarmed around Babylon and the other urban population centers of the Middle East, causing what Otis called the "greatest demonic ingathering in human history" to assemble over the Tower of Babel.[35] To put a stop to this gathering, God proceeded to confuse the single language that the builders spoke and create multiple new ones. As the ancient builders of Babel spread from the tower, God separated them by breaking up landmasses.[36]

While on the surface this story might appear to paint a relatively calm transition from a single culture to multiple ones, Otis depicts the shift as anything but peaceful. The original unity of humanity was violently disrupted. The people of Babel fled their city, took harrowing journeys to new homelands, faced natural disasters, suffered disease and pestilence, and endured famine and warfare. Humankind experienced what we understand today to be some form of collective trauma.

And all of this allowed demons to pose as gods to develop pacts with the survivors. According to Otis, "the deal was simple. In return for allegiance pledged to these masquerading demons, the community would receive immediate trauma relief as well as restored access to the power, wisdom, and deities of their forefathers."[37] In order to make their lives more manageable, humans created pacts with demons that would follow their ancestors into the modern world.

From Theory to Practice

And there you have it. In the worldview of the NAR, religious beliefs other than Jews and Christians are the result of a demonic pact that was set up by demons thousands of years ago as the people who hold those beliefs left Babel or, in the case of the New Age movement or other modern religious practices, a more recent form of manipulation and temptation made by these same demons. From ancient animism to modern humanism, Otis teaches in his chapter entitled "The Art of Shadow-Ruling" that demons maintain this hold over humanity by causing people to falsely worship them as gods,[38] by feeding people lies about the natural world,[39] and by directing human rulers.[40] Through these pacts and methods, demons establish strongholds and lord over humanity, necessitating the use of strategic-level spiritual warfare to break their influence.

When viewed in this light, it's clear that any competing religious beliefs or political ideologies must necessarily be seen as a threat to those who believe in the principles of spiritual mapping, that is, as a demonic manipulation that keeps people away from God. Given that these same individuals often strongly believe in the idea of the Great Commission, the idea that the Gospel should be spread to all peoples and nations, this problem of demons presents a seemingly overwhelming oppositional force. A natural question then presents itself to those with these beliefs: How is it possible to undo centuries of demonic influence and right the world before the end of time?

The answer is simple.

You need a game plan.

CHAPTER NINETEEN

Dominion, He Wrote

Consider for a moment the totality of the world view laid out in the last chapter: In this line of thinking, demons have been an omnipresent force since the dawn of time. And by successfully manipulating humankind—through their ability to alleviate the suffering caused by trauma and, seemingly, to restore elements of the lost golden age of Eden—they have been guiding the development of the world toward nefarious ends. They engage in spiritual warfare against us on multiple levels. They lure and infect us on an individual level through lies and coercion. They spread disinformation and blind us to God's truth on an occult level. They rule over our identity groups and territories from on high on a strategic level.

But that's not all. Compounding all these problems is the fact that the end of the world is swiftly approaching and humans do not have centuries to make slow and calculated decisions regarding this new knowledge about demons; we have only a few short years to turn the tide of a battle that has raged since Creation itself before the End of Days. As Otis says in his work, *The Last of the Giants: Lifting the Veil on Islam and the End Times*, "there are . . . increasing signs that God may be leading His people deep into the autumn season—a time of final harvest before the onset of winter darkness."[1] Otis then goes on to discuss possible apocalyptic scenarios, making it clear that the "winter darkness" is the end of time.

A bleak picture indeed. And one that followers of the NAR and the people they've influenced feel compelled to address. In order to understand how their theology has come to impact our contemporary political world, you and I would do well to, for a moment, put ourselves in their shoes.

Consider with me: If you believed this world view, how would you approach your place in the world? I suspect that I'd set about trying to fix it. Seeking to simplify these complex ideas for the masses, I'd find a way to distill them down into a few talking points. No more four-hundred-page Otis works required!

I'd also recognize that it would be great if these talking points came with an implied plan of action, some element that begged the people hearing it to do something. Since many of the people I would want to convert no doubt would be skeptical about demons, I would want to save that part for later. The talking points would need to require no discussion of demons to be understood, and the action plan, no talk of demons to be implemented. If the whole thing was to be memorable and catchy, it should include some alliteration too; not too much, just a little.

The Seven Mountain Mandate

Welcome to the "Seven Mountain Mandate" (often referred to as "7MM" or "7M" as shorthand), which is just such a set of talking points. The idea of the Seven Mountain Mandate began in 1975 with Bill Bright, founder of Campus Crusade for Christ, and Loren Cunningham, founder of Youth with a Mission. As the story goes, both individuals received the same revelation from God about areas to focus their evangelism upon, and both had been given approximately the same seven areas (just with different wording). Cunningham referred to these areas as "mind molders" and Bright as "world kingdoms."[2]

Yet, it wasn't until Cunningham met with Lance Wallnau, the influential NAR leader and author of *God's Chaos Candidate* whom you may remember from the introduction, that the idea began to gather steam. While the first three figures seem to have viewed the idea of the seven mountains as areas upon which to focus evangelism, Wallnau appears instead to have viewed them as a means to dominate areas of culture. In his 2013 book *Invading Babylon: The 7 Mountain Mandate*, coedited with Charismatic pastor and key NAR figure Bill Johnson, Wallnau lays out a way to think about the mountains as demonically dominated strongholds that must be taken back from Satan.

The book was a hit.

First, we'll talk about the mountains. Then we'll get into the mandate.

Broadly speaking, the idea behind the Seven Mountain Mandate is that there are seven "mountains" of worldly influence. While these mountains can be identified by different terms depending on the understanding of the person teaching about it, modern interpretations roughly correspond to (1) religion, (2) family, (3) education,

(4) government, (5) media and arts, (6) science and technology, and (7) business. The numerical order does not indicate importance: Each of the mountains is just as important as the others. As you can probably see from looking at these designations, more or less the totality of human experience in the modern world is covered by these mountains.

In his contribution to *Invading Babylon*, Lance Wallnau speaks of these areas of authority when he says that there are "kings," or influential people, who do the following:

> . . . [they] occupy the high places, the spheres of influence in the seven mountains of culture. They write the songs you sing and make the movies you watch. They tell you what's in fashion and what's out. They design the iPhone and determine the price of gas. They craft the legislation you live with, and they send your sons to war. They straddle the thrones at the top of the seven mountains . . . we might . . . [call] them gatekeepers. Simply stated, a mountain king is someone with a significant sphere of authority.[3]

And here, we begin inching toward the need for a mandate. The problem with these seven mountains, as many modern conservative Christians see it, is that very few of the kings who rule them are ("true") Christians! According to Wallnau, Christians have for too long believed that the only mountain that is holy, and thus, the only one that they as Christians imagine that they are allowed to occupy, is the mountain of religion. Not so! "The shocking truth," he teaches, "is that each mountain is a spiritual mountain!"[4]

When Christians fail to understand this truth, Wallnau explains, they cannot wield cultural influence effectively to modify the world around them. "The Church lacks cultural power because it focuses on changing the world from within the Church Mountain."[5] And here at last, we come to our mandate: In the eyes of proponents of 7M, it is high time that Christians occupy *all* the mountains.

Once Christians have become the new "mountain kings,"[6] according to Seven Mountain Mandate thinking, then they will be able to exert authority over the culture and political structure of the world. This belief clearly sets up what Wallnau says must happen next:

"The world is a matrix of overlapping systems or spheres of influence. We are called to go into the entire matrix and invade every system with an influence that liberates that system's fullest potential."[7] Following this reason, each Christian then must discover in what area they have been called by God to act and work to claim that mountain and its attendant cultural influence for the Church.

If that sounds kind of like a plan for a hostile takeover, that's because it is. The full realization of the Seven Mountain Mandate would mean that conservative Christian values fill educational spaces, heterosexual marriages are the only legally recognized form of union in the United States,[8] godly media entertains the world, science bends a knee to conservative Christian worldviews, and "workplace apostles"[9]—individuals who evangelize at work or earn capital for godly projects—spread throughout the work-a-day world. And, of course, the NAR and groups like them (that is, religious and political organizations who share their beliefs) control the government.

As Wallnau points out, this result does not require a mass change in religious practices or spiritual beliefs. "The business of shifting culture or transforming nations does not require a majority of conversions. We make a mistake when we focus on winning a culture in order to shape a harvest."[10] In other words, there's no need to convert a whole population in order to control the mountains. All you really need is a few determined believers who are willing to bend the world according to God's will.

This does not, however, mean that every Christian can't participate. In fact, Wallnau says to his presumably Christian reader:

> all believers can become deliverers who arise like Joseph or Esther to save their nations and preserve the heritage of faith in their communities. You, more than any other person who does not know God, are uniquely called out from among others in your nation to be a citizen of Heaven with authority to bring Heaven and its unique resources and solutions into the earth. You can do this through the power of the Holy Spirit made manifest in your specific calling and assignment![11]

What a tantalizing call to action! The message, essentially, is the same as Billy Graham's: The world is broken, you can fix it, and (this part is just a bit different) you'll become enriched through the process as well. Truly, God has created a situation where you can have your cake and eat it too!

And all that without having to mention the demons! Though of course in his book Wallnau does. As I noted in the previous chapter, when NAR members or those assisting them create communications intended to ensnare those not already in the movement, these communications include a fair bit of dog-whistling. But he appears to assume that if you've bought his book, you must be there for the good stuff. And he delivers.

Not surprisingly given the world view we saw laid out in the last chapter, in Wallnau's accounting of the issue, every mountain that isn't controlled by Christians is dominated by Satan. Wallnau confidently claims, "High places, the spheres of influence where kings position themselves, are the specific target and habitation of darkness. In fact, the apostle Paul revealed to the Ephesians that much of their wrestling was not with rulers made of flesh and blood, but rather against 'spiritual hosts of wickedness in the heavenly places.'"[12]

For Wallnau, Satan's temptation of Jesus in the wilderness is evidence that spiritual powers guard the mountains of influence. In light of this conclusion, Wallnau suggests to his audience that there are really only two options: either we (Christians) occupy the mountains of influence or Satan does.

His chapter concludes with a note about spiritual warfare. Since humans are living at the end of time, Wallnau says, "we are entering a bigger battle than most of us appreciate. Something is emerging in the earth that seeks to rob nations of their ability to stand up in the freedom of their unique autonomy and reveal the glory God has deposited in them."[13] He follows this claim with a warning that believers will have to be cautious, for they stand against "an increasingly hostile devil who knows that he has but a short time."[14] That is, it is a short time until "the last great chapter of the journey of the church into the Kingdom Age," the Kingdom Age likely being a reference to the millennial reign of the saints at the end of time. However, until that blessed day arrives, believers are "engaged in a real war."[15]

Before the next chapter, a full page of text in large type reminds the reader that "cultural transformation can only come about by strategic prayer and spiritual warfare."[16] A final reminder to the reader about who currently rules over the culture in the United States: demons.

This chapter from Wallnau's book represents a dramatic new recontextualization of the idea of spiritual warfare. Evangelicals have long thought of spiritual warfare and a person's "calling" or "vocation" from God (both words emerge from the Latin *vocatio*, a calling)—that is, a sense of occupational purpose that God directs them toward and that is aligned with God's will—as being two separate domains. Wallnau, on the other hand, is now combining vocation and a battle against the Devil. By participating in your occupational calling, he tells his readers, you are fighting against the demonic hold over the seven mountains and precipitating cultural change. Your vocation is *also* a battle against the Devil.

And this battle has a desired shape and outcome. Wallnau's argument is simple: Christians should take over all walks of life, from business to government. The only way to stop the Devil is to ensure that Christians control *everything*.

In the abstract, it can be difficult to picture Wallnau's vision of spiritual warfare; to see how alarming a realization of this vision can be. So let's zoom in and look more closely at some examples of how Wallnau sees the Seven Mountain Mandate and American culture interacting today. In a live post to Facebook, on August 14, 2025, Wallnau stated the following:

> I'm telling you, man. Stephen Colbert's out. Howard Stern's out. . . . this is what you're praying for. The seven mountains of influence: culture. If all we do is have our little parties over here in revival land, and we don't see the grenades going over there into the top of academia, in the top of Wall Street, in the top of business, in the top of government, in the top of the intelligence firm, in the top the Kennedy Center. If we don't go after these high places. . . Jesus said it. He said, "When the Enemy is swept out, if you don't occupy that territory, he will come back seven times worse.". . . [Some Christians say] "When the Democrats come back, they're going to—they're going to come after us." Yeah, of course. They're going to come up with a vengeance if they have anything left to use. But right now, God's letting you be a wrecking ball. . . . Trump is smiting them arrows like, like Jehu riding a chariot. . . . He's got principalities and powers all befuddled right now. The Devil never should

> have tried to kill him because when the Devil overreaches, God says that's going to cost you. You want to take his life like that? When I told you not to touch his body and you tried to take his skull and fragment it with a bullet, that's going to cost you. . . . There's a spirit of God on him like Jehu, because his ear throbs every couple of days to remind him you should be dead. I spared your life to save America.[17]

Wow, that's a lot to take in.

In this speech, Wallnau is claiming that figures like Colbert and Stern are being ousted from their mountain king positions in the media mountain. While Wallnau's message is a bit disjointed and off-the-cuff, he seems to be implying that additional "grenades" (note the warfare language) are being lobbed into other mountains as well, presumably at the behest of the Trump administration, which Wallnau paints as being led by God to oust the Devil.

In Wallnau's description of what he sees happening in America, Christians' prayers are working. So, what needs to happen next? Christians must press the attack! Here the insinuation seems to be, at least, that Christians cannot possibly be Democrats, and, at most, that the Devil and Democrats are the same. Regardless of which, *both* will retake their territory if allowed to, so they have to be stripped of anything and everything they might use to do so. Wallnau even cites the image of "Jehu riding a chariot," Jehu being the Hebrew Bible king who dispatched the ungodly house of Ahab, an allusion that seems to link the Democrats to this idolatrous biblical house. Oh, and don't forget, the Devil tried to assassinate Trump. These are a lot of moving pieces to tie together. But Wallnau does so, linking them in a way that seems intended to prove that, as many a conspiracy theorist has claimed, "It's all connected."

Dominion!

While those outside the NAR movement may find Wallnau's ideas about culture and Christianity's role within it alarming, they are at least limited in scope. Wallnau presents an imperative: Christians must take over all elements of human functioning. He also gives a simple rationale for why such action is necessary: If you don't do it the Devil will. Still, his published teachings on the subject don't stretch much beyond this basic framework, which is, as of the time of this writing, confined to a single chapter in one book.

The teachings of another key NAR figure we already know, however, go further.

Several years before Wallnau and Johnson's book was released, C. Peter Wagner (the nominal NAR founder and missiologist from Fuller Theological Seminary) published, in 2008, a book of his own about dominion theology, titled *Dominion! How Kingdom Action Can Change the World*. Wagner had become aware of the Seven Mountain Mandate through a meeting with Lance Wallnau,[18] and while many of his ideas resemble Wallnau's, his plan is more developed and alarming.

At the book's core, Wagner writes primarily about a theological framework known as "Dominion Theology." The framework of dominion theology, which (as we'll see below) emerged in the mid-twentieth century, argues that Genesis establishes God's intention for humans to govern all aspects of society. Let's look at Wagner's interpretation of the idea.

Wagner notes that in Genesis 1:28, the "first thing God said to Adam and Eve was, 'Be fruitful and multiply; fill the earth and subdue it; have *dominion* over [all the creation].'"[19] Yet, Satan—appearing as that pesky serpent, yet again—steals dominion of the earth from them in Genesis 3, a dominion that Wagner sees encoded in the symbol of the apple.[20] Here, Wagner tells the reader that Christians' "traditional interpretation is that Satan wanted to . . . introduce original sin, which would then be transmitted genetically to all their human progeny through the ages so that people would not go to heaven but to hell."[21]

Wagner conveys his agreement that this is indeed one of Satan's intents, but he argues that, more than that, the Devil's *primary* goal was to wrest the dominion of the world from Adam's grasp.

Two Kinds of Redemption

In Wagner's view, the apple was "simply the visual symbol of Adam's choice" to disobey and not an actual fruit. When Adam accepted it, he essentially transferred dominion of the earth to another: "Adam put himself and the whole future human race under the authority of Satan."[22]

However, Wagner argues, when Christ died upon the cross, he defeated the Devil, making it possible for humankind to reacquire dominion over the earth. In Wagner's words, Christ died not just to redeem humankind; "The Savior," he says, "is also dealing with dominion. . . . God sent Jesus in true human flesh to do what Adam failed to do. Jesus lived a human life of purity and obedience to the Father."[23] This acted as a corrective measure: it ended the dominion of the Devil on earth and returned dominion to human beings. Once Christ left the earth, Wagner says, he "delegated" the responsibility for dominion to Christians.[24]

In Wagner's vision, although the Devil no longer had legitimate authority over the earth, a passive mindset in the Christian church had unfortunately allowed the Devil to continue to exert dominance over the world, nonetheless. In order to reverse this and bring the earth back under God-intended human control once more, he argues, Christians need "to become spiritual and social activists until Satan's dominion has ended."[25] They must recognize that dominion is what God has wanted for Christians all along.

A Change of Mindset

Wagner ascribes this passivity to a problem he refers to as "the Greek mindset" vs. "the Hebrew mindset." As he describes it, the Hebrew mindset represents a worldview in which "God and accompanying spiritual principles permeate all of life here on earth." A Greek mindset, by contrast, is one in which the natural and the spiritual are separated.[26]

Wagner wants to see the Hebrew mindset as the mindset of original Christianity while the Greek mindset is a later addition to the Christian tradition. From a historical perspective, this is an odd claim. It completely ignores the fact that the New Testament was written in the Roman Empire, largely by authors who were trained in Greek educational environments. Contrary to this well-known historical context, Wagner wants to see the Greek mindset as a later addition to Christianity. It is only centuries later that, Wagner claims, Greco-Roman culture increasingly "crept" into the Church "until Emperor Constantine finally hijacked the Church"[27] and, unfortunately, the dualistic Greek mindset became the norm.

This division between spiritual and material, Wagner says, leads to a passive mindset that separates the spiritual world of principalities and powers from real-world politics. On the contrary, he argues, Christians need to see the world as being connected, much as he claims the Hebrews did. Christianity, he argues, needs to be just as much about dominating culture as it is about saving souls, and the goal of Christians should be "social transformation."[28]

Dangerous Theonomy

According to Wagner, the theological framework of dominion theology aims to accomplish this social transformation. In explaining dominion theology's origins, he says "it's history can be traced through [theologians] R. J. Rushdoony and Abraham Kuyper to John Calvin."[29] Blink and you'll miss the subtle political dog whistle buried in this reference. What's important to note here is that Abraham Kuyper is the father of neo-Calvinism, a theological and cultural movement that emerged in the late nineteenth century and is famous for (among other ideas) its idea of the "cultural mandate,"[30] a view of reality which shares much in common with dominion theology.

Both emphasize the importance of Christian influence on society. There are key differences, though: While dominion theology asserts a cultural mandate of authority and dominion, neo-Calvinism promotes the ideas of stewardship and influence. Still, there's a point here that's important not to miss: As Wagner points out earlier in his book, Kuyper also served as prime minister of the Netherlands during a time that it underwent significant reform-oriented changes, which were influenced by his neo-Calvinist worldview, so Wagner is signaling to his readers that Christian takeovers of government have already been historically accomplished.[31]

Now let's look at another of the names that Wagner cites when writing about the origins of dominion theology: R. J. Rushdoony. The founder of a twentieth-century movement called Christian Reconstructionism, Rushdoony is an even more controversial figure than Kuyper to point to (which might explain why Wagner only does so once in his book). Rushdoony is controversial because he is the author of a massive, three-volume work, *The Institutes of Biblical Law*, that is at its core what is called a theonomic work: *theos* for God and *nomos* for law. Meaning that Rushdoony advocates a legal system that is grounded in biblical law, with the Ten Commandments serving as the foundational framework for legal governance.[32]

This idea of using the Ten Commandments as a basis for legal governance becomes disturbing very quickly. As scholar Michael McVicar writes in *Christian Reconstruction: R. J. Rushdoony and American Religious Conservatism*:

> Of all the crimes [e.g., "blasphemy, propagating false doctrines, sacrificing to foreign gods, and witchcraft"], however, Rushdoony spent most of the book outlining those that amounted to war against the family and therefore necessitated death. Murder, cursing a parent, kidnapping, adultery, incest, bestiality, homosexuality, rape, and habitual delinquency all struck out against the propagative, future-oriented nature of the family. *Death was necessary in these cases because each crime asserted the sovereignty of humanity over God's law.*[33]

Historian Kerwin Klein names the danger even more succinctly in his 2011 book *From History to Theory*, in which he states that "Moral Majority leader Jerry Falwell attacked Rushdoony for planning to execute homosexuals and drunkards" and further notes that Rushdoony replied indignantly to this attack that "he had never endorsed the execution of *drunkards*."[34]

The fact that dominion theology has roots that can be traced to theonomy perhaps explains the alarm I feel over the fact that both Wallnau and Wagner cite LGBTQ+ issues as go-to examples for concern. Consider the following examples.

In writing about the Seven Mountain Mandate, Wallnau claims that "Together, Protestants and Catholics make up a 70% majority in the U.S. population, and as such already have a majority consensus on key matters affecting marriage and abortion. Yet they are still incapable of being more than a firewall to the minority, who are advancing a same-sex ideology."[35]

There are several things wrong with this statement. First, it presumes that all Protestants and Catholics agree on issues surrounding marriage and abortion. This is far from the truth. Given that, even if Protestants and Catholics make up 70 percent of the population, they cannot be said to have a "majority consensus" regarding these issues, only to be a populational majority. Second, this imagined majority consensus that Wallnau claims to exist is clearly an anti-gay view, else it would not be possible for it to function as a "firewall" against the minority view that he paints as pro-gay. The implication of this message is clear: the reader (in Wallnau's mind) stands in opposition to gay rights, and those rights are on a trajectory toward acceptance in the United States due to an impassioned minority. Thus, it stands to reason that an equally impassioned opposition could correct this trajectory.

When discussing the differences between a theocracy and a democracy, Wagner makes a similar claim, stating that "If a majority [of the population in a democratic society] feels that heterosexual marriage is the best choice for a happy and prosperous society, those in the minority who disagree should conform . . . because they live in a democracy."[36] Nor is this confined to Wallnau and Wagner. In his book *The New Apostolic Reformation: History of a Modern Charismatic Movement*, author John Weaver notes that "[prominent NAR figure] Cindy Jacobs used Rousas Rushdoony's *Institutes for Biblical Law* (1973) as one of her prime research tools for her work *The Reformation Manifesto* (2008)"[37] and many individuals in the movement have commandeered Reconstructionist language. It is hard to imagine that the movement would so significantly integrate Rushdoony's work and rhetoric if it did not also share his lethal views toward gay men and women.

From Classical Theism to Open Theism

From these dubious origins for a spiritual concept, Wagner goes on to carefully craft an idea that he calls "open theism."[38] Before we discuss what open theism is, let's define the concept it modifies. Wagner defines classical theism as a theological framework with ancient roots in both philosophy and Judeo-Christian theology in which God is both omniscient (all-knowing) and omnipotent (all-powerful).[39] In this world view, because God is both, the bad things that happen in the world are either directly or indirectly God's doing. For example, in classical theist thought, God knew the Devil would turn bad when he made him (because he's omniscient) and also had the capacity (omnipotence) to prevent this rebellion. He chose to both invent the Devil and allow the rebellion anyway. Similarly, God knew that Adam and Eve would give in to the Devil's temptation and cause the entirety of humanity to Fall, and he allowed that too.

By contrast, Wagner proposes an open theism in which God is able to limit his sovereignty. That is, God is able to give himself a kind of selective amnesia about the future so that he can be surprised by the outcome of certain beings' choices. In this paradigm, God effectively says to himself "I hope Adam and Eve choose Path A" and limits his sovereignty so that he doesn't see the outcome. Once the outcome plays out differently than anticipated, God then creates an alternative plan.

Whether or not this is a sound theological system is up for debate. But let's set aside that question and ask instead why Wagner might propose such a thing. He seems to settle this issue himself at the end of the chapter when he claims: "Yes, God has an open mind. Yes, prayer makes a difference!"[40]

For Wagner, who is operating in a kind of Latter Rain framework that emphasizes an outpouring of holiness in the present day, this explanation means that the Holy Spirit's presence in the early days of Christianity, its dwindling presence in the Middle Ages, and the resurgence of its presence in the twentieth century has a clear explanation: people just needed to ask (that is, pray to) God for the power of the Holy Spirit to be given to them. Those who have prayed thusly, he notes, "can do the same or greater things than Jesus did because [they] have access to the same power source."[41] In Wagner's humble opinion, this was already happening: those in the "Global South"[42] (i.e., South America and Africa) were already seeing miraculous occurrences happen. Wagner seemed even to believe that raising the dead was a common occurrence there.[43]

Given that promise, a question naturally presents itself: *How do we ensure that these miraculous occurrences begin in America?* The answer, for Wagner? We go to war. In his mind, Jesus's death and resurrection were essentially Satan's D-Day: From that day forward, the war was effectively over, but that doesn't mean that spiritual warfare's "Hitler" figure was giving up.[44] I won't belabor the point here about the importance of the idea of spiritual warfare in NAR material: Wagner spends the next twenty pages articulating in additional ways the same ideas that we've already seen.

"Do Whatever It Takes"

At this point, Wagner has established his framework: He's told his readers what dominion theology is, why it's important, and how demons factor into it. Now, he gets to the nitty-gritty. In the next chapter, he shifts to the same topics that Wallnau would write about in 2013 in *Invading Babylon*. (He even credits Wallnau with bringing the idea of the Seven Mountain Mandate to his attention.[45]) However, in *Dominion!*, Wagner explores them in even greater depth.

Specifically, he advocates for the activation of "workplace apostles."[46] That is, he encourages individuals to see their workplace (not just those in the industry of business but in jobs on the other six mountains) as an extension of the church. Wagner argues that Christians imagine that when they gather together on Sunday, they are participating in the "nuclear church,"[47] and they behave accordingly. Then, after they leave, they act according to a different "rule book":[48] They operate in a secular manner.

Wagner advocates for this to change. By acting in ways that treat the workplace as the "extended church,"[49] he says, workplace apostles would be able to turn those mountains over to God. In a passage of the book with the heading "Overthrowing a Government," he argues that each of the mountains already has its own governmental structure, which Satan has established. "It takes a government to overthrow a government,"[50] Wagner states. That is, Christians must create a new governmental structure on each of the mountains to oppose the governmental structures previously established by Satan. By activating various workplace apostles on each of the seven mountains to form a government, that mountain can be reclaimed from Satan and dominion can be established.

But Wagner has his sights set on more than just figurative governments of metaphorical mountains. In his eyes, it is the city that is the core element of transformation, and it is by claiming cities (that is, by converting all the mountains in a particular geographical area) that Christians can bring about social transformation. This strategy provides a benchmark for success that people in the movement, like George Otis, Jr.—the key figure from the spiritual mapping movement whom we discussed in Chapter 18—had already begun to use to weigh the success of their efforts to bring about social transformation through spiritual mapping and strategic prayer.

All of this sounds innocent enough. Wagner has thus far signaled no reason for concern about his intentions. Yet, he tips his hand when he begins talking about the importance of money in elections. In one graphic that appears in the book, the words "social transformation" are supported by a pillar labeled "The Great Transfer of Wealth."[51] It is important to note that he is not talking here about the relatively benign "Great Wealth Transfer" that economists have pointed to in recent years, in which the wealth of older generations has moved to younger ones. No, Wagner is pointing to something else entirely: effectively, a transfer of wealth from the ungodly to the godly, one precipitated by the activities performed by workplace apostles. "As long as those who are pleasing Satan remain in charge of the world economy, we can expect little progress,"[52] Wagner opines. This shift in wealth is, in his opinion, essential to the goals of dominion theology.

In the very next section, "Buying a Nation?", Wagner tells the story of being asked by an apostle in South Africa whether he would like to "buy a nation." The apostle goes on to tell Wagner that at a cost of "US$50,000 for each provincial governorship and US$1 million for the presidency"[53] Christian candidates would be installed on the ballot in the Democratic Republic of Congo. Despite the title of the section, Wagner is quick to clarify that the conversation was not about buying votes but instead about acquiring money to place candidates on ballots. Yet, this seems to me disingenuous. Wagner clearly realizes the role that money plays in elections when he states later "the more serious we get about social transformation, the more serious we need to get about the realistic price tags."[54]

This focus on money reflects a practical, brass tacks approach that Wagner promotes, one that is chilling in its rhetoric. In a section titled "Clarifying Our Goals," he states:

> The first step toward determining a strategy is to set a viable goal. The goal, of course, is what counts. The strategy is only a means to accomplish the end. I mention this because somehow a large number of people have become programmed with the ridiculous notion that "the end doesn't justify the means." It does not require much hard thinking to realize that nothing can possibly justify the means except the end.[55]

What possible reason could Wagner have to invoke this Machiavellian idea? (It is, literally, the philosophy of Niccolo Machiavelli, who argued in his 1513 work *The Prince* that rulers must use any means at their disposal—even deception, manipulation, fear, and cruelty—to achieve their goals.) The only reason I could think of to personally invoke the phrase is if someone else suggested that the means I was putting forth to accomplish something were not morally justifiable based on the end. Wagner does not seem unaware that he could face such accusations; he even addresses this concern in advance, if in a wishy-washy sort of way, claiming:

> Some will respond that we cannot use immoral means to accomplish a given end, even though it might be a moral end. This is true. Let's agree that we must be ethical in everything we do. Having agreed on that up front, I suggest that we now move out of the realm of ethics and into the realm of practical strategy.[56]

Let's sit with those words for just a moment. Wagner began by making blithe use of one of the most loaded phrases in the English language, "the ends justify the means." Then, with what I read as the guile of a toddler attempting to rationalize having stolen candy, he says in so many words, "Ok, I agree that it's bad to be unethical. So, let's just agree that we'll all be ethical, yeah?" From here, he argues that there are "ethically neutral"[57] (not good, but ethically neutral) ways of accomplishing goals. Out of these, he says, people should "naturally choose the strategy that will best accomplish the goal. Another way of saying this is 'Do whatever it takes!'"[58] To sum all of this up, a theologian who has basically laid out a step-by-step plan for Christians to take over all walks of life—and who appears to follow a teacher who would advocate the death penalty for a variety of offenses—has just told his followers to accomplish these goals by whatever means necessary.

This Was All in the Past

As familiar as all of these scenarios and dynamics might seem to you and me today, both Wallnau and Wagner have been, in the quotes we've read, discussing them as if they will happen in the future. The reason for this is simple: Wagner's *Dominion!* was published in 2008 and Wallnau and Johnson's *Invading Babylon* in 2013. At the time of this writing, it's 2025, and the earliest that you might be holding this book is 2026.

Unsurprisingly, the movement has not stood idly by during this time. Wagner's "Great Transfer of Wealth" has already begun. Most of the mountains of the Seven Mountain Mandate have started their shift toward dominionist influence in the United States. NAR social goals—which are echoed in Project 2025 (a conservative plan to restructure the federal government that's associated with the right-wing think tank the Heritage Foundation)—are being implemented in the United States, with the project's own website claiming that, as of August 2025, the various goals of the plan have reached 47 percent completion.[59] And so, the Reconstruction project of Rushdoony marches forward under new names.

It would have been difficult to predict all of this happening so quickly after Wagner and Wallnau wrote. Then again, it would have been difficult to predict Trump's election when Wagner published in 2008 and Wallnau in 2013. While none of this may have been predicted, however, 2016 and subsequent years would prove themselves to be high times for dominionism and the Seven Mountain Mandate. And we're still being impacted by the influence of these demonic doctrines.

CHAPTER TWENTY

Whatever It Takes

THERE ARE MANY places where we could start the story of the elections that propelled Donald J. Trump to the presidency (and subsequently removed him from it and then propelled him back there again). We could talk, as many authors have, about currents of racism that flow through American history, ideas of gender that permeate American evangelical groups, or anti-immigration sentiment over the course of our nation's history, all of which certainly played a role in the outcomes of these elections (in which he faced two female opponents, one of them a woman of color). We could discuss the unease that some Americans still feel over the Sexual Revolution and other changes that unfolded throughout the 1960s, an unease that was largely responsible for the formation and rise of Christian Reconstructionism, which advocates for a return to biblical law. In some respects, we've already covered many of these subjects.

Instead of diving into historical context, however, I want to start with the elections themselves, and also examine how everything we've learned brings us back to the topic of demons. In this chapter, we'll be looking at how the idea of demons, either as a conscious formation for many Americans or as an influencing factor for powerful movers and shakers behind the scenes, influenced the three elections in which Trump was on the ticket, as well as the fallout from these elections.

2016

God's Chaos Candidate

In 2015 and 2016, evangelical leaders had multiple meetings with then-candidate Trump. If the attendance list at one such closed door meeting, as recorded by NPR, is a representative sample, then such meetings were well-attended by high-powered evangelical figures such as in the person of ordained Southern Baptist minister and former Governor of Arkansas Mike Huckabee and Focus on the Family founder James

Dobson.[1] Many of these meetings appeared intended to either allay fears the evangelical community had about the candidate or to sell him to them as being an ideal one.

It wasn't until C. Peter Wagner, whose health was failing him in 2016, took to Facebook, however, that the NAR mobilized fully. Through a simple endorsement that began with "I like Donald Trump" and ended on the claim that the status quo wouldn't change if nothing new was done, Wagner encouraged his readers to stand up against what he called "establishment politics."[2] At that point, the NAR (and NAR-adjacent) tide clearly, and steadfastly, turned. Wagner died on October 21, 2016, less than a month before the election that he helped to turn in favor of Trump.

As religious scholar Matthew D. Taylor wrote in his book *The Violent Take It by Force: The Christian Movement That Is Threatening Our Democracy*, "From the point of Wagner's endorsement up until the present, the NAR leaders became the trailblazing Christians championing the political career of Donald Trump."[3] Yet, one attendant of these meetings arguably did a more effective job than any of his peers at championing Trump: Lance Wallnau.

According to Wallnau's book *God's Chaos Candidate*, which he released just over a month before the 2016 election, Wallnau had been invited to meet the future president on September 14, 2015, with Kim Clement (another NAR prophet). After Wallnau left the meeting, he became convinced that Trump was destined by God to become the president and wrote the book.

I suspect part of the research he conducted involved figuring out how to couch the language of the demonic as subtly as he could, so that he could avoid alarming nonbelievers while still dog-whistling effectively enough to catch the ear of true believers. Consider the example of one of Wallnau's most oft-quoted lines, found in the first chapter of his book. "I heard in my spirit: *Donald Trump is a wrecking ball to the spirit of political correctness.*"[4]

Many who read his book, and many who heard this line from those who had, assumed this mention of "spirit" was a metaphor. That is, they read it as meaning "Donald Trump will put an end to political correctness." The journalist Chris Mitchell, writing for the Christian Broadcasting Network, seems to have approached the phrase in this way when he titled a postelection article "Trump: A 'Wrecking Ball' for Political Correctness."[5] This interpretation isn't necessarily wrong; it is clear that Wallnau was, in part, making this exact point.

But let's zero in on those last four words: "the spirit of political correctness." As we saw with the Hammonds and NAR members like Cindy Jacobs, there are times when individuals have addressed demons not by proper names but by more general names like "the spirit of X." Here, I would argue that Wallnau is maintaining this naming convention.

Much like Cindy Jacobs's reference to "the Robbing Spirit" (mentioned in "The Third Level: Strategic-Level Spiritual Warfare" section, in Chapter 18), we would first look to confirm that the "spirit of political correctness" has been used publicly in a demonic context before. Our search might point us to a post Wallnau made on his Facebook page on October 27, 2015, in which he says that "the spirit of political correctness . . . has been like witchcraft muzzling and intimidating the Christian community."[6] Or perhaps to Hal Lindsey, author of the 1970s end-times theology bestseller *The Late Great Planet Earth* and host of *The Hal Lindsey Report*, who stated also in 2015: "as we see the demonic spirit of 'political correctness' take firmer hold on all areas of our society, I'm convinced that the decision by true Christians to stand up for Jesus on certain issues and claims will spark an onslaught of derision and discrimination against us."[7] That is, Wallnau appears to be invoking the notion that a demon is attacking the Christian community via means of political correctness, silencing them and preventing them from standing up for what they believe in. Nevertheless, as we see with Mitchell above, a Christian can easily miss this potential reference.

As I've said before: Blink and you'll miss it.

Wallnau next begins to weave a conspiracy theory about an entity he calls "The Shadow Cabinet," which he claims is "the best kept secret of the Progressive Left."[8] He switches to calling this supposed covert organization "the Thunder Road Group" and makes the following claim:

> Thunder Road built a siege engine, a machine whose infrastructure now dwarfs conservatism's in size, scope and sophistication. It has been setting and helping to impose the national agenda that has changed America since 2000, and it kicked into high gear with President Obama in 2008. Since then it has morphed and expanded like Professor Moriarty's [the criminal mastermind from Sir Arthur Conan Doy's Sherlock Holmes stories] underground web.[9]

Now, you might imagine that all of this talk of Thunder Road and Sherlock Holmes means Wallnau has abruptly abandoned the demonic overtones of his book. If so, you would be wrong! On the next page, Wallnau claims "In the very place where God wants a harvest, Satan plants people who attempt to disrupt the harvest!"[10]

Wallnau then launches into a discussion of the Seven Mountain Mandate. As we have seen, 7M theory relies profoundly on ideas of the demonic, and in this new book, Wallnau doesn't disappoint readers who want to go there. At the time of his writing, he says, the "gates of hell"—or demonic strongholds—are located on the top of the mountains, or spheres of influence. Why? Because "the devil himself takes an interest in who rules kingdoms" and established them there.[11]

After this discussion of the mountains, we're back to conspiracies. "We are witnessing the first phase of the 'unraveling,'" Wallnau claims, "—race wars, class wars, and religious wars as Islamic terror incidents at home add to the combustion. All of this is the intentional destabilizing prelude to the great economic 'reset.'"[12] By this term, he means a deliberate transformation of American economic systems by progressive elites. To ensure his readers don't dismiss this perceived threat, Wallnau adds: "Radical progressives are trying to ride the wave of social unrest in order to trigger a socialist reset of America. It is up to you and me to resist this remaking of America."[13]

And then, it's back to demons! Just remember, Wallnau warns, that the "'doctrines of demons,' 'false Christs,' and 'false teachers'. . . [that] Scripture is talking about" aren't within the Church, they're the "nutty professors in schools and universities," "progressive politics," and "the myriad of well-funded, single-issue activist organizations on the Left."[14] Here, Wallnau is creating a warning for his, presumably, demonically inexperienced, audience: What you've read about in the Bible doesn't stay on the page. Right now, there are demonic ideologies circulating in your backyard, all engineered by the Left.

Stumping for Cyrus

From here, Wallnau begins to lay out his case for Trump, which is essentially: He's really a good guy, and he's actually Christian at heart. Paradoxically, Trump is simultaneously, to Wallnau, a "Cyrus figure" like Cyrus the Great, referred to in the book of Isaiah, who God chose to free the Jews from their Babylonian captivity. That is to say, Wallnau sees Trump as someone from outside of the faith who was specially selected by God for a particular purpose. In fact, Wallnau argues, God has selected Cyrus figures throughout history—like Winston Churchill, George Patton, Margaret Thatcher, and Abraham Lincoln—to do his work in times of need. Is it a coincidence, he asks, that Cyrus the Great appears in Isaiah 45 and Trump, if elected, would become the forty-fifth president of the United States? Of course not, he concludes. After all, everything is connected.

The goals that Wallnau accomplished by publishing his book prior to the 2016 election are remarkable. Two, especially, are noteworthy. First, the Cyrus moniker stuck. It became a rallying cry to evangelical Christians, an idea that conservative Christian voters could get behind. It no longer mattered that Trump wasn't a lifelong Christian or even seemingly a good man! Cyrus the Great had been a pagan and not a good man, but he still had accomplished God's work. Even Trump himself seems to have later assimilated part of this language: When discussing the US trade war with China in 2019, Trump looked briefly toward the heavens and declared "I am the Chosen One."[15] Prime Minister of Israel Bejamin Netanyahu similarly compared Trump to the biblical figure in a 2018 speech that addressed the topic of the relocation of the American embassy from Tel Aviv to Jerusalem.[16] Not only did this excuse Trump's questionable past and present behaviors—after all, Cyrus needn't act as a Christian does—but it also meant that Trump's actions could be interpreted as carrying out God's will, just as Cyrus carried out God's will in freeing the Jews from Babylon.

The second and less obvious accomplishment is that the combination of spiritual warfare and conspiracy theory Wallnau set forth resonated with a lot of Americans. The idea that the Democratic Party had somehow nefariously manipulated public perception and used "political correctness" to stifle discussion was a heady wine that could be passed around the Republican Party. This blend of spiritual warfare and conspiracy dovetailed nicely with Trump's frequent campaign trail invocation of the "silent majority," a term coined by President Richard Nixon in 1969. Nixon had claimed that those who did not publicly protest the Vietnam War could be taken to agree with his policies. Trump similarly argued that the majority of the people agreed with his policy positions and statements but did not speak about this openly because they felt muzzled by social pressures.[17]

QAnon—a conspiratorial set of ideas about demonic Democrats and child-devouring cults that we talked about in "The Modern Takeaway: Satanic Panic Redux, Into the New Millennium"—also began to take shape in the post-2016 environment. Perhaps not surprisingly, adherents of the QAnon conspiracy theory and the anonymous figure Q himself all have demonstrated a tendency to use the language of spiritual warfare. Both groups, QAnon and the NAR, would find themselves at the Capitol on January 6, 2021.

2020

Spiritual Warfare over the Capitol

From 2016 through much of 2020, the NAR and adjacent groups were all alight with a newly kindled fire. From their perspective, an apparent underdog had seized the presidency of the United States, championing a set of ideas that were at last in line with God's. Access to the presidency had been granted to the faithful, and a group that had long felt they were on the political outs suddenly had real clout in Washington.

To those who believed in spiritual warfare, this must have seemed like a profound victory of prayer over the territorial forces of Satan. How else could one explain such a profound upset? The miraculous had occurred.

Not surprisingly, the same group that had organized to bring about a Trump presidency mobilized to protect it once it was established. In *The Violent Take It by Force*, Matthew D. Taylor notes that a week before Trump's 2017 inauguration, a number of key NAR figures including Cindy Jacobs and Lance Wallnau—as well as charismatic pastor Dutch Sheets, spiritual warfare teacher Rebecca Greenwood, and prayer rally organizer Lou Engle—created an organization that they named POTUS Shield.[18] In the group's parlance, POTUS is used both as an acronym for "President of the United States" and to mean "Prophetic Order of the United States,"[19] a nod to the idea of charismatic Christians spiritual intercession on behalf of the nation. The website for the group (potusshield.com), which still exists as of this writing, makes clear that the protection of the Trump presidency is a matter of spiritual warfare: the "shield" in question is a spiritual shield against the demonic.

POTUS Shield teaches that these spiritual shields are created by Christians who participate in "prayer watches," that is, eight scheduled three-hour periods of time each day in which people volunteer to pray. In describing the prayer watches, the website employs the language of spiritual warfare. The description of the third watch, for example, claims that "Witches, warlocks, satanists, and anti-christ spirits make their moves while people are entering deep sleep. Shields are down and they strike. Warriors employ their spiritual armor and weapons, boldly tearing down strongholds, dismantling satanic attacks, and attacking evil forces fearlessly in the power of God."[20] Once more, we see a key element of the NAR movement, the idea of the primacy of demons. For the members of POTUS Shield, creating a defense for the president against demonic influence is a top priority, one that requires round the clock prayer.

Then in 2019, Trump spiritual advisor Paula White (mentioned in the introduction as the person who started his 2020 campaign with an exorcism) established a religious-political initiative called the "One Voice Prayer Movement." Officially, "OVPM's mission was to unite [people] with 'one voice' in prayer on 'national issues which are important to God in the United States.'"[21] Of course, most of these national issues were issues that were of special interest to the NAR and other evangelical Christians, such as restricting access to abortion or adopting anti-LGBTQ+ political stances. It therefore is not surprising that White was joined in these efforts by other key NAR figures, including Jacobs and Sheets.

The Christian Broadcasting Network told a slightly more demon-focused story about the group's founding. In *American Evangelicals for Trump: Dominion, Spiritual Warfare, and the End Times*, Canadian theologian André Gagné writes that, according to CBN, "The OVPM was established to combat spiritual opposition that posed a threat to President Trump. This prayer network sought to bring about social transformation by freeing secular society from demonic forces. The Charismatic group involved in this network believed that they were chosen by God to fight against these demonic spirits that hindered the spread of the Gospel message."[22] Now, President Trump had both a means of defending against the demonic and a method of defeating it to bring about social transformation.

It wasn't enough. By late 2020, the dream had fallen apart. Trump lost the election, one that many "prophets" had foretold he would win, to Joe Biden. Those who had expected the opposite outcome wondered:

What could possibly have happened? What nefarious force could have possibly put an end to the prayerful protection the OVPM and other groups offered?

The answer, of course, was demons. Abruptly in the wake of the 2020 election, many NAR and NAR-associated groups initiated a pivot toward interceding for a Trump win. But only a small one was needed. OVPM, for example, launched a series of Zoom based prayer meetings named "Global Prayer for Election Integrity" that were virtually attended by 1.1 million people who either joined the calls live or watched them at a later time. These calls were led by an assortment of NAR and Republican leaders and strategists who came together to create what Taylor called, in *The Violent Take It by Force*, "one of the most important vectors for gathering Christians to oppose the legitimacy of the 2020 election."[23]

The first sign that NAR related groups were not going to back down following Trump's election loss was the emergence of the Jericho Marches, a series of protests that were organized by activist supporters of Donald Trump. The name alludes to the sixth chapter of Joshua in the Hebrew Bible, in which the Israelites march around the city of Jericho in an act that eventually brings down the city's protective outer walls: a passage that is frequently cited as validation for strategic-level spiritual warfare. The first of these marches was held in November 2020, just a few days after the election.

The Jericho Marches took place in a variety of different cities, but arguably the second most important one occurred on December 12, 2020, in Washington, DC, where a motley seeming crew assembled—from far-right radio host and conspiracy theorist Alex Jones to disgraced National Security Advisor Michael Flynn to NAR leader Lance Wallnau. Participants at these meetings at times blew shofars—ram's horn trumpets associated with the Jericho narrative. (While these were not NAR-organized events, it's worth noting that the shofar is associated with spiritual warfare in NAR thought as well, because the fall of Jericho is seen as an example of strategic-level spiritual warfare in the Hebrew Bible.)

The most important of the Jericho Marches occurred in Washington, DC, on January 6, 2021: the day that members of the US Congress had gathered at the US Capitol for the purpose of certifying the results of the 2020 presidential election, of which Biden had been the winner. As Matthew D. Taylor writes in *The Violent Take It by*

Force, January 6 had been billed to charismatic Christians as being "another Jericho March—the ultimate Jericho March, in fact."[24] Taylor notes, too, that "One of [OVPM's] prayer calls occurred at the exact time [on January 6, 2021] that the Capitol was breached."[25]

On that day, the Capitol Police issued six permits for protests outside the Capitol: two to organizers of the Stop the Steal movement, one to an anti-COVID conspiracy theory group, *and the other three to "Independent Charismatic groups."*[26] As attendants chanted "Jesus is my savior and Trump is my president" and protestors began to break through the barriers surrounding the Capitol building, NAR members like Cindy Jacobs and Rebecca Greenwood were just outside performing strategic-level spiritual warfare while shofars were blown and things slowly escalated to violence. In the words of Taylor,

> It is difficult to imagine that a more direct line could be drawn between the NAR and the theology of [NAR founder] Peter Wagner and the Capitol riot. Here two of Wagner's spiritual daughters [Jacobs and Greenwood] are praying and doing strategic-level spiritual warfare against "territorial spirits," just steps away from the intensifying violence of the insurrection.[27]

Thankfully, the Jericho Marches, and even the frightful Capitol Riot, were unsuccessful in turning the tide for Trump. Donald Trump was forced to leave office on January 20, 2021, when Joe Biden was sworn in. It might have been the end of the first Trump presidency, but it was not the end of the NAR's influence on politics.

Readying for 2024

Ziklag

The NAR was now down but not out. As the United States settled into an uneasy peace following Biden's assumption of the presidency, the NAR and adjacent groups needed to figure out a way to preserve whatever momentum from their movement remained. It seems almost silly at this point to assert what is by now the obvious answer: They turned to demons.

Back when Trump won the 2016 election, the time for dominion had seemed at hand. To help those seeking this outcome achieve this end, Ken Eldred, a Silicon Valley evangelist and author whom Wagner loves to quote in *Dominion!*, in 2018 established a Christian dominionist entity named Ziklag, after a town in the Hebrew Bible in which David builds his military might.

As an organization, Eldred's Ziklag has its fingers in a lot of pies. More to the point: It has its fingers on a lot of mountains. By this, I mean that the stated goal of the organization according to internal documents is to "take dominion over the Seven Mountains."[28] This reference to dominion is also clearly couched in the demonic. According to Andy Kroll, a national reporter for ProPublica, "a strategy document that lays out Ziklag's 30-year vision to 'redirect the trajectory of American culture toward Christ by bringing back Biblical structure, order and truth to our Nation'" further makes the claim that "'We are in a spiritual battle and locked in a terrible conflict with the powers of darkness.'"[29] If those sound a lot like the words of Lance Wallnau to you, you're on to something. Care to guess who one of the major forces behind and advisors to Ziklag might be? That's right: Wallnau again.

Heading into the 2024 election, both Ziklag (operating as a nonprofit under the name "USATransform") and Lance Wallnau Ministries Inc. were (and at the time of this writing and to the best of my knowledge, still are) officially registered as 501(c)(3) nonprofit organizations. According to the IRS's official website:

> Under the Internal Revenue Code, all section 501(c)(3) organizations are absolutely prohibited from directly or indirectly participating in, or intervening in, any political campaign on behalf of (or in opposition to) any candidate for elective public office. Contributions to political campaign funds or public statements of position (verbal or written) made on behalf of the organization in favor of or in opposition to any candidate for public office clearly violate the prohibition against political campaign activity.[30]

Both ProPublica and the Freedom from Religion Foundation have noted that this group's actions seem shockingly political given its nonprofit status. Internal documents obtained by ProPublica and Documented reveal plans to influence swing states in 2024 through anti-transgender messaging. In its private newsletter, Ziklag touted its influential role in Amy Coney Barrett's confirmation to the Supreme Court, and other documents detailed a $12 million dollar funding plan designed to support "a constellation of groups working on the ground to shift the 2024 electorate in favor of Trump and other Republicans."[31]

The group's endgame appears related to Wagner's idea of dominion. According to ProPublica's read of the internal documents:

> The Ziklag files detail not only what Christians should do to conquer all seven mountains, but also what their goals will be once they've taken the summit. For the government mountain, one key document says that "the biblical role of government is to promote good and punish evil" and that "the word of God and prayer play a significant role in policy decisions."
>
> For the arts and entertainment mountain, goals include that 80% of the movies produced be rated G or PG "with a moral story," and that many people who work in the industry "operate under a biblical/moral worldview." The education section says that homeschooling should be a "fundamental right" and the government "must not favor one form of education over another."
>
> Other internal Ziklag documents voice strong opposition to same-sex marriage and transgender rights. One reads: "transgender acceptance = Final sign before imminent collapse."[32]

The group's goals appear, predictably to mirror Wallnau and Wagner's shared goal: the transformation of every area of culture to reflect their narrowly defined interpretation of Christianity.

Given the group's focus on anti-transgender narratives, it seemingly would behoove them to have a demon associated with transgenderism that they could deploy during the then-upcoming 2024 election cycle.

Enter the Jezebel Spirit.

The Jezebel Spirit

Since the late twentieth century, conservative Christians concerned with the demonic have been gradually developing a detailed concept of what they have come to call the Jezebel Spirit: so named after the figure of Jezebel, who is described in the Bible as being a manipulative seductress who rebels against God's spiritual authority. In these Christians' eyes, this demonic influence can be for everything from transgenderism to feminism to pornography, and even sometimes the Democratic Party and its members. The trait that all of these entities, and others that get slapped with this label, have in common is a lack of submission. The Jezebel Spirit is the spirit of those who refuse to submit to a God-given role or position.

In addition to the biblical queen Jezebel who appears in the Hebrew Bible books of 1 Kings 18 and 2 Kings 9, another biblical figure called "Jezebel" emerges in Revelation 2:20, when Christ instructs John to write to the church of Thyatira: "Nevertheless I have a few things against you, because you allow that woman Jezebel, who calls herself a prophetess, to teach and seduce My servants to commit sexual immorality and eat things sacrificed to idols." The implication here seems to be that there is a woman who has encouraged behaviors which John rejects, and whom he has named Jezebel in echo of the Hebrew Bible figure who rejects God.

Given the Jezebel Spirit's associations with feminism, you might (as I do) find it unsurprising that conservative Christians frequently apply the term to women who don't "know their place" according to the people leveling the accusation. In the context of Donald Trump's presidential campaigns, the idea of Jezebel was first deployed against Hillary Clinton. Although others made the comparison, it arguably was articulated most completely by the author Jonathan Cahn.

Cahn is a messianic rabbi—meaning, he practices Jewish traditions while also believing that Jesus is the Messiah—as well as *The New York Times* bestselling author of such books as *The Harbinger: The Ancient Mystery that Holds the Secret of America's Future* (2012) and *The Return of the Gods* (2022). In 2017, Cahn produced a work entitled *The Paradigm: The Ancient Blueprint That Holds the Mystery of Our Times*, which sought to articulate "the Ancient Reason Trump Won."[33] In *The Paradigm*, Cahn attempts to draw parallels between biblical figures and political figures in the 2016 election, a comparison he makes using the term *antitypes*: by which he means the latter is a modern fulfillment or echo of a biblical character represented in Scripture.

While Cahn never overtly depicts Hillary as a "Jezebel Spirit" in his book or claims that she has been influenced or taken over by one, he does suggest that Clinton is an antitype for Jezebel and that she is therefore linked to the Canaanite god Baal (commonly viewed by some Bible interpreters as being a demon), whom the biblical queen Jezebel worshipped.[34] Cahn also associates Hillary Clinton with Astarte/Ishtar, another biblical deity often read as a demon and one that occupies the same intellectual space as the Jezebel Spirit in NAR and adjacent groups' thought.[35]

In 2020, four years after Trump's first election win, the rhetoric of the Jezebel Spirit was deployed once more: this time against then vice-presidential nominee Kamala Harris. In a candid video recorded for his followers that was seen by nearly four hundred thousand people, Lance Wallnau reported having a prophetic dream that causes him to discern that Harris is aided by the Jezebel Spirit. Wallnau asserts that in the dream "she [Harris] was going to be the one that the Devil was going to try to use to take Trump out."[36] Invoking rhetoric from the 2016 election, Wallnau then claims "Kamala is Hillary 2.0. It's . . . Jezebel Spirit 2.0." Here, Wallnau is drawing a connection between Clinton and Harris, suggesting that both were influenced by the demonic Jezebel Spirit.

Fast forward to the presidential election of 2024. Given the fervor surrounding accusations of the Jezebel Spirit, it must have almost seemed like a gift to NAR political strategists when Kamala Harris took over the Biden/Harris presidential campaign from the then-sitting president. Suddenly, the imagined threat of the Jezebel Spirit took on real gravity, and pundits could really kick the rhetoric up a notch.

Cahn was one of the key speakers at a Washington, DC, protest: the "A Million Women" march.[37] During the event, held on the National Mall in October 2024, Cahn and several other men destroyed a symbolic altar of Ishtar/Astarte that was meant to represent the evils in US society. Regarding this performance, journalist and senior research analyst at Political Research Associates Frederick Clarkson writes:

> Cahn and others described Ishtar as a demonic spirit that dominates our culture and is responsible for a broad range of evils that have kept our country "in bondage," including feminism; abortion; pornography; "sexual immorality" and all matters concerning LGBTQ people, especially the "transitioning of children . . . mutilating them"; divorce; the destruction of families; "the trafficking of women and children";

> and more. The smashing of the altar of Ishtar was intended to liberate the people, the capitol, and the nation from the bondage of Ishtar.[38]

During the same march, NAR apostle Ché Ahn collapsed the distinction between Harris and the Jezebel Spirit when he proclaimed, "I decree . . . that Trump will win on November the 5th. He will be our 47th president and Kamala Harris will be cast-out and she will lose." As he spoke, the crowd blew shofars.[39]

Meanwhile, Wallnau continued to repeat his claims that Harris was imbued with the Jezebel Spirit. In a discussion with the head of the eponymously named Mario Murillo Ministries on his podcast and video series *The Lance Wallnau Show*, Wallnau claimed that "Republicans [who were] like Ahab in the Bible" were allowing the Jezebel Spirit free reign and that Harris is aided by "a Jezebel Spirit . . . the personification of intimidation, seduction, domination, and manipulation."[40] On another episode of the show, Wallnau claims that the Jezebel Spirit is active in the United States and that the demon has performed an "emasculating move of lesbian, gay, bi, trans—go down the alphabet. . . . It's all about emasculating men."[41]

Thinking about Wallnau's claims from 2020 and 2024, there is very little to connect Hillary Clinton and Kamala Harris other than the fact that they are both Democrats with progressive policy positions, and both ran against Donald Trump in a bid to become the first female president of the United States. Below the surface of Wallnau's accusations, however, we can see that the Jezebel Spirit is seen here being associated with powerful women, women who threaten to occupy powerful roles—president and vice president—that have historically been held by men. There is an unease here that the demon personifies, an unease at sharing the reins of power. We see this masculine uneasiness reflected in Wallnau's plea to interpret the Jezebel Spirit as a force of emasculation, a demon that is stealing the manhood of American men.

Political Demons

It would be intellectually dishonest to suggest that the last three elections were all about demons. Obviously, the political-spiritual landscape of those periods is much more complex than can be reflected in such a simplistic stance. However, it *would* be accurate to say that the ideas of demons played a major, perhaps even decisive, role in the 2016 and 2024 elections that went to Trump. It would also be reasonable to state that the insurrection at the Capitol included a component of spiritual warfare against Trump's failed election bid in 2020 that slid into actual violence. Decades into the twenty-first century, we see, demons continue to exert a shocking hold over the political mind in America. And it doesn't look like that's going to change any time soon.

As you might imagine from given how well-developed the idea of the Jezebel Spirit is and how frequently it is evoked, political demons take up a good bit of room in the diabolical stable of the NAR and related groups. That is to say, there is a whole host of demons that they have developed and point to. And those of us who want to understand the boogeymen the NAR call upon to land their political-spiritual punches would do well to acquaint ourselves with them.

To that end, in the next chapter, we'll explore this veritable "monster manual" that the NAR and adjacent groups subscribe to. We'll also see how the NAR uses these demons to create a defense against outside criticism from other Christian groups, and how the NAR and related groups use them as a means to safely protect their ideas from political opposition without ever having to really engage with arguments leveled by their opponents. Let's take a look inside the protective box that insulates and protects the NAR and related groups from the outside world, one that relies upon demons for its protection.

CHAPTER TWENTY-ONE

The Monster Manual

As WE HAVE seen, the NAR and related groups have developed a host of new ideas about human interactions with demons. Many of these interactions are either implicitly political in purpose (as in the case of strategic-level spiritual warfare, i.e., the dismantling of demonic strongholds, as in spiritual mapping) or explicitly political in nature (as with the Seven Mountain Mandate).

One way that they managed to develop these spiritual concepts so effectively was by creating new ideas about old demons—for instance, by associating Baal with the Clintons, as Cahn did in *The Paradigm*—or inventing new demons from whole cloth, such as the Jezebel Spirit, named after an Hebrew Bible figure but decidedly not spoken about as a demon until the late twentieth century. But that hasn't been their sole approach. They've also given new demonic life to some other figures in the Bible.

For instance, while the historical identity of Leviathan, widely understood to be a mythological sea creature who symbolizes chaos, has been fairly well-established by biblical scholarship, the NAR movement generally eschews this interpretation, preferring to instead view him as a demon whose purpose is to divide people in churches and political organizations, using the tools of pride, confusion, and division.

And why wouldn't a spiritual-political organization like the NAR want to view him this way? After all, this interpretation supports one of their key ideas: that strategic-level spiritual warfare must be used to combat demons who have authority over whole geographic areas or institutions. In fact, most of these demons have specific political uses.

Of course, attempting to trace the countless tracks of how these demons have been employed in the media would be hellish indeed. We would have to wade through a labyrinthian maze of audio recordings of local church groups, Facebook posts, YouTube videos, conspiracy forums, podcasts, and a host of other sources that would represent literally tens of thousands of hours' worth of material. An infernal effort from which I will spare us both.

Instead, I'm going to provide a bird's eye view of the weird beasts slouching toward Washington, DC, that the NAR and NAR-influenced groups have created (and that sympathetic believers have helped spread), focusing on four purported demons that have been used for specific political purposes. I'll then shine some light on some ways that those who are inclined to do so are using such demons to inform a political stance that is resistant to change.

Leviathan

In 2018, Lance Wallnau went on televangelist Sid Roth's program *It's Supernatural!* to discuss the so-called Leviathan spirit.[1] In the episode, he describes this demon as the "Prince behind mind control" that seeks to divide "people against people."[2] Wallnau goes on to equate the behavior of Leviathan with a crocodile that twists and snaps off its victims' limbs or drags them underwater so that they're unable to breathe. He then links these ideas of crocodile-like behavior to Psalm 56:5: "All day they twist my words; All their thoughts *are* against me for evil."[3] In this way, Wallnau claims, Leviathan is the demon behind the so-called fake news of a demonically influenced mainstream media;[4] the being who seeks to twist words and press humans into situations in which they can't see reason.

In an episode of his own podcast entitled "Breaking the Power of Leviathan: Spiritual Warfare," Wallnau further argues that this spirit is responsible for the increasingly socially "toxic" world that we live in. For Wallnau, the gift of spiritual discernment (that is, the ability to tell the nature of a spirit, fair or foul) is of the utmost importance in our current environment since there is what he calls "so much conspiracy news . . . in traditional news dealers"[5] That is, Wallnau is calling attention to the popular conservative idea that traditional news outlets are peddling conspiracies, rather than the other way around. The effect of this is to drive his listeners further away from balanced news sources that might offer critiques of the Trump administration.

As religion scholar S. Jonathon O'Donnell writes in *Passing Orders: Demonology and Sovereignty in American Spiritual Warfare*, Leviathan is often depicted—as Wallnau did in the previous paragraphs—as "a divisive spirit" but the nature of this division can take a variety of forms.[6] Elsewhere, O'Donnell notes that Wallnau has claimed that the

Leviathan spirit is responsible for such progressive political movements as Occupy Wall Street, Code Pink, and Black Lives Matter.[7] (Cindy Jacobs appears to echo this sentiment about Occupy Wall Street.[8]) Ron Phillips, a charismatic Southern Baptist preacher and the author of *Everyone's Guide to Demons & Spiritual Warfare: Simple, Powerful Tools for Outmaneuvering Satan in Your Daily Life*, argues that this spirit is able to attack conceptual formations as well.

> Leviathan has attacked motherhood. A twisted form of feminism through the media appears to empower women innocently, but in reality women are shunning the responsibility of child rearing in the name of freedom. Women are escaping motherhood either altogether with the diabolical practice of abortion or simply giving their kids to ex-husbands and grandparents to raise.[9]

Phillips goes on to argue that Leviathan is also impacting school systems, saying: "Leviathan begins to twist historical records, twists testimonials from professing homosexuals, and twists community support until a school is buried beneath the waves of so-called tolerance."[10] Philips seems to ascribe the most power to Leviathan yet: painting him as an entity capable of warping historical records and manipulating popular sentiment to such a degree that those oppressed by the spirit are walking around in bubbles completely separate from reality.

Jennifer LeClaire of the Awakening House of Prayer, a charismatic Christian ministry that is theologically aligned with the NAR[11] (and that has connections with such NAR figures as Cindy Jacobs, Dutch Sheets, and Ché Ahn) claims in the third chapter of her book *The Spiritual Warfare Battle Plan*, that Leviathan is a power that convinces other people they are right and others are wrong; this, then makes them intractable when engaged in arguments.[12] In LeClaire's telling, Leviathan is the being behind gossip and chaos,[13] one that prefers to manifest around coastal areas, due to its watery nature. LeClaire asserts that Leviathan especially likes to manifest in South Florida, where her ministry is based.[14] The correlation is clear: The majority of coastal states and cities go blue in elections, with Fort Lauderdale often perceived as one of the most liberal cities in the state; LeClaire is implying that Leviathan's influence is to blame for this political effect.

Let's return once more to the question of brass tacks: What result does this demon get for those who believe in it? This time the answer is appallingly easy: Opponents who disagree with NAR ideas or members can be demonized and depicted as deceived or confused. After all, if the spirit of Leviathan is the one who twists words and makes people think things other than what occurred, then Leviathan is also the one who is manipulating people's perceptions of events. In this way of thinking, those afflicted with the Leviathan spirit are incapable of seeing the truth because of its demonic manipulation of them. This is the spiritual equivalent of the often touted "Trump Derangement Syndrome," the accusation that those on the political left have a psychologically warped view of reality that makes them behave irrationally toward Trump and his policies.

But that's not the only benefit. Belief in the demonic Leviathan also allows people to accuse specific political or educational movements of also being evil. If you don't like what the school is teaching, as Phillips essentially says when discussing Leviathan, the problem isn't that you're being intolerant; it's that Leviathan is active in the school. Does your political opposition disagree with you? Of course they do! That acknowledgment, however, doesn't require attempting any honest understanding of the other person's positions. What would be the point in trying? They're being governed by Leviathan.

Molech

The biblical identity of Molech (also spelled Moloch or Molek) has long been contested. Traditionally, Molech has been understood by Christian interpreters to be a Canaanite God, a kind of evil deity. People came to associate this deity with child sacrifice thanks to Bible verses such as Leviticus 18:21 ("And you shall not let any of your descendants pass through *the fire* to Molech, nor shall you profane the name of your God: I *am* the Lord") and Leviticus 20:2 ("Again, you shall say to the children of Israel: 'Whoever of the children of Israel, or of the strangers who dwell in Israel, who gives *any* of his descendants to Molech, he shall surely be put to death. The people of the land shall stone him with stones.'") However, there appears to be a growing consensus among biblical scholars that the term Molech (in Hebrew: *mlk*) refers not to a *being* to whom things are sacrificed but rather to a particular *type* of sacrifice.

As you might imagine, NAR and adjacent groups reject this shift and stand by the notion that Molech is an actual being who is a demonic agent. One who, like Leviathan, has a specific identity and purpose. And what is Molech's area of specialization? The author and messianic rabbi Jonathan Cahn writes in *The Return of the Gods* that "Molech was associated with the darkest of sins—the sacrifice of human beings and, in particular, the sacrifice of children. Even darker, Molech is associated with the sacrifice of children by their parents."[15] This description offers what I believe to be the clearest articulation of this supposed being and its purview.

In his book, Cahn argues the idea that the dark gods of the Bible, Baal, Ishtar, and Molech, have returned to present-day America. Now, you and I might imagine that if this were the case, we would be unable to miss that this was happening. Wrong, Cahn tells us via the following example: "it [Molech's return] began in the late 1960s, when a handful of American states opened the door by legalizing the killing of unborn children. Then, on January 22, 1973, the Supreme Court legalized the murder of unborn children. Molech had come to America."[16] As a result, Cahn says, "America, the shining *city on the hill*, had now become a blood-soaked high place of Molech."[17] In other words, the spirit of Molech is alive in contemporary America, in the medical practice of abortion and, by extension, in the advocacy for reproductive rights that supports a woman's right to choose.

This narrative of a demonic influence over the reproductive rights battle is difficult if not impossible to challenge, in part because many people aren't even aware of its existence. In my discussions with more hopeful pro-choice friends, I sometimes hear the notion articulated that the two sides of the debate are likely closer than they may appear, or the speculation that once misunderstandings about what constitutes an abortion are cleared up, pro-choice individuals may find more people on their side.

My understanding of the concept of Molech as a modern-day US demon leaves me dubious. I doubt that those hoping for increased understanding between the two sides envision what I know: that on the so-called pro-life side of the issue some people believe that a demon god is greedily consuming the willing sacrifices of unborn babies as a way to empower itself to work evil in the United States.

The Spirit of Poverty

We've already established that the NAR and NAR-associated groups seek to reassert dominion of key spheres of society. But how does one establish dominion without the financial means to do so? As Wagner pointed out in his book *Dominion!*, it's impossible to change the world without money.[18] But there's a problem: How do you convince a population of people of the need to become wealthy when they hold a book in their hands that includes verses like Mark 10:25, in which Jesus says "It is easier for a camel to go through the eye of a needle than for a rich man to enter the kingdom of God?"

One answer is: You might offer reinterpretations of this position, arguing that God, in fact, wants your life to be bountiful and prosperous. You'd likely come up with something like "Prosperity Theology," which is taught by famous charismatic evangelicals like Oral Roberts and Kenneth Copeland,[19] but also famously seemed to leak into the messages of megachurch pastor Joel Osteen.[20]Another option is a more radical one.

You could invent a demon.

The Spirit of Poverty is the outcome of this latter option. As we've already seen, the defeat of demons is an essential aspect of the social transformation that Wagner seeks. Let's look closer at how his teachings about spiritual warfare intersect with another of his key ideas, which he calls the "Great Transfer of Wealth."

In Wagner's world view, God plans to bring about a miraculous redistribution of global financial resources that will put wealth into the hands of the faithful. This transfer, Wagner says, will break the power that the Spirit of Poverty exerts on Christians. It is clear that he does *not* intend this phrase to be taken as a metaphor for an abstract discussion of poverty:

> Satan's desire is for poverty to prevail. He knows that "the poor man's wisdom is despised, and his words are not heard" (Ecclesiastes 9:16). In heaven there is no poverty, only prosperity. Aiming for "Your will to be done on earth as it is in heaven," implies that we do all we can to see that people prosper. The spirit of poverty is a demonic agent of Satan, intent on preventing people from enjoying God-given prosperity.[21]

Wagner goes on to dismiss the idea that poverty is somehow noble, claiming that the "Global South"—South America and Africa—is breaking the influence of the Spirit of Poverty quite effectively. For those living in the United States the next step must necessarily be to "bind and neutralize the spirit of poverty."[22] That is, the influence of a demon, the Spirit of Poverty, which causes poverty must be removed.

Other believers in this spirit are quick to point out that this redistribution of wealth isn't (just) about becoming personally wealthy. In his 2003 book *Overcoming the Spirit of Poverty*, charismatic NAR leader and leader of multiple Christian ministries Rick Joyner uses the two sentences in Luke 16:13—"No servant can serve two masters; for either he will hate the one and love the other, or else he will be loyal to the one and despise the other. You cannot serve God and mammon"—to distinguish between the act of acquiring wealth and one's internal motivations for doing so.

Joyner tells his reader, "That we cannot serve God and mammon means we cannot combine the motive of serving God with the motive of making money."[23] He then instructs them on how to differentiate between "good" and "bad" money and introduces the idea that "REPENTANCE + OBEDIENCE = FREEDOM." In presenting this formula, Joyner tips his hand: The following quote seems to indicate that in this context, obedience means tithing (the practice of giving a percentage of your income to the church):

> I have the testimony that the only times I have suffered financially since becoming a Christian were when I neglected to tithe. This was usually done out of carelessness, because I have always believed in tithing. However, every time I have suffered financial trouble and have gone back and checked my records, I found that my troubles began when I became careless in this one thing. When I repented and started giving the firstfruits of my income to the Lord again, the windows of heaven always quickly opened just as He promised.[24]

For Joyner, the relationship is clear: When one abandons Mammon—often interpreted by medieval and later Christians as a demon associated with money—and instead tithes generously of their income to a ministry, that person will receive financial enrichment from God.

(Perhaps such a person would even choose to tithe to Joyner's Morningstar Ministries.)

Bill Johnson, Lance Wallnau's coeditor on *Invading Babylon*, makes similar claims in his 2019 book *Breaking the Spirit of Poverty*. Here, as in Wagner's work, the Spirit of Poverty is depicted as a demonic entity. Speaking to his parish in Redding, California, in Shasta County, Johnson declares "Listen to me, it is a demon power, and it's a demon power that has exercised an incredible amount of authority over Shasta County."[25] He then relates an experience from preaching at a church in Malawi in Africa (where Wagner claimed the Spirit of Poverty was breaking).

According to Johnson, after the people learned to practice "radical generosity" toward their churches, the economy of the entire region, and not just their individual finances, had begun to change.[26] Naturally, he argued, when it came time to offer at the church "These folks gave like they were running to a war. That thing had to take 10 or 15 minutes for people just to get down the aisle, and they were dancing the entire way. They were going down the aisle. The dust filled that place."[27] The message is clear: Deliverance from the Spirit of Poverty is easy; you just have to give money generously to the church and it will be returned to you!

It is hard not to read Wagner's dominion schema into these teachings. In the ninth chapter of his book *Dominion!*—titled in part "Money Answers Everything!", Wagner introduces the idea of a Great Transfer of Wealth that is achieved through a series of links in a chain. The first link in the chain is the "providers" who create and give the wealth, and the second is the "managers" who steward that wealth and turn it into more.

The money next goes to the "distributors" (third link) whose job is to allocate resources. While speaking about these distributors, Wagner claims: "In the old wineskin [model of church growth], distributors were typically denominational executives, mission board directors or leaders of specialized ministries. In the new wineskin [the new NAR-esque model for church growth], distributors are, for the most part, apostles."[28] (That is to say, spiritual leaders.) Finally, once they are armed with all this wealth, the apostles then become the vectors for social transformation by distributing funds to the fourth link: "field marshals" (more spiritual leaders) who carry out "on the ground" missions for change.

To my untrained eye, this all sounds a little like a pyramid scheme. But that's probably just Leviathan talking.

The Religious Spirit

All of this may sound well and good to those inclined to favor a global transfer of wealth to the Christian faithful. But what if you were to disagree with this idea of wealth? Or, for that matter, what if you were to disagree with any of the new ideas that the NAR is pumping out? There's a demon for that too.

In the 2005 book *Freedom from the Religious Spirit*, editor C. Peter Wagner claims that the spirit of religion is "an agent of Satan assigned to prevent change and to maintain the status quo by using religious devices."[29] He then invites the reader to "imagine that Satan's kingdom has something like a Luciferian Department of Religion and that there are two major divisions of that department: the Division of Non-Christian Religions and the Division of Christendom."[30] It appears that both of these divisions would be staffed by Religious Spirits.

In this allegory, the Religious Spirit that inhabits the Non-Christian "department" is responsible for keeping people stuck in their current choices that are, in Wagner's eyes, heresy. (The examples he gives are Islam and Buddhism.) Meanwhile, the next department over, Christendom, is managed by two types of demons: one who targets individuals and another, "corporate" spirit that afflicts churches and even denominations.

As you might guess, this means the demons in the Christendom department cause people or organizations to act in a fashion that is unlike how teachers like Wagner believe they ought to behave. In a chapter entitled "The Corporate Spirit of Religion in Action—A Case Study," contributor Jim Anderson recounts what he calls a "personal encounter" with the spirit of religion that appears to have stemmed from a disagreement concerning the Evangelical Lutheran Church of America's (ELCA) stance toward gay people.[31]

In 1986, Anderson and other charismatic Lutherans had been contemplating aligning themselves with a planned merging of three major Lutheran church bodies, a process that would eventually result in the formation of the Evangelical Lutheran Church of America in 1988, but some felt concern that "the new denomination would drift toward unbiblical positions on issues like same-sex unions and the ordination of homosexuals."[32] Anderson was shocked to hear some leaders were willing to overlook what he clearly saw as a major theological issue in favor of not offending church leaders and a desire to make life easier for those charismatic Lutherans currently in ELCA-leaning congregations.[33] Anderson blamed the corporate Religious Spirit for creating in people what he calls "an irrational loyalty to their denomination."[34]

Other contributors to the volume offer their own assessments of traits that they say are evoked by the Religious Spirit. However, to many observers (including myself), many of these—from an "undue emphasis on tradition" to "rejecting spiritual manifestations they don't understand" to "moving believers to depend on reasoning and intellect rather than on guidance, power, and revelation of the Spirit"—simply sound like a way of demonizing people who don't agree with the NAR.

Resistance to Change

We've now met Leviathan, Molech, the Spirit of Poverty, and the Religious Spirit. And there are a lot, and I mean *a lot*, more demons that we could discuss if we continued in this vein, including the Queen of Heaven (a spirit of religious deception), the Anti-Christ Spirit (a spirit seen as generating social justice movements),[35] the Python Spirit (a hindrance to prophetic ministry), the . . . well, you get the idea. Likewise, we could talk about how these spirits interact with one another and hypothetically aid one another in their tasks. (I am reminded of LeClaire's discussion about the Jezebel Spirit in *The Spiritual Warfare Battle Plan* in which she claims that people afflicted by the demon are incapable of humbling themselves. "They may seem humble, but it's false humility stemming from a religious spirit."[36] Here, we see two spirits, Jezebel and the Religious Spirit, working in tandem.)

But rather than expanding on our list, let's instead stay with just this handful of spirits—many of which are considered within the NAR to be "major principalities" or high-ranking demons—and consider what conditions the ideas of them, taken together, might create. This process will lead us to two ideas, both of which constellate around a resistance to change.

Are We Actually Talking About Demons?

But first, a caveat. Before we explore key outcomes of one group's ideas about demons, we would do well to examine our own stance toward their claim that, at this moment, in the United States, demons are manifesting in ways that they have never before been historically understood to do. You or I might reject this idea and wish for another explanation. We might ask: What is *really* the cause for our country's upheaval, since it surely can't be demons?

Rather than try to answer that question, I suggest that we reject this way of thinking and instead return to the premise that demons are to blame. In a sense, I'm asking you to accept the idea that our country's current upheaval actually *is* "really" about demons! By that I mean, to a significant segment of our population, that belief is the truth. And rejecting that fact out of hand will get us nowhere in our attempts at understanding that population.

Put another way: If we try to excise from our country's collective narrative an important part of another group's explanation about how the world works, we turn away from something important. Something that's vital to understanding both where we are and the forces that got us here. You and I and our fellow citizens can't fix the problems that currently plague our communication as a nation unless we're willing to accept what people say and try to understand why what they say makes sense to them. That doesn't mean that any of us must accept the idea that demons *exist* if we're not inclined to do so. But it is important for us to accept the idea that—at least for the people we're trying to understand—this political-spiritual upheaval we are witnessing in the twenty-first century really is about demons.

Demons and the Sexual Revolution

With that settled, let's return to the question at hand: Do these ideas of demons that we've discussed tend to constellate around a particular focal point? To my mind, the answer is yes and based on my reading of material by and about the NAR, I have in fact concluded that these ideas about demons strongly coalesce around, and serve as a response to, two such points, and that those responses reflect a deep resistance to change.

The first focal point for NAR thought about demons is the Sexual Revolution of the 1960s. This was a time in which women began to further separate from the "traditional" roles of wife and mother; LGBTQ+ individuals began their march toward equality; and white men gradually saw themselves losing some of their social capital. Those are all pretty threatening shifts for people whose identities rely on maintenance of traditional power dynamics.

Crucially, the Sexual Revolution also serves to link the events of part 3 (the Satanic Panic) and this section. That is, as we saw in chapter 16, the idea of a satanic conspiracy seemed to target daycares and ideas of abortion, two ways in which women could take advantage of the opportunities for educational and occupational equity that had recently begun to emerge. (It just so happens to also be a link between Christian Reconstructionism, which advocates for a return to governance by biblical law. As Michael McVicar makes clear, R. J. Rushdoony's three-volume work about biblical law was a response to a "perceived lawlessness" that permeated the United States after the '60s. Likely, Wagner's and Jacobs's use of Rushdoony discussed in chapter 19 can be linked to this shared sense of lawlessness.[37])

We've seen examples of this obsession with sexuality throughout these chapters, but nowhere is it articulated more starkly than in Jonathan Cahn's *The Return of the Gods*, which explores the topic of demonic presences in the West, especially in the United States. In its pages, Cahn frequently alludes to the Sexual Revolution of the '60s, particularly the Stonewall Uprising, the series of protests in New York in 1969 that resulted from a raid on the gay bar, the Stonewall Inn.

In Cahn's worldview, the ancient biblical deities Baal, Ishtar, and Molech (which Cahn reads as demons) wormed their way into the United States through openings created by the Stonewall events. He devotes countless chapters to a detailed analysis of the Stonewall Uprising and the riots surrounding it. In Cahn's view, Ishtar (again, often read as the same as the Jezebel Spirit) was present during the protest:

> It was there in the streets of New York City that the goddess would make her stand and bring what had been hidden in the shadows out of the spotlight of American culture, then Western culture, and finally the world. Her agenda was ultimately to take a Christian civilization, alter its values, its perception of marriage, gender, and sexuality, until it had been transformed into a pagan civilization.[38]

Cahn next attempts to reconstruct the events of the uprising in exacting detail. The interpretive methods he applies to the historical accounts of the uprising swing from the weirdly literal to the deeply symbolic. For instance, he claims "The goddess . . . is a stone . . . that buckles out the *stone wall*."[39] Presumably, he expects his reader to gasp at the similarity of the translated phrasing—presumably Akkadian to English since he appears to be quoting the *Epic of Gilgamesh*—to the actual name of the Stonewall Inn.

Yet elsewhere, he doesn't shy from suggesting that Stonewall is a figurative gateway that could stand in place of a literal "Gate of Ishtar": the biblical inner city of Babylon. Following this line of thinking, Cahn concludes that the modern-day pride parades that started at Stonewall and continue today are actually parades of worship to the goddess Ishtar.[40]

My favorite example of Cahn's interpretive efforts is his attempt to link the protestors at Stonewall to the *kezertu*, a class of cultic officials in ancient Mesopotamia that Cahn sees as exclusively linked to Ishtar. He claims that the term *kezertu* comes from the word *kezeru* meaning to curl hair, and that dancing and singing girls were a common element of Ishtar worship. He attempts to link this back to one portion of the riots in which a group of protestors performed a kick line and a song before police:

> Those engaged in the dance had no idea. But it was as if the spirit of the kezertu had taken them over. They were men, but now they became as women, dancing women, singing girls. Their song was a lewd taunt of the police officers. But the lyrics were most significant. They began, "We are the Stonewall girls." And then came the words that stretched back to the Akkadian of ancient Mesopotamia and to the goddess; they sang, "We wear our hair in curls." In the Akkadian tongue it was equivalent to saying, "We are the kezertu."[41]

Setting aside for the moment the fact that these protestors were certainly *not* speaking Akkadian, that the *kezertu* were a phenomenon of more than just Ishtar worship, and that many religions (including denominations of Christianity!) incorporate into their practices singing and dancing performed by girls, we still have a problem: Cahn doesn't even provide his reader with the context for the chant. Lined up in a chorus-girl-style kick line, the dancing men rolled up their socks and sang to the tune of the Howdy Doody Show theme song, "We are the Stonewall girls/We wear our hair in curls/We don't wear underwear/ We show our pubic hairs."[42] One can guess at why Cahn didn't include these lyrics in his argument; the clearly ridiculous nature of the chant may well have broken the spell he hoped to cast over his audience.

This is just one example, but it's an illustrative one. Adding this to the history we've read throughout the book, it seems reasonable to read these and other ideas about demons held by the NAR and adjacent groups—if not the formation of the groups themselves—as a response to the Sexual Revolution. The world was changing, but not everyone wanted to change. If the source of the upheaval was demons, though, and if one was fighting the demons, one didn't have to.

In this way, belief in demons reflects an unwillingness to change along with the rest of America, and to see equal personhood in women and LGBTQ+ people.

Demons and Dissent

All of this brings us to the second focal point for modern ideas about spiritual warfare and demons: the relationship between demons and dissent. As we read about the Sexual Revolution, when demons are to blame, one doesn't have to succumb to change. The same thing holds true for outside criticism: If the criticism itself is demonic (or is leveled by someone who is being influenced by demons) it stands that one doesn't have to seriously consider or even listen to it. This too creates a hedge against the necessity of change.

Let's return to the major players we've discussed so far: the Jezebel Spirit, Leviathan, the Religious Spirit, the Spirit of Poverty, and Molech. We'll start with the two who are most clearly related to the Sexual Revolution: the Jezebel Spirit and Molech. LGBTQ+ issues are the purview of the Jezebel Spirit, and Molech is localized around the issue of abortion, which, as we've already seen, is an option that is often credited with providing women with a way to live a life that is not dictated by motherhood and traditional sex roles.

Believing in the Jezebel Spirit and Molech does something important for individuals who believe in literal demons: It gives them a powerful excuse to resist change, one that is grounded in the supernatural and thus seemingly beyond reproach. Faced with challenges to their political stances, these people can say: "God is real, demons are real, and they're active in the world. LGBTQ+ rights and abortion are obviously the work of demons. That means I'm not being prejudiced; I'm being faithful."

But what happens when other Christians disagree? What if other churches say one's teachings aren't biblical or even that they're influenced by the Devil? That resistance could create a kind of deadlock or even make a person question whether they're really fighting against demons, or helping them. That's where the idea of the Religious Spirit comes in.

For a moment, put yourself in the shoes of the person being challenged. Someone disagrees with you about something. No problem. The trouble isn't what you believe or do, it's the Religious Spirit that's acting in your opponents and causing them to question you. Given the long lists of traits that have been ascribed to the Religious Spirit—traits that even authors who advocate for the spirit, like Rick Joyner, admit seem contradictory[43]—you should have no trouble finding *something* about the individual, church, or denomination rejecting your worldview that shows that they're being influenced by the Religious Spirit. From your perspective, the problem takes on a new configuration: It's not you who's resisting change, it's the other side who is resisting change due to demonic interference!

With this as your goal, you need a way to radically transform the world around you to match the vision in your head, a way to "encourage" others to share your view. Wagner's dominionist ideas are just the ticket. They're hard to realize without money though.

Time for the Spirit of Poverty! Now, with this tool in your toolkit, you can convince people of the necessity of regular tithing. A quick survey of the landscape reveals that tithing is a clear means to wealth: the Church of Jesus Christ of Latter-day Saints (Mormons) has required compulsory tithing since the early nineteenth century and it has a net worth (as of 2024) of $293 *billion*.[44] Imagine what would be possible if your group benefited from regular tithing? How swiftly you could advance the Kingdom toward dominion!

Plus, there's zero benefit not to tithe. Not tithing is actually the thing that's keeping individuals back in their finances. This "Mammon mentality" of holding on to one's money is essentially a form of greed that stops God from depositing the fullness of his blessings. Tithe, and

God will more than make up for the difference. Plus, you'll be defeating a demon to boot.

Of course, when the work of reestablishing dominion starts intensifying, some people will definitely put up a fuss. They'll criticize your candidate, your policies, your beliefs, anything they can get their hands on. When that happens, don't worry: That's just the Leviathan spirit doing its work of sowing division and confusion. You know that your cause is righteous, so there's no need to reflect or doubt. Just pray against this spirit and hope that its influence over your neighbors, coworkers, family, old friends, and others is broken. While you pray, stay the course.

No need to change a thing.

The Intersection of Demons and Conspiracies

Could you make these arguments to an NAR proponent? Absolutely. Would they convince the person? Let's hope! However, I wouldn't hold my breath.

While a lot of the ideas of demons we've discussed so far in this section are relatively new in their current forms, they're not all that different conceptually from older, equally poisonous ideas that have circulated within the West for centuries. From ideas of Jewish blood drinking conspiracies (a centuries' old antisemitic myth known as the Blood Libel) to the notion that witches held secret meetings to inflict harm (just to name two),[45] people who supported such ideas all shared the NAR's ability to see an invisible hand at work that they claimed profoundly impacted the world, to resist evidence that might contradict their claim, and to see a hidden, nefarious hand working in the world. In the modern day, the same ideas are at work when people see Jewish media conspiracies, the Rothschilds, or the Illuminati, rather than demons, as that malevolent force.

The modern world has a term for those people.

Conspiracy theorists.

CHAPTER TWENTY-TWO

Conspiracy!

As you may recall, I started the book by suggesting that believing in demons isn't *necessarily* a bad thing. Rather, I singled out a conspiratorial mindset as a "bad way" to believe in them, one whose adoption is intrinsically harmful. The harm caused by conspiracy theories impacts democratic institutions and nations, all of which are built either implicitly or explicitly on the notion that an informed populace can make decisions that benefit everyone. But what happens when that populace is fed questionable information and taught to see their fellow citizens as unredeemable sources of evil? In a word: disaster.

In this chapter, we're going to be considering what makes information bad or good, that is, built on sound principles, judgment and expertise instead of simply being an opinionated claim. While it doesn't deal overtly with the idea of demons, the significant connection between demons and conspiratorial mindsets in the United States warrants at least a brief discussion of these ideas, not the least of which so that you, as the reader, can be informed enough to respond when someone tries to make such a claim. To begin to understand how conspiracies are formed and spread, we first need to understand how knowledge is formed and spread.

How Do You Know That What You Know, You (Really) Know?

There's a branch of philosophy that tries to answer questions about belief, such as *What is knowledge? How do we acquire knowledge?* and *Is it possible to ever be truly certain about one's beliefs?* This philosophical discipline is called epistemology (*episteme*—knowledge; *logos*—the study of something). Now, like any field of study, this topic can get a bit abstract and theoretical, so for our purposes we're going to distill it down to its essential elements.

The first item that we should note is that knowledge is a social phenomenon. That is to say, if someone made a claim to knowing something (let's call it "Claim X") then individuals around them likely wouldn't *agree* that the person knew Claim X until they'd verified it through what they believed to be a trustworthy source. Corroboration could occur through something as simple as seeing something with one's own eyes (after which some might say something like, "I also agree that objects fall when you drop them"), through a report by a widely accepted authority ("*The New York Times* said it was so, so it must be!"), or through data produced by credible producers of reliable information (for instance, journals such as *The Lancet* and *Nature* have been producing peer-reviewed—to be discussed in a moment—journal articles for over a century).

Now, let's zoom in on the verification process above.

Not All Knowledge Is Equal

At first glance, all accepted knowledge may appear to be equal. But in fact, there are grades to the quality of information that exists in the world. At the highest level is the data that is produced by people who are working in very specialized areas of academic research, such as college professors, professional scientists, and other individuals who have undergone highly specific and extensive training in their area of expertise. These people typically publish their work in periodicals known as peer-reviewed journals, which are publications that usually require other researchers in the author's field to check over the claims made in a scholarly article. (*The Lancet* and *Nature* mentioned above are two such peer-reviewed journals.)

If any inconsistencies are found or issues raised by the reviewers, the author-researchers are then required to revise their work or to provide evidence that supports a decision not to make a reviewer's suggested change. Sometimes a review process can unfold over multiple rounds; it can sometimes take years for a single article to go from being written to being published! As a result, these publications are considered the gold standard for trustworthy, reliable information. However, the accessibility of this information is an issue; the articles in these journals often include ideas, theories, and vocabulary that only those within the field understand. In fact, it's not uncommon for only a handful of people to read and understand a particular issue of a peer-reviewed journal in its entirety!

Yet, the information that's included in these publications is immensely important. The data often represents small but significant strides that are being made in the fields of study in which the researchers are publishing. How then do these important tidbits of information get condensed and disseminated in ways that everyday people can consume and understand?

The answer is journalists. When new information is published in academic journals, journalists with expertise in relevant fields distill that information and communicate it in a format that other people who don't share their specialized training can understand. This process can occur several times, with each journalist distilling ideas from other journalists so that the ideas become more and more accessible. This process is one reason a free press is so vital in democratic societies: In theory, the average person bases their choice of political candidates on the candidates' positions and their own understanding of the issues. If their understanding of the issues is flawed, then their understanding of what's at stake and their ability to decide wisely will be too. The result is that they may not choose the candidate who is working in their or their communities' best interests.

This is why journalism is so vital.

"Do Your Own Research"

And here is where things get tricky. For all this to work, everyone involved needs to do their part: Researchers need to provide reliable information, journalists need to report it in a trustworthy and understandable way, and people need to trust them. One of the key pieces of this framework has to do with the issue of bias.

The people toward the top of the verification pyramid, that is, peer-reviewed researchers, and below them, journalists, are trained to account for the existence of *bias*: a preference to favor a certain set of ideas or outcomes over others, particularly in ways that distort a person's judgment or objectivity. That doesn't mean that they always keep bias from influencing their findings, but they're much better at watching out for it than most.

If someone has ever told you to "do your own research," you've bumped up against the issue of bias. Usually, when someone says this, they're attempting to refute a particular argument, position, or way of thinking, and they're hoping that you'll search for articles or data that aligns with their conflicting viewpoint, which will in turn lead you to material that will support their conclusions.

Put another way: They've given some indication or hint of what the outcome of your thinking should be and are sending you in search of data that will support it. Generally speaking, those who are trained to do research tend to do the exact *opposite*. That's why when someone tells me they've done their own research, I often reply, "Do you do your own surgeries too?" There are good reasons that both surgeon and researcher are occupations that require significant investments of time. Both vocations involve the acquisition and use of skills that the average person doesn't have, at least not on their level.

The fact that the person on the street is not trained to undertake the task of serious research doesn't mean that those people aren't intelligent individuals capable of critical thinking: it just means that their occupation is not *researcher*, *professor*, or *journalist*. Similarly, I'm not able to act as a plumber, a dental hygienist, or an air traffic controller: I'm not trained to do so. It's worth noting that even those who operate at the highest levels of the verification pyramid have their limits. For example, I am trained to perform research and to read journal articles in a few areas of the humanities; however, that doesn't mean that my experience is transferable to reading medical journals. Research areas are highly specialized, and we need individuals to be providing reliable information in every field. And they do. For the most part. But not always. And there's the rub.

In an ideal world, researchers would always produce top-notch analyses, journalists would report on all topics in as bias-free a manner as possible, and the resulting data would be made easily accessible to the general public so that everyone could make informed decisions about everything in their lives. Unfortunately, it doesn't always work that way. Sometimes researchers make mistakes or get influenced by bias, as can happen, for example, when money is involved. For example, in 2015 *The New York Times* reported on substantial donations that the Coca-Cola corporation made to the now defunct Global Energy Balance Network (GEBN). These donations seemed to have been made for the purpose of getting or encouraging the GEBN to advance an idea of weight loss that downplayed or eliminated the role of sugary beverages in obesity and type 2 diabetes.[1] Money for research has to come from somewhere and caution has to be observed lest strings are attached.

Sometimes journalists also make mistakes. Luckily, there are *other* researchers and *other* journalists who are keeping an eye out for such abuses. One example is an organization called Retraction Watch, which as "a window into the scientific process,"[2] tracks papers that have been retracted from journals. Without the work of organizations like Retraction Watch, violations of research ethics and lapses in scholarly standards that are part of larger patterns of malfeasance could instead be taken as isolated offenses. Accessing this data, which has been collected and made accessible in a centralized location, can help people to draw larger conclusions about how, for example, AI use is influencing journal articles as well as creating a collaborative space in which such problems can be reported.[3] Both researchers and journalists participate in this excellent resource.

The back and forth that occurs between researchers and journalists in the academic area of the history and philosophy of science on *Retraction Watch* unfolds as an ongoing and ever-evolving conversation. In fact, researchers often use the term *conversation* to denote ongoing research in particular academic areas because, much as in a typical conversation between individuals, pauses and asides occur, corrections and adjustments are made, and shifts in thinking unfold as new considerations are weighed. In fact, it's pretty common for academics, researchers, journalists, and others to refer to this process informally as "*the* conversation," which is where the excellent academic news platform and expert commentary site *The Conversation* gets its name.[4] In addition to the give and take nature of this ongoing exchange, the term also points to the inherently social aspect of communicating knowledge.

Which brings us to where we are today.

A Flourishing of Conspiracies

Next, let's consider the fact that every conversation that humans have tends to follow social guidelines. For example, our conversations with our romantic partners are generally very different in vocabulary choice, tone, and content than those we have with, say, our bosses. Likewise, conversations that we have with our childhood friends are different than ones we share with our coworkers, and we speak differently to children than we do to adults, and to people in a bar than to those we meet on the street. Even if we might not be able to verbalize those rules, we have been taught to follow them; for example, most of us are aware that we should communicate respectfully to our direct supervisors and to speak with care when we're addressing our partners and our kids.

Academic conversations, too, often function by some fairly specific rules, and one of those rules could be summed up as: "If you're going to make a claim, you had better have evidence or clear reasoning." Different fields of knowledge tend to evaluate evidence and reasoning in different ways, but there are three principles for assessment that tend to hold weight across the various disciplines:

1. *More is Better than Less*: In academic disciplines, arguments gain strength when they're backed by a plethora of supporting evidence. That evidence might, for example, take the form of more experiments, more textual attestations (meaning, more articles and sources), or more grounding of claims to credible authority. Likewise, having a greater number of experts agree that the evidence is reliable is better than having fewer. Regardless of the form it takes, though, the result is the same: arguments that are built upon more (and more reliable) evidence are more trustworthy and resilient than those that are founded on less.
2. *No Circular Reasoning*: Circular reasoning is a logical fallacy—that is, an error in reasoning—that occurs when a person relies on a claim that they've made to validate that same claim. Such an argument might look something like "X is true because X." If you're a parent, you might have used this one before. If you ever told your child "It's bedtime" only to have them ask "Why?," and then you responded, "Because it's time for bed!" then you've used circular reasoning.
3. *Occam's Razor*: The fourteenth-century theologian and philosopher William of Ockham formulated a useful principle for evaluating explanations and constructing arguments that has resonated for more than eight hundred years (and counting!). In its original form, his

> idea said, essentially: Don't multiply entities (that is, assume more entities or explanations than are needed) to account for the evidence. This is sometimes summarized today as "The simplest explanation is usually the best" or "When you hear hoofbeats, think horses, not zebras." In other words, when faced with multiple explanations, a person should favor the one that involves the least amount of complication and requires the fewest assumptions.

These principles likely sound reasonable. After all, they've been tested by time! Often times, however, a conspiracy theory violates all three of them. Let's look at an example of how this occurs.

From Reliable Evidence to Stigmatized Knowledge

We'll start with an example that isn't immediately related to demons. How about the belief that there are sentient, human-like reptiles that have invaded the government? You might laugh, but there actually are people who believe that "Reptilians"—shape-shifting lizard-like beings who can make themselves look like people—have occupied government positions around the world. This is the claim. Now, let's assess it using the three principles above.

First, we'll ask: Is there evidence that supports this claim, and if so, how much of it? Proponents of this theory say that it's there, but notably all of the things that you and I might think would be good evidence (DNA, documents, unbiased reports, etc.) have not yet been forthcoming. So where does this belief find its grounding?

Rather than building upon the kind of reliable evidence that we have been discussing in this chapter, the so-called evidence that conspiracies rely upon (including the conspiracy about Reptilians) is what political scientist Michael Barkun, the author of *A Culture of Conspiracy: Apocalyptic Visions in Contemporary America*, calls "stigmatized knowledge."[5] This refers to knowledge that falls outside of the trustworthy framework we've outlined above. It may be considered stigmatized because it has been superseded (no longer considered accurate, as in science's transition from belief in alchemy to the study of chemistry), ignored or dismissed by much of the population (as with folk medicine), rejected by experts after analysis, or even theorized to have been forgotten or suppressed (claims that we allegedly once knew but lost, or that powerful organizations allegedly are keeping hidden).

Conspiracy theorists often use these forms of stigmatized knowledge to construct their claims. For example, ideas about the Reptilians draw on rejected knowledge such as New Age vibrational principles and forgotten knowledge, through the interpretation of mythic texts as evidence of a supposed conspiracy plot. When asked why there's no conventional evidence forthcoming, a proponent of the theory might claim, "Because the lizard people are so good at hiding their tracks!" And here, we find circular reasoning: (1) There's a conspiracy! (2) Where's the evidence? (3) There is no evidence because there's a conspiracy!

Finally, we get to our third principle for evaluating evidence and reasoning: Occam's multiplication of entities. And here is where the Reptilian theory's most egregious offense takes place. To explain the lack of evidence for shape-shifting lizard people, believers must suggest a lot of additional wrinkles to their theory, from underground bases to human collusion to interbreeding between humans and reptilian beings.

Needless to say, believing all this takes a rather large leap of faith. Now, does this mean that it's *impossible* for the claim to be true? Crucially, no. I say crucially because this is an important principle to grasp: Academia works in terms of interpretations of evidence and sound reasoning, not in unassailable truth that will never be overturned.

Let's return to our earlier topic of knowledge and research. The conversations that emerge from academia don't tell us what *is true*. Instead, they give us best practices and well-developed ideas for thinking *about* truth and point us toward what is most probably true. Working within this framework, it hypothetically could be true that shape-shifting lizard people control the world.

Given all this, the question most worth asking is not whether Reptilians are real, but why anyone would accept the idea of the Reptilians (or other conspiracies) as being true. Or put another way: When someone offers no concrete evidence valued by any academic body, can't respond to contrary claims in any significant way, and relies on an idea that can be more easily explained in a conventional manner, what possible reason could there be to accept these ideas as true?

The answer is simple: Comfort.

Conspiracies of Comfort

As strange as it might sound, I would argue that a lot of conspiracy theories, despite their often frightening nature, have more to do with shoring up people's feelings of comfort than anything else. This pursuit of comfort often takes the form of two goals: warding away chaos and gaining a greater sense of belonging.

First, it can be scary to live in a world that's as chaotic a place as ours, in which everyone is just trying their best to hold on for dear life. For some folks, though, the idea that some secret clandestine entity runs the world, such as "the Rothschilds" or a "secret Jewish conspiracy," provides a sense that *someone* is in charge. In the minds of these individuals, there is at least a hidden hand of order in all the seeming chaos, a singular force to contend against, rather than endless random chances and petty squabbles.

And what about the second goal? What if you feel out of step with the rest of a world that doesn't agree with you? Not to worry. It's not you that's the problem: it's, for example, the "Deep State" controlling the media. If it weren't for this extra-governmental entity manipulating the facts, so the theory goes, everyone would see the rightness of what you believed and think just like you! Secure in this mindset, you can believe that your views actually match up with those of the majority of people, or, at the very least, of a minority whose special knowledge has elevated you and your peers, the only group worth belonging to, above the *hoi polloi*.

Of the two goals, the first, warding away chaos, is arguably the most motivating. Barkun suggests as much when he writes:

> The essence of conspiracy beliefs lies in attempts to delineate and explain evil. At their broadest, conspiracy theories "view history as controlled by massive, demonic forces." The locus of this evil lies outside the true community, in some "Other, defined as foreign or barbarian, though often . . . disguised as innocent and upright." The result is a worldview characterized by a sharp division between the realms of good and evil.[6]

Put another way, as Barkun argues, "the conspiracist worldview implies a universe governed by design rather than by randomness."[7]

Even the conspiracist worldview, it would seem, follows a consistent design. Barkun points out three elements that appear in nearly all conspiracy theories and underscore this essentially ordered cosmos. First, he says, conspiracy theories reject the idea of random chance; in these beliefs, an ordered hand is everywhere, influencing outcomes that at first appear chaotic or random. Second, nothing is ever what it first appears to be; the ordered hand can be seen consistently working behind the scenes, if one is only perceptive enough to detect it. Finally, there is an idea that we've seen alluded to already: "everything is connected." In this mindset, there's no such thing as random chance, and patterns can be found in even the tiniest and most inconsequential events or coincidences.

The problem, particularly as it relates to politics and the demonic in modern day America, is that these elements—the ordered hand, the work occurring behind the scenes, the idea of otherworldly connection and order—are also beliefs shared by a significant number of Christian groups.

Demonic Conspiracies Are the Worst

Let me be clear: I'm not implying here that Christianity is a conspiracy theory. Rather, I am suggesting a relationship between the two that's not unlike the one between music and math. Consider the fairly well-known phenomenon that people who play music tend to be better at math than those who don't. What's the connection? Some have suggested that it's that both disciplines teach pattern recognition, emphasizing certain executive functions and relying upon shared reasoning skills.

In much the same way, the teachings that a particular church, denomination, group, or movement instills in their adherents can predispose them to be "good" at conspiracies as well. Consider the following comparison between Barkun's principles and notions that are common in many Christian groups in the United States.

Just as Barkun suggests about conspiracy theories, many Christian groups also accept and teach the idea that there are sharp divisions between good and evil. Likewise, many of these same groups believe in an ordered hand (God), the work occurring behind the scenes (God working), and the idea of otherworldly connection and order (God's plan). This idea of order and connectivity is reinforced by the notion that patterns occur in nature and the Bible that are not immediately perceptible to a casual viewer but that are important to understand. Such believers claim that rather than focusing on plot structure and general narrative goals in Scripture, those who want to discern these patterns can and must do so by employing interpretive methods that pay attention to tiny minutiae and secret correspondences. Again, this is the very same thing that many conspiracy theorists might claim.

Then, add to all that, the question of demons.

We talked earlier about the conspiracy of Reptilians as a non-demon example. But now, we're back at demons once again. And demon conspiracies truly are the most problematic conspiracies of all.

Why are demonic conspiracies the worst? Because they can effectively enfold *all other conspiracies* within their parameters. Let me explain.

In his book, Barkun makes a distinction between three types of conspiracies: event conspiracies that focus on a specific, one-time event; systemic conspiracies that allege that a powerful organization or institution controls an entire system; and superconspiracies that tie all of the other conspiracies together as being part of one, big plan that is designed and controlled by a particular someone or something. Examples of each type include theories about Kennedy's assassination (event conspiracy), the notion that Freemasons control the government (systemic), and the idea of Reptilians taking over the world (superconspiracy). Each individual conspiracy presents challenges of its own. Yet, each one can also be enfolded easily within the framework of a demonic conspiracy by recognizing each conspiracy as true and attributing its events to the cosmic actions of the Devil. In effect, this joining of conspiracy theories allows believers in demons to draw a variety of groups under their banner, swelling their numbers and the seeming authority with which they speak. And more bad political actors means more bad politics.

You could even say the ideas that necessarily undergird the idea of a demonic conspiracy are ideas that encourage a "reaching across the aisles" to other conspiratorial camps. Perhaps not surprisingly, this is exactly the type of activity that occurs in QAnon, which has been the conspiracy *du jour* in the United States for the past decade or so. The fact is, there are lots of popular conspiratorial ideas flying around various websites, chat rooms, and forums, many of them seeming on the surface to be entirely unrelated. But they often don't stay that way. Because both Q himself and many QAnon proponents seek to link them through the idea of spiritual warfare and demons.[8]

Unfortunately, this present moment in our country is especially susceptible to conspiracy theories: Many of our fellow citizens are denigrating education, the foundation of making and distributing good information, more than has ever happened before; the internet acts as a distribution mechanism for bad information, one with no safety features by which to limit or control its multiplication; and the advent of AI has sharpened humans' ability to produce false "evidence" like no previously seen technology has had the capacity to do. Put simply, we're in a bad way.

But we don't have to stay this way. It is possible to move from bad to good, but to do so, we need to rise to the challenge of this present moment in American history. As I've argued in this book, this work will require us to break the conspiratorial hold that the idea of demons is exerting over present-day America. In order to do that, we need to be armed with our own history, a history that has a surprisingly rich set of intersections between demons and politics. This knowledge then allows us to identify and counter the conspiratorial assumptions that have become so deeply entwined in the American political experience. This is the knowledge you have been engaging with throughout this book.

But we cannot stop there. If we are to address the need for belonging and abatement of chaos that is at the beating heart of every conspiratorial view of the world, we also need to find a way to return to our shared humanity.

CHAPTER TWENTY-THREE

What Happens Next

On June 14, 2025, in the middle of the night, a gunman drove to the homes of two state lawmakers and shot and killed Minnesota House Representative Melissa Hortman and her husband and shot Minnesota State Senator John Hoffman and his wife. The shootings precipitated the largest manhunt in Minnesota history for the suspect, Vance Luther Boelter. Acting US attorney for the district of Minnesota Joe Thompson said that "Boelter was disguised as a police officer, drove a black SUV with emergency lights turned on, and had a license plate that said 'police.' He carried a 9mm handgun, wore a black tactical vest and was disguised with a realistic silicone mask."[1] According to local TV station KARE11, Boelter allegedly sent a text message to his family after the shootings that read "Dad went to war last night."[2]

What could that message mean? At the time of this writing, Boelter appears to have had ties with organizations linked to the NAR. Boelter attended the Christ for the Nations Institute in Dallas, Texas, a college connected to the Latter Rain movement through one of its founders, James Gordon Lindsay, and graduated in 1990 "with a Diploma in Practical Theology in Leadership and Pastoral [studies]."[3] After getting additional education, Boelter founded a nonprofit company with his wife called Revoformation Ministries.[4]

It has been reported that he had traveled to the Democratic Republic of Congo, where several times he spoke at a local church. Some of his sermons could still be found online in the year after the shooting. In these sermons Boelter engages the language of the NAR: speaking about the return of modern day prophets and apostles in the United States, framing "gender confusion" in a demonic manner,[5] and addressing what he sees as the evils of abortion.[6]

This last grievance provides a window into what may have been the rationale for the attack. According to a statement from Melissa Fowler, Chief Program Officer for the National Abortion Federation, "It is clear that these were politically motivated attacks—police found the suspect's list of over 70 targets, which include a number of abortion providers and pro-abortion advocates."[7] Given the focus on abortion providers and abortion advocacy on his list of targets and the NAR-esque intellectual framing of his sermons, it seems likely that Boelter's "war" was spiritual warfare against Molech, the demon associated with abortions that we discussed in chapter 21.

Boelter's attacks provide a horrific and terrifying example of how politics and spiritual warfare can, and have, come together in violent ways in the twenty-first century. But he's far from the only person in the United States today who's embracing an overlap of the two.

From Spiritual to Actual Warfare?

All over the country today, the gap between spiritual warfare and actual warfare and violence is beginning to narrow. Consider the following example: In April 2024, journalist Dominick Bonny reported an affiliated church and ministry located in Cashmere, Washington, The Collective and Kingdom Defense Ministries, were offering upcoming workshops that featured firearms training and education about tying tourniquets and other doomsday preparation-type activities.

> In a promotional video that cuts between footage recorded during worship services in Cashmere and scenes from a drag queen story hour, pro-choice marches and what appears to be Islamic terrorists preparing to execute hostages, a male narrator explains the need for Christians to partake in training sessions like these. "We must be pioneers in a world that just wants to bully us into the consensus," [the narrator] said.[8]

The website for The Collective bills itself as being "unified under the mantle of turning the heart of our nation back to the Father. This calling is to the 'Now Generation', *to lay down our lives for the sake of all future generations.*"[9] The fact that a church is preparing young men and women for what appears to be war alongside a claim that it is time to lay down one's life is a disturbing combination.

Here's another example from the other side of the country. On July 13, 2025, a new branch of the Moscow, Idaho, Christ Church founded by self-described "Christian nationalist" Doug Wilson, held its inaugural service in Washinton, DC.[10] (Wilson, who has said that he wants

America to become fully converted to Christianity,[11] holds ideas about a government guided by biblical principles that have been connected to the ideas of R. J. Rushdoony and Christian Reconstructionism.) That morning, pastor Jared Longshore made the claim, "We understand that worship is warfare." He paused for a moment, then added: "We mean that."[12]

Many people have found it disconcerting that Pete Hegseth, the US Secretary of War, was in attendance that day. There's no need, though, to get hung up on that one visit: Hegseth had already closely associated himself with Wilson's network of Communion of Reformed Evangelical Churches, known for its "hard-line theology and . . . embrace of patriarchy and Christian nationalism."[13]

And, since I enjoy closing a loop, let's consider one more example. Remember Amanda Grace? The Trump supporter from the introduction who, at a ReAwaken America Tour event, foretold of upcoming spiritual warfare with mermaids? Well, she also published a book in 2025 titled *The Revelationary War: The Epic Battle Against False Prophecy and Deception*. In it, she makes a variety of claims, from the old (Karl Marx, the father of Marxism, was in league with Satan)[14] to the nouveau (the "Kingdom of Darkness" is using AI for its purposes)[15] to the so-often-repeated-and-refuted-as-to-be-banal (Obama is a "closet Muslim").[16] Both the title and overtone of the work suggests a brewing conflict, and Grace very clearly paints the two sides as being Democrat versus Republican.

But she doesn't stop there. In a June 2025 episode of *Encounter Today*—part of the multimedia ministry of pastor and media host Alan DiDio—Didio asks Grace to comment on whether a new "Civil War" is coming to America. In a confusing construction of purported parallels between the present and the past, she asserts that the United States is currently in the exact same position that it was in before the Civil War, and that the Democratic Party has been trying to "literally . . . put America on the slave block themselves and sell America to the highest bidder."[17] As a result, she predicted, they would experience a "backdraft," an "implosion" from the "brokenness and lawlessness and disorder and chaos" which they had sown.[18]

Nor is Grace alone in this idea of a new Civil War, and in fact, many more NAR and NAR-adjacent speakers and organizations have been much more explicit in their speech.[19] While violence frequently seems to be explicitly rejected by such speakers, there is a disturbing way in which these rejections seem hollow. Perhaps, Wagner's "do whatever it takes" has developed a chilling aspect, one that seems to beg violent conflict.

The Problem

Given all this talk of another Civil War, it might seem like evidence that as a country we're cruising toward some kind of bloody confrontation divided along political lines. Such conflict might even seem inevitable to some. However, I doubt that this is the case. I don't buy the idea that violence is unavoidable or that our differences are so great in the United States that there's no solution.

If we want to prevent this outcome, however, we do need to correct our trajectory. As we've seen through our tour of demons and politics in American history, a limited historical perspective can sometimes make things seem like the time a person is living in is unique—even hopeless. And as we have also seen, it's not: the Revolutionary War, the Civil War, and the Satanic Panic all offered similar dynamics between politics and demons. And from these examples in history, we've also seen that we as a country are not destined to remain stuck here.

That's the good news. And now, the question: How do we go about fixing things? That's a complex question that can benefit from a historical perspective (which this book offers), though solid answers necessarily will be informed by a range of disciplines. We'll talk about a solution in a moment. But first, I suggest we briefly step outside the confines of this book's topic of politics and demons and consider four larger societal problems that are contributing to our current sociopolitical climate.

The Internet

In today's climate of "fake news" and accusations of bias in the media, a lot of people find themselves longing for the days when media was believed to depict middle of the road positions and news programs were considered repositories of "the truth." Ever wonder how all that changed?

Journalist and scholar of religion and media Diane Winston offers an explanation. In her book *Righting the American Dream*: *How the*

Media Mainstreamed Reagan's Evangelical Vision, she points out that being successful as a media outlet in the age before the internet required significant financial investment: "Since owners needed large audiences to attract advertisers, editors sought the widest common denominator rather than the fiery extremes. As a result, news was more standardized and less polarized than it would become in the digital era."[20]

Today, however, much media distribution has shifted to the internet. Since such titanic overhead is no longer required, news outlets can be financially successful while targeting what are known as niche audiences: that is, narrow groups of individuals who share a particular set of interests or preferences. Many people also now get their news from social media, a move that has contributed to this shift as specialized niche content delivered to them via algorithms further polarizes both the right and the left.

The problem with algorithmic content is that few of us ever think about the algorithm. When I go to YouTube, I'm not necessarily thinking *This is my YouTube; the algorithm is pushing content to me that it suspects I will agree with and enjoy.* I just think essentially *This is YouTube; it's the same YouTube that everyone sees.* So, when it gives me only things that I agree with, it can seem to me like everyone else agrees with me too. I don't realize that it's just catering to me as a member of the niche audience to which it thinks I belong.

The Best Drug

As I frequently remind my students, someone agreeing with you is the best drug there is. The reason for this is that we are social animals with tribal instincts, and when another person appears to wholeheartedly share our worldview, we get an instant high in that feeling of camaraderie.

Unfortunately, the effect is even greater when that agreement involves watching someone who doesn't share our worldview get taken down a peg. Think about how much media content we consume on a daily basis that is in some way a takedown of a person we disagree with, or of other people being "owned" in various ways. Consider the growing popularity of such figures as the late Charlie Kirk on the right, who famously debated students on college campuses about conservative issues in what has been described by critics as a "gotcha" style of debate, and liberal TikTok creators known for their confrontational split-screen debates with conservatives on the issues of the day.[21] As we consume, we feel the hit of righteous anger as our opponents are seemingly demolished. And we seek this dynamic out again and again.

Anti-Intellectualism

Arguably, all of this is a substitute for actual discussion (not "gotcha" debates, but meaningful discussion) about the issues at hand. Generally speaking, as a population, we are increasingly not seeking to be informed, *really* informed on things. Instead of being curious and seeking to learn more about a problem or issue we're facing, many of us commonly become upset and critical, without seeking to learn more or to embrace a broader understanding.

For example, you may have heard people take a dig at higher education, saying that it doesn't teach people how to do a job, when that's only part of the point of a college education (which is also designed to teach critical thinking, help create good citizens, facilitate personal growth, and improve communication skills, all of which help build well functionating individuals who are better able to contribute to a healthy society). Ideally, higher education is precisely the place where we are supposed to learn how to broaden our understanding, to work constructively with others to discover solutions to complex problems, and where we learn to lead in a way that projects respect, authority, and goodwill.

We needn't all attend college to feel the benefits of higher education on our society; quite the contrary, it's possible for anyone to see the effects that the devaluing of intellectual leadership is having on us as a nation. We make snap judgments because the world is just moving so fast. We allow niche media to tell us what to think rather than just give us information about the world because at the end of a hard day at whatever job we're working, it's just too much effort to create an informed opinion of our own. We find that we don't have any place to turn for good information or that can provide guidance for the difficult course of our lives. It's not because these sources don't exist or because people aren't teaching them, but rather that we are collectively getting what we put into our education: by focusing on occupational outcomes, we miss what I would argue is the *majority* of the good that higher education offers.

A Feeling of Powerlessness

And finally, we reach the fourth problem, a feeling of powerlessness, which is where the first three problems all lead. We don't know who to trust for good information, so we turn toward bad sources of information. Those sources of information offer us a picture of the world in which everything is on fire, and where there's no hope of civil discussion with those who don't agree with us. In this place, we can't influence politics through traditional channels because no one will listen to us or we don't have the time because we're struggling just to get by. From here, there is only one thing we can do to change anything, and that is to go into battle against the opposition.

And that makes us feel good. It feels good to fight back against an ethos or set of ideas that we consider bad for the world. We want to feel like we make a difference, that our voice matters.

Sometimes, that leads us to demons.

Once More, Demons

The four problems described above all create an environment in which the cesspool of conspiratorial demonology does its best work. Let's look at how that happens, beginning at the top.

We'll start at the internet, which has contributed significantly to the spread of misinformation. When we're misinformed, it becomes easy to manipulate our sense of reality. That brings us to the best drug: when others agree with us, we feel as though we live in a shared world; and this manipulated sense of reality seems justified and right. Our third problem, anti-intellectualism, frequently causes us to abandon or neglect opportunities for intellectual pursuits and personal betterment, and keeps us from the educational endeavors that are the primary way most of us learn the perspectives of others outside of our in-group. Once these outside perspectives are removed from our view, the small slice of the world we live in becomes absolute and correct in a way that it could never be if we allowed ourselves access to them.

Finally, our sense of powerlessness makes us vulnerable to wanting to believe there must be something more than simple social forces at work. Everyone agrees with us, after all. So how could it possibly be that we can't change the broken things about the world? The answer is simple: It must be because an entity that transcends the human is at work. In a Christian matrix, the obvious answer is demons.

Once we realize all of the above, all our bad feelings leave us, and the idea that we're impacted by the four problems above seems absurd. Powerless? Absolutely not! We are cosmic warriors fighting on the side of God; we've been chosen by the Almighty to combat the demonic threat through intercessory prayer (or more extreme measures . . .). Others might be powerless, but we have the capacity to change the world. And every time that you fight that battle, you get that hit of the best drug in the world: righteous correctness shared with your in-group.

Uninformed? Anti-intellectual? Hardly. So many people have gotten wrapped up in academic jargon and the academic deceits of demons that they've missed the obvious: God is in control and the world is organized according to simple biblical principles. The complexity of the world arises from demonic deceptions, deceptions that I have now seen through.

A discouraging picture, no? And one that brings us back to our original question: What's the solution? Before I answer, a caveat: I noted earlier that I am a historian. I like to "practice what I preach" as best as possible, so I'm not going to claim that, from my perspective, I have *all* the answers. There are no doubt many good large-scale ideas for change, especially in other fields, that I am partially or wholly ignorant of. But within the field of subjects I know fairly well—that is, conspiratorial thinking, religious studies, and research practices—I have drawn the following three suggestions that I think are fine places to start. Three steps that, if taken on a wide scale, could significantly improve our current trajectory in the United States. The best part is that you don't need to be part of a group that's focused on enacting these changes nor do you need to spend all your free time laser-focused on these tasks. On the contrary, integrating these changes into your life as one individual can make a difference, and you can easily spread the information about how to do so to others while you're modeling this behavior.

It may seem like it will take a miracle to get our country back on solid ground—back to our regular, run-of-the-mill American fascination with demons, and away from the dangerous, conspiratorial variety we're facing today—but it really won't. It's just a matter of getting back to the basics of what makes us human.

Quit the Conspiracies

The first thing we as a country, and that begins with us as individuals, need to do is quit believing conspiracies. The previous chapter provides a much more comprehensive view of the subject, but its main points are worth reiterating again: (1) do not take the absence of evidence as evidence; (2) find experts, journalists, and news outlets that are trustworthy; and (3) accept their conclusions—however much you may not like them—with regard to areas that fall outside your expertise.

There's another aspect of believing in conspiracies that's also worth noting: this practice often goes hand-in-hand with an indifference to other people's suffering. That's why, if we are to move away from belief in conspiracies, we also need to move toward the cultivation of empathy and kindness. Unfortunately, in recent years a new movement has begun to spring up among some practitioners of Christianity—generally these are individuals who belong to or feel affinity with the groups discussed in this book—that attempts to get their fellow Christians to see empathy as a kind of sin. I cannot overstate the danger of this belief.

Let me be clear, rejecting empathy as a necessary component not just of our political process but as a part of our daily lives is how we come to see our neighbors as evil, nefarious, or the emissaries of demons. Once that happens, we've sacrificed something that is essential to our democracy—let alone our humanity. This is true not just for those who believe in demons; those who don't are equally as likely to fall prey to demonic thinking if they are unable to understand and hold space for both the hurt and happiness of their opponents. If we make monsters out of our opponents instead of treating them like human beings, then as history shows us, we will eventually find a reason to engage in violence.

A good first step in this process of protecting, and even restoring, our empathy is to limit our contact with social media. In its current form, social media is an inexhaustible source of fuel for the engine that feeds conspiratorial thinking. Its algorithms create artificial communities that feel absolute, as within them there are no dissenting voices. The growing prevalence of AI-generated material blurs the lines of reality even further, often in ways that are difficult to detect, and the existence of bad political actors on social media, often representing foreign governments, seeking to undermine democratic thought has been proven time and time again.[22]

To be clear, I'm *not* saying you should stop consuming or sharing silly cat videos, random knock-knock jokes, or pictures of your family. What I *am* saying is that the moment a political meme, a video clip in which someone professes to "own" a particular group, or any other content makes you feel a deep sense of anger or triumph on the part of your community, it's time to navigate away from the site or even put down the phone. I'll even go one step further: If the only thing you find on a particular app is that kind of content, it's time to uninstall that app.

Finally, the main thing we need to do in order to quit conspiracies is to become better informed. The only real inoculation against misinformation is an education that has both breadth and depth. The more examples that we have to draw from, the less likely one line of conspiratorial thinking will weave through all our avenues of critical thinking without us catching it.

The most immediate way to make an impact on your information pipeline? Change your news sources. As we noted earlier, journalists can rank very high in the information verification hierarchy; but not every one of them does the work that puts them there. At its core, journalism is about the dissemination of information for profit. It's a current truism that this information doesn't have to be *accurate* to be *profitable*. This means that you may have to do some digging in order to find sources that are profitable due to accuracy and not some other reason, such as sensationalism.

Luckily, there are a lot of organizations that can help you do this work, as entities responsive to this consumer need have developed options to help people find and choose better sources of news. I'm a particular fan of Ad Fontes Media, which publishes on its site an easy to use static and interactive chart that has evaluated different news sources for bias and reliability. Choose ones that lean toward the center and are high on the reliability scale.[23]

All of this will help us transition away from bad information and toward good information, away from conspiracies and toward knowledge and understanding. Once we've addressed what we're willing to talk about, then we have to address what we've been *unwilling* to talk about. Which brings us to our next two suggestions.

Think About Religion

Another step that we can take is to become better at how we think about religion. We have to stop being so squeamish about talking about it or confronting its influence. The problem we face in this area is well illustrated by the 2025 confirmation of Pete Hegseth as Secretary of Defense, a role that, starting in September 2025 and still at the time of this writing, is now being referred to in our government instead as Secretary of War.

There are many who, for a variety of reasons, question whether Hegseth should have been confirmed to this position at all. I want to focus instead on the religious persona that he presented leading up to and during the confirmation process.

Let's begin with his comments about the Crusades, the religious wars that began during the Middle Ages and were fought between Christians and Muslims. Hegseth is reported to have verbally stated that he shared the sentiments of some of these medieval Christian warriors. A coworker "lodged a complaint against Hegseth after he and an associate began chanting 'Kill All Muslims! Kill All Muslims!' in 'a drunk and a violent manner' at a bar while on official travel for a work event."[24] In another example, *The New York Times* reports that he once wrote that if someone enjoys the various benefits of "Western civilization" that they should "thank a Crusader."[25]

He even named his 2020 book *American Crusade: Our Right to Stay Free* and argued in it that these benefits were under threat and that a new Crusade was needed—this one against "leftists." Claiming that the "American experiment" is under threat of death, Hegseth calls for an "American Crusade" a "holy war for the righteous cause of human freedom."[26] Disavowing violence half-heartedly ("No, I'm not calling for violence, I'm just pointing out the reality"[27]), Hegseth encourages his audience to contextualize a holy war as a violent conflict through violent language.[28]

Hegseth believes these ideas strongly enough to have them inked permanently on his body. Pictures of him running around shirtless (an occurrence that, given the number of photos circulating, appears to happen relatively frequently) allow for the easy identification of five Jerusalem crosses on his right pectoral and a sword with the phrase "Deus Vult" (the popular "God wills it" command that supposedly started the Crusades) on the inside of his right arm.[29]

I've already noted earlier in this chapter his associations with the Christian Nationalist and Christian Reconstructionist Doug Wilson. I know of no repudiation of Wilson's beliefs from Hegseth, and it is a safe bet that it would be impossible for Hegseth to have missed these elements of the church he attends. Ergo, we must assume he agrees with these ideas, a reasonable likelihood considering the content of his own writings.

Given all this evidence, if I were a Democratic senator who didn't want to see Hegseth's candidacy pushed through, I would have leaned into all of these elements in my questions. Yet, during Hegseth's hearing, only one person asked a single question about his religious ideas. Even more shockingly, it was not a hardball question from a Democrat trying to sink his candidacy, but rather a gentle nudge for Hegseth to defend himself, delivered by a Republican. In this revealing exchange, Senator Kevin Cramer (R-ND) asked after the Jerusalem Crosses on his pectoral. Hegseth answered by identifying it as "a historic Christian symbol. . . . It is a Christian religious symbol."

I have seen no evidence of any other questions being asked about his religious beliefs. With that, the matter was closed.

What could possibly have compelled this response, or lack thereof? I speculate that once Hegseth identified the symbols as "Christian," no one dared challenge it. If this is the case, it's a bet he won. This is a favorite strategy of conservative American Protestant denominations because identifying something as "Christian" generally has one of three effects. The word may elicit a positive response, a dismissal response, or a withdrawal from engagement. Let's explore these using a specific claim that you're intimately familiar with by now: Demons influence human governments.

First, for those that agree that the idea that demons influence human governments is "Christian," the use of that word has a buoying effect. Slapping the label *Christian* on an idea can make it sound as if 2.4 billion Christians and two thousand years of tradition agree with the person presenting it. After all, how could so many people and so many years of tradition be wrong?

The problem of course is that the term *Christian* doesn't indicate significant agreement throughout time and space, it simply signals that someone has adopted the term as a part of their identity. The term *Christian* applies to a diverse range of people, including early Docetic Christians who thought Christ's body was an illusion sent from a higher realm (and so he could not have died on the cross); Arian Christians who saw the Father, Son, and Holy Ghost not as a coequal Trinity but a hierarchy;

the so-called Hidden Christians of the Edo period in Japan whose Bible began with "In the beginning Deusu was worshipped as Lord of Heaven and Earth. . . . [And] Deusu has two hundred ranks and forty-two forms."[30]; and the contemporary Ecclesia Gnostica (Gnostic Church), which believes that this world is a prison administered by inferior spiritual powers to a transcendent spiritual manifestation and the entities it manifested (whew!). These are just a few examples; it is extremely difficult to say exactly how many "denominations" there are within the broad historical trend we consider Christianity. When I ask students to estimate, they often say something like "a couple dozen." In fact, many scholarly estimates exceed ten thousand and some approach fifty thousand. The diversity that has developed in Christianity is astounding.

Now, let's return to the idea that someone makes a claim and calls their belief "Christian." What happens if you identify as Christian and don't agree with the statement? For example, imagine that someone says to you that "demons influence human governments." If you disagree with this theory, more often than not, you'll simply shrug or roll your eyes. After all, if you're Christian and what the person is saying doesn't match your understanding of Christianity, you may well conclude that the other person is not a Christian, even if they claim otherwise. You may see this as just a case of mistaken identity. Thus, their claim, whatever it is, is not your problem; best not to make things uncomfortable by confronting them.

Finally, those who live in the United States (Christian or not) are impacted by intellectual traditions that often frame religion as a personal matter, rather than a social or political one. Because of this, those who don't identify as "Christian" often dismiss the significance of religious ideas in public debates, thinking of the person who's speaking, *That's just their opinion*. After all, do we not believe in the separation of church and state in America?

This assumption, however, has consequences, and we are reaching a critical point in America. If we continue to ignore religion's role in public life—as we've learned the groups in this last section would like us to—then we create opportunity for bad political actors to undermine our democracy. And here at last, we arrive at a possible solution, or at least a first step toward one: understanding.

For those of us seeking to course correct a country that is being steered by those on a mission to battle demons, the answer lies not in excluding religion from the political arena, but rather in our becoming educated about what different groups believe and what their goals are. It is this understanding that allows us to strip away the plausible deniability that these bad political actors require to thrive. It also allows us to build a more equitable future in which everyone feels heard and understood, even if they don't wind up getting their way. And that is a strong step toward lasting civil conversation, government, and peace.

Demand Transparency

Realizing this vision will require us to have more information. At this point in our nation's history, it is absolutely essential, more so than it has ever been, that we understand the religious proclivities of the candidates that we elect and the groups which support them.

But this won't happen unless we demand it. It is part of the nature of our political engine to withhold excess information. This isn't necessarily nefarious in nature or by design. It's what we pay our lawmakers to do: represent our interests in a bureaucratic web that must be complex in order to serve a country of three hundred and fifty million people. We want outcomes, not details.

However, if there is reason for us to suspect that a politician will act against what we consider to be our best interests then we deserve to know. For instance, if a candidate believes—I'll just choose something off the top of my head—that demons are swarming around Washington, DC, and controlling his or her fellow lawmakers, then that is information we have a right to have. That fact means that their judgment is compromised by conspiratorial thinking and compromised in a way that could be disastrous for democracy.

In order to identify these questionable political actors, we need to demonstrate our interest in transparency. We need to attend local meetings of political candidates and inform ourselves well beforehand so we can ask the hard questions. We need to write to news sources and request coverage of an individual's religious beliefs in large enough numbers that reputable news sources feel it necessary to respond to the demand.

And finally, once we have this new information, we need to have well-reasoned discussions in which we walk a fine line. On the one hand, we can't flinch from the hard truths. We need to be willing to say that someone's beliefs are destructive and problematic. On the other, we cannot shout down those we disagree with and leave them feeling silenced.

Decades of Demons

As we do this work, there is one thing we must keep in mind, and that is that these ideas about demons and politics are not going to go away. They will change and mutate over time, just as we have seen happen throughout this book and just as all ideas do. But they will not go away.

Coexistence is key. Democracy thrives when people share a variety of different viewpoints and use reliable information to work through their differences. It dies when conspiracy, enforced silence, and ignorance thrive.

If we're lucky, we have decades of demons yet ahead of us. Along with a tradition of clear and intelligent discourse, belief in demons appears to be a core pillar in the American experience. It is only when we turn toward conspiratorial ideas about them, and away from hard conversations, that demons emerge as a threat. To invert Lincoln's famous saying, when we give in to the worse demons of our natures, then we all lose.

Like I said in the introduction, I can't tell you whether demons exist or not. What I can tell you is that two historical things seem clear. The first is that how we Americans believe in demons has changed the political climate of the United States in the past, is still changing it, and will continue to do so in the future.

Second, this doesn't have to be the End of Days: We have surmounted these challenges before, and we can do so again. Modern day beliefs about demons are not a battle cry to another Civil War, they are a clarion call for us to rise above our problematic thinking and come back better than ever before.

The first step to doing so is dealing with our demons.

ACKNOWLEDGMENTS

I'll be honest with you: This is my least favorite part of a book. I'm always afraid that I'm going to leave someone off my list of people to thank, or that I won't say the right thing about someone. I'm also positive that in writing about how this book came about, I'll also have to incidentally do something that most scholars dread: Write about myself. Or at least, about what inspired me.

The truth is that this book emerged from hope. You might think that to someone who has focused a lot of attention on demons and monstrosity in their career, hope would be in short supply. For me, it's exactly the opposite: I study these topics because I think we as human beings can be better than we've been in the distant (and not so distant) past. I think we can be kinder, gentler, and more understanding with every passing year; we just need to be reminded that that's who we are. Some of my friends might suggest that's the Midwesterner in me talking; I choose to think that it's the realist in me.

My first set of thanks goes to Giles Anderson, my agent, who was the first to advocate for this book. His recommendations and suggestions were invaluable to developing the proposal and selecting Broadleaf Books as the publisher.

And the main reason I chose Broadleaf was because of my editor Shari MacDonald Strong. Her excitement about the book from its nascency to completion kept my spirits high, even after the fifth cup of coffee on late nights. And she was more than up to the Herculean task of refining my rough draft into a work that I'm confident conveys what I have to teach about this subject to the world.

I've also had the privilege in my career of teaching, and being taught by, groups of students at two excellent academic institutions. At the University of South Florida, I taught a course entitled "The Religious Quest in Contemporary Films" (not my title), and my discussions with students in that course were instrumental in my initial thoughts about ideas of demons being influenced by media depictions. At Lycoming College, I've had the chance to teach "Religion and Film" (*that's* my title) and "Angels and Demons." Over the years, these courses have gradually incorporated more political material, and I'm grateful to students for their interest and feedback. Lycoming College has also been generous in their support, and this book has benefited from conference funding support from the institution as well as sabbatical funds for the 2024–25 academic year.

I've also benefited from an incredible set of colleagues over the years. Kate, Mike, Vince, and Zach: I'm so glad that I can continue to benefit from your friendship and advice even though we live in different parts of the country. For Robin and Steve, thanks for taking a chance on a guy with a plan; I couldn't ask for better people to share a department with. For Andy, Chris, Cullen, Sascha, and Todd: I'll see you at 2.

Outside the two institutions at which I've worked, I've also been blessed with an abundance of friends both inside and outside academia. To Brandon: Thanks for sharing your experience and your kind words over the course of the project. To Dave and Mike: It would be impossible to find more supportive friends.

This book is dedicated to my family. My father Edward, my mother Linda, and sister Beth who helped to shape me into the person I am today. I would be nothing without them. My spouse, Stacey, has been a part of every accomplishment in my life and more responsible for many of them than she's willing to acknowledge. I would be lost without her. To my children, Xander and Luna, and my niece, Evie, and nephew, Wesley: I hope this book helps make the world you grow up in a better place.

NOTES

INTRODUCTION

1. "About Us," Ark of Grace Ministries, accessed October 8, 2025, https://arkofgrace.org/about-us.
2. Patriot Takes (@patriottakes), "At Trump Doral, Prophet Amanda Grace warned of technologically advanced 'mermaids and water people' spreading perversion and told the crowd, 'we are meant for hand to hand combat,'" Twitter (now X), May 14, 2023, https://x.com/patriottakes/status/1657868909716951041.
3. David Corn (@DavidCornDC), Twitter (now X), May 15, 2023, https://x.com/DavidCornDC/status/1658063620721311745.
4. The most complete transcript I have found appears on Tim Dickinson, "Trump Doral Re-Awaken America Tour: Prophets, Demons, and Mermaids," *Rolling Stone*, May 15, 2023, https://www.rollingstone.com/politics/politics-features/trump-doral-reawaken-america-pastors-mermaids-1234735924/, but this portion of Grace's speech can also be viewed at Patriot Takes (@patriottakes), "At Trump Doral."
5. Lance Wallnau, *God's Chaos Candidate: Donald J. Trump and the American Unraveling* (Killer Sheep Media, 2016), 143, 142.
6. Tara Law, "Trump Advisor Calls for Miscarriage of 'Satanic Pregnancies,'" TIME, January 26, 2020, https://time.com/5771920/trump-paula-white-miscarriage-satanic-pregnancies/; Mihir Zaveri and Johnny Diaz, "Paula White Says Video About 'Satanic Pregnancies' Was Taken Out of Context," *The New York Times*, January 27, 2020, https://www.nytimes.com/2020/01/27/us/politics/paula-white-miscarriage-video.html. Some have unintentionally misrepresented her words, a correction that can be found in André Gagné, *American Evangelicals for Trump: Dominion, Spiritual Warfare, and the End Times*, trans. Linda Shanahan (Routledge, 2023), 48–51.
7. Jason Lemon, "Trump Spiritual Adviser Paula White Prays Against President's Opponents, Suggests They 'Operate in Sorcery and Witchcraft,'" *Newsweek*, November 6, 2019, https://www.newsweek.com/trump-spiritual-adviser-paula-white-prays-against-presidents-opponents-suggests-they-operate-1470197.

8. Brandon W. Hawk, "Stella Immanuel's Theories About the Relationship Between Demons, Illness and Sex Have a Long History," The Conversation, July 29, 2020, http://theconversation.com/stella-immanuels-theories-about-the-relationship-between-demons-illness-and-sex-have-a-long-history-143587.
9. Emily Brumfield-Hessen, "Millions of Americans Believe Trump Is Fighting Literal Demons," *Foreign Policy*, June 10, 2020, https://foreignpolicy.com/2020/06/10/trump-evangelicals-charismatics-paula-white-demons/.
10. Right Side Broadcasting Network, "WATCH: Pastor Paula White Delivers Opening Prayer at President Trump's Reelection Rally," June 18, 2019, 05:15, https://www.youtube.com/watch?v=MY4MYPCzAfk.
11. Molly Olmstead, "The Wisconsin Priest Who Performed Exorcisms Against Election Fraud," *Slate Magazine*, January 29, 2021, https://slate.com/human-interest/2021/01/father-z-election-fraud-exorcism.html.
12. Amanda Arden, "Portland Exorcism: Archbishop Prays Away Evil of Social Unrest," *Koin 6 News*, October 23, 2020, https://www.koin.com/news/special-reports/a-portland-exorcism-archbishop-prays-evil-away-after-months-of-unrest/.
13. Associated Press, "San Francisco Archbishop Performs Exorcism at Marin Church Where Junipero Serra Statue Was Toppled," *ABC7 News* San Francisco, October 17, 2020, https://abc7news.com/7115234/.
14. "Donald Trump Holds Texas Rally Under Shadow of Indictment—Donald Trump Live Speech—USA News," *Rev*, accessed September 18, 2023, https://tinyurl.com/3z3vakvt.
15. Michael E. Heyes, "The 'Jezebel Spirit' Isn't (Just) Bible-Based Misogyny, It's a Literal Demon—So What Happens When They 'Stop Tolerating' It?" *Religion Dispatches*, November 1, 2024, https://religiondispatches.org/the-nars-jezebel-spirit-isnt-just-bible-based-misogyny-its-a-literal-demon-so-what-happens-when-they-stop-tolerating-it/.
16. For example, see Joseph Essig, Ping Xu, James Garand, and Ceren Keser, "The 'Trump' Effect: Political Elite and Support for Free Trade in America," *American Politics Research* 49, no. 3 (2021): 328–42, https://doi.org/10.1177/1532673X21992124; Benjamin Newman, Jennifer L. Merolla, Sono Shah, Danielle Casarez Lemi, Loren Collingwood, and S. Karthick Ramakrishnan, "The Trump Effect: An Experimental Investigation of the Emboldening Effect of Racially Inflammatory Elite Communication," *British Journal of Political Science* 51, no. 3 (2021): 1138–59, https://doi.org/10.1017/S0007123419000590.
17. Brian Levack, *The Devil Within: Possession and Exorcism in the Christian West* (Yale University Press, 2013).
18. Stuart Clark, *Thinking with Demons: The Idea of Witchcraft in Early Modern Europe* (Oxford University Press, 1999).
19. Jeffrey Burton Russell, *The Devil: Perceptions of Evil from Antiquity to Primitive Christianity* (Cornell University Press, 1987); *Satan: The Early Christian*

Tradition (Cornell University Press, 1987); *Lucifer: The Devil in the Middle Ages* (Cornell University Press, 1986); and *Mephistopheles: The Devil in the Modern World* (Cornell University Press, 1990).

20. See Ruth H. Bloch, *Visionary Republic: Millennial Themes in American Thought, 1756–1800* (Cambridge University Press, 1988), 55–60.
21. Edward J. Blum, "'The First Secessionist Was Satan': Secession and the Religious Politics of Evil in Civil War America," *Civil War History* 60, no. 3 (September 1, 2014): 234–69, https://doi.org/10.1353/cwh.2014.0056.
22. Alfred Gale, *Pictorial History of the Cause of the Great Rebellion*, vol. 1 (Asbury, NJ: n.p., 1865). Over three broadsheets the author argues that Spiritualists are consorting with the demons, not the dead, and that these practices are directly responsible for the Civil War.

CHAPTER ONE: IN THE BEGINNING . . .

1. I'm going to use "Hebrew Bible" throughout the book instead of "Old Testament." That latter term smacks of what we call *supersessionism* in biblical studies, or the idea that Jews have been replaced by Christians as the chosen people of God.
2. Just a little smattering of the incident (Numbers 22:28–30): Then the Lord opened the mouth of the donkey, and she said to Balaam, "What have I done to you, that you have struck me these three times?" And Balaam said to the donkey, "Because you have abused me. I wish there were a sword in my hand, for now I would kill you!" So the donkey said to Balaam, "*Am* I not your donkey on which you have ridden, ever since *I became* yours, to this day? Was I ever disposed to do this to you?"
3. NET: "Then I looked, and I heard an eagle flying directly overhead, proclaiming with a loud voice, 'Woe! Woe! Woe to those who live on the earth because of the remaining sounds of the trumpets of the three angels who are about to blow them!"
4. Bill T. Arnold, *Genesis* (Cambridge University Press, 2009).
5. If you want to read more about Leviathan and other biblical monsters, I'd recommend Esther Hamori's excellent book, *God's Monsters: Vengeful Spirits, Deadly Angels, Hybrid Creatures, and Divine Hitmen of the Bible* (Broadleaf Books, 2023). If you want a bit more meat on just Leviathan and you don't mind a denser read, you can't beat Andrei A. Orlov, *Supernal Serpent: Mysteries of Leviathan in Judaism and Christianity* (Oxford University Press, 2023).
6. See for instance, Philip Almond, *The Devil: A New Biography* (Cornell University Press, 2014), 17–18.
7. You can read 1 Enoch online at https://www.ccel.org/c/charles/otpseudepig/enoch/ENOCH_1.HTM.
8. Samyaza and Azazel spring to mind. Samyaza is called out in 1 Enoch as the leader of the rebel angels, a position that seems to situate him naturally in a

"devilish" mode. On the other hand, Azazel is the angel that teaches all the most reprehensible things to humankind, including how to craft weapons, how to make war, and I kid you not, in 1 Enoch 8, how to put on makeup (i.e., the arts of using makeup and ornamentation).

9. Also online at https://www.pseudepigrapha.com/jubilees/index.htm.

CHAPTER TWO: DEALING WITH DEMONS

1. A similar occurrence appears in Matthew 8:28–34, but there are two demoniacs for the price of one!
2. Matthew 9:33: "And when the demon was cast out, the mute spoke. And the multitudes marveled, saying, 'It was never seen like this in Israel!'" Matthew 12:22: "Then one was brought to Him who was demon-possessed, blind and mute; and He healed him, so that the blind and mute man both spoke and saw."
3. Matthew 8:16: "When evening had come, they brought to Him many who were demon-possessed. And He cast out the spirits with a word, and healed all who were sick."
4. Richard Kieckhefer, *Forbidden Rites: A Necromancer's Manual of the Fifteenth Century*, Magic in History (Penn State University Press, 1998), 14.
5. Kieckhefer, *Forbidden Rites*, 25.
6. "... supervacaneis vel curiosis interrogationibus, praesertim de rebus futuris et occultis, ad suum munus non pertinentibus. . ." J. Murphy, *Rituale Romanum*, [Baltimore: J. Murphy, 1873], 386).
7. For example, Acts 5:3: "But Peter said, 'Ananias, why has Satan filled your heart to lie to the Holy Spirit and keep back *part* of the price of the land for yourself?'" And Acts 13:10: "O full of all deceit and all fraud, *you* son of the devil, *you* enemy of all righteousness, will you not cease perverting the straight ways of the Lord?"
8. Brian P. Levack, *The Devil Within: Possession & Exorcism in the Christian West* (Yale University Press, 2013), 39.
9. Ephesians is actually a Deutero-Pauline epistle, meaning that it might be an authentic letter of Paul or it might be someone else writing a letter as if they were Paul (this writing as someone else is called "pseudepigraphy" and the material written is "pseudepigraphic").
10. Augustine's City of God is available online at https://www.newadvent.org/fathers/1201.htm.
11. Most often the mouth but use your imagination; despite what we may think, medieval people certainly weren't prudish! An excellent treatment of this and other medieval topics can be found in Nancy Caciola, *Discerning Spirits: Divine and Demonic Possession in the Middle Ages* (Cornell University Press, 2006).

12. Institutes 6.7. A translation of the hard-to-find-section can be found here: http://www.ldysinger.com/@texts/0415_cassian/02_inst-06.htm.
13. If you're interested in all the sordid details, there's no better source than Walter Stephens, *Demon Lovers: Witchcraft, Sex, and the Crisis of Belief* (University of Chicago Press, 2003).
14. Christopher S. Mackay, *The Hammer of Witches: A Complete Translation of the Malleus Maleficarum* (Cambridge University Press, 2009).
15. ". . . it is true that to beget a human is the act of a living body. When it is said that demons cannot give life because it flows in a formal sense from the soul, this again is true, but it is emitted as matter from the seed and the demon incubus can send it in with God's permission through sexual union, doing so not as if the seed were emitted by him but with another human's seed that he has taken for this purpose. . . . For the same demon who is a succubus in terms of the man becomes an incubus in terms of the woman. (This is also how they take up the seeds of some things for the generation of other things. . . . When it is concluded that the demon can both receive and pour in seed invisibly, this is true, but he instead does this work visibly as a succubus and incubus, so that in this way he may use a foul act like this to taint the body and soul in each person (both the man's and the woman's)" (Mackay, *The Hammer of Witches*, 128–29).
16. See an image of Giovanni da Modena's *The Inferno* on Wikimedia Commons here: https://commons.wikimedia.org/wiki/File:Giovanni_da_Modena_-_The_Inferno,_cropped.jpg; an image of Jörg Breu's "Idol of Calicut" is also on Wikimedia Commons here: https://commons.wikimedia.org/wiki/File:*%22The_Idol_of_Calicut,%22_in_a_depiction_from_1516*_(Univ._of_Zurich).jpg.
17. This often occurs by associating names with their supposed meanings, numerology, or relating events that occur within a person's life to those in the Bible. For instance, one popular notion of Barack Obama as Antichrist was based on the idea that the name Barack (meaning "blessed") was instead Barak (meaning "lightning"). Such interpreters then sought to connect the name to Luke 10:18 when Jesus tells the seventy disciples "I saw Satan fall like lightning from heaven."
18. Tacitus, *Annals*, 15.44.
19. For example, 2 John 1:7: "For many deceivers have gone out into the world who do not confess Jesus Christ *as* coming in the flesh. This is a deceiver and an antichrist." Here it seems we are to take the deceivers as being antichrists. And 1 John 2:18: "Little children, it is the last hour; and as you have heard that the Antichrist is coming, even now many antichrists have come, by which we know that it is the last hour." Here we get a definitively plural *antichrists*, as well as another clear indication that the author of 1 John thought the world was imminently facing the End in his lifetime.

CHAPTER THREE: THE PAPAL BEAST AND THE FRENCH AND INDIAN WAR

1. Scott H. Hendrix, *Martin Luther: A Very Short Introduction* (Oxford University Press, 2010), 4. Those looking for a readable account of Luther's life will find it here as well!
2. These and many others can be found in Jeffrey Burton Russell, *Mephistopheles: The Devil in the Modern World* (Cornell University Press, 1990), 39.
3. Henry F. French, *Martin Luther's Table Talk: Abridged from Luther's Works*, vol. 54 (Augsburg Fortress Press, 2017), 128.
4. Martin Luther, *Works of Martin Luther: With Introductions and Notes*, vol. 3, ed. Adolph Spaeth and Henry Eyster Jacobs (Muhlenberg Press, 1930), 60.
5. Martin Luther, "Treatise on the Power and Primacy of the Pope," in *Book of Concord*, accessed December 10, 2025, https://thebookofconcord.org/power-and-primacy-of-the-pope/.
6. Individuals such as Joachim of Fiore (a twelfth-century medieval mystic), John Wycliffe (one of the first individuals who clamored for reformation in the Church in the fourteenth century), and Jan Huss (another pre-Luther reformer) all claimed that the Antichrist would be associated with the papacy (see for instance, Anthony C. Thiselton, *1 and 2 Thessalonians Through the Centuries* [Wiley-Blackwell, 2020]).
7. For example, Puritans, Anglicans, Quakers, Lutherans, Presbyterians, and Baptists, but also a minority of Jews, Muslims, and even a smattering of Roman Catholics, despite the persecution they experienced.
8. While a significant amount of the population was English, there were a variety of other European groups like the Dutch, Swedish, and French. Likewise, there was a large population of enslaved Africans forced to live and work in the colonies by the transatlantic slave trade.
9. See, for instance, Jonathan Edwards's *Sinners in the Hands of an Angry God*, which can be accessed online at https://digitalcommons.unl.edu/cgi/viewcontent.cgi?article=1053&context=etas.
10. John Cotton, *The Pouring Out of the Seven Vials: Or an Exposition of the 16th Chapter of the Revelation, with an Application of It to Our Times . . . Preached in Sundry Sermons* (R. S.; to be sold at Henry Overtons shop, 1645), 38.
11. Cotton, *The Pouring Out of the Seven Vials*, 41.
12. Cotton, *The Pouring Out of the Seven Vials*, 60.
13. Massachusetts, *The General Laws and Liberties of the Massachusets Colony: Revised & Re-Printed, by Order of the General Court Holden at Boston. May 15th. 1672. Edward Rawson Secr. : [Two Lines from Romans]* (1672), accessed December 10, 2025, http://name.umdl.umich.edu/N00114.0001.001.
14. Ruth H. Bloch, *Visionary Republic: Millennial Themes in American Thought, 1756–1800* (Cambridge University Press, 1988), 20.

15. See for instance, Bloch, *Visionary Republic*, 20, 85–86, 92–93.
16. See for instance, Christopher Smyth, "'Chastisements of a Heavenly Father': The Meaning of the London Earthquakes of 1750," *Religion in the Age of Enlightenment* 2, no. 1 (2011).
17. James Allin, *Thunder and Earthquake, a Loud and Awful Call to Reformation. Consider'd in a Sermon Preached at Brooklyn [i.e., Brookline, Mass.], November the First; upon a Special Fast, Occasion'd by the Earthquake, Which Happen'd in the Evening after the 29th Day of October 1727.* (Printed by Gamaliel Rogers, for Joseph Edwards at the corner shop on the north side of the town-house, 1727), 28, http://name.umdl.umich.edu/N02390.0001.001.
18. Allin, *Thunder and Earthquake*, 39.
19. Bloch, *Visionary Republic*, 26.
20. David Imrie, *A Letter from the Reverend Dr. David Imrie* (Re-printed and sold by S. Kneeland, in Queen-Street, 1756), 10.
21. Imrie, *A Letter from the Reverend Dr. David Imrie*, 17.
22. For example, the edition printed in London in 1795 promised the culmination of all the prophecies by 1805 rather than by 1763. Christopher Love, *The Strange and Wonderful Predictions of Mr. Christopher Love* (Printed for the booksellers, 1795).
23. Bloch, *Visionary Republic*, 39.
24. Aaron Burr, *The Watchman's Answer to the Question, What of the Night* (Boston: S. Kneeland, 1756), 27; as well as Bloch, *Visionary Republic*, 40.
25. Samuel Finley, *The Curse of Meroz, or, the Danger of Neutrality in the Cause of God, and Our Country* (James Chattin, 1757), 31.
26. Bloch, *Visionary Republic*, 3–37.
27. Samuel Davies, *The Crisis; Or, the Uncertain Doom of Kingdoms at Particular Times, Considered with Reference to Great-Britain and Her Colonies in Their Present Circumstances* (London: J. Buckland, 1757), 26.

CHAPTER FOUR: A REVOLUTIONARY APOCALYPSE

1. Steven Sarson, *The American Colonies and the British Empire, 1607–1783, Part 1*, vol. 1 (Routledge, 2010), xxviii.
2. Massachusetts Historical Society, "Letter from Cyrus Baldwin to Loammi Baldwin, 15 August 1765," *Collections Online*, accessed October 17, 2025, http://www.masshist.org/database/601.
3. An image can be seen here: "A Warm Place—Hell," *Encyclopedia Virginia*, accessed December 11, 2025, https://encyclopediavirginia.org/a-warm-place-hell/.
4. The image can be viewed at https://collections.americanantiquarian.org/revere/i1f20.jpg.

5. Richard Connors and Colin Gow, eds., *Anglo-American Millennialism, from Milton to the Millerites*, (Brill, 2004), 129.
6. Connors and Gow, *Anglo-American Millennialism*, 131.
7. John Adams, "'A Dissertation on the Canon and the Feudal Law,' No. 4, 21 October 1765," Founders Online, University of Virginia Press, accessed October 18, 2025, http://founders.archives.gov/documents/Adams/06-01-02-0052-0007.
8. Peter Oliver, *Peter Oliver's Origin and Progress of the American Rebellion: A Tory View*, ed. Douglass Adair and John A. Schutz (Stanford University Press, 1967), 65.
9. "Address to the People of Great Britain, 21 October 1774," Founders Online, University of Virginia Press, accessed October 18, 2025, http://founders.archives.gov/documents/Jay/01-01-02-0071.
10. "Address to the People of Great Britain."
11. "Address to the People of Great Britain."
12. All quotations from "Address to the People of Great Britain."
13. Judah Champion, *Christian and Civil Liberty and Freedom Considered and Recommended: A Sermon, Delivered before the General Assembly of the Colony of Connecticut, at Hartford, on the Day of Their Anniversary Election, May 9th, 1776.* (Printed by E. Watson, near the Great-Bridge, 1776), 18, accessed December 11, 2025, http://name.umdl.umich.edu/N11613.0001.001.
14. Parker C. Thompson, *From Its European Antecedents to 1791: The United States Army Chaplaincy* (Office of the Chief of Chaplains, Department of the Army, 1978), 102.
15. Thompson, *From Its European Antecedents to 1791*, 102.
16. Thompson, *From Its European Antecedents to 1791*, 103.
17. Casca, "To His TYRANNIC MAJESTY.—the DEVIL.," *The Crisis: A British Defense of American Rights, 1775–1776*, No. 23, June 24, 1775, accessed October 19, 2025, https://oll.libertyfund.org/titles/the-crisis-a-british-defense-of-american-rights-1775-1776.
18. Robert C. Fuller, *Naming the Antichrist: The History of an American Obsession* (Oxford University Press, 1995), 71.
19. James Purves, *Observations on Prophetic Time and Similitudes. Part Second.* (Edinburgh, 1778), 3 (unnumbered).
20. Bloch, *Visionary Republic*, 77.
21. "The Church's Flight into the Wilderness: An Address on the Times, by Samuel Sherwood (January 17, 1776)," *Political Sermons of the American Founding Era*. Vol. 1. Ed. Ellis Sandoz. Indianapolis: Liberty Fund, 1998. 497–527, https://www.consource.org/document/the-churchs-flight-into-the-wilderness-an-address-on-the-times-by-samuel-sherwood-1776-1-17/.
22. Samuel West, *An Anniversary Sermon, Preached at Plymouth, December 22d, 1777.* (Draper and Folsom, at their printing-office, at the corner of Winter-Street, 1778), 5 (unnumbered), http://name.umdl.umich.edu/N12791.0001.001.

23. West, *An Anniversary Sermon*, 6.
24. West, *An Anniversary Sermon*, 6.

THE MODERN TAKEAWAY: AMERICAN APOCALYPSE

1. Joseph Franklin Rutherford, *Millions Now Living Will Never Die!* (International Bible Students Association, 1920), 97.
2. Massachusetts Historical Society, "John Winthrop: A Modell of Christian Charity, 1630," Hanover Historical Texts Collection, accessed October 20, 2025, https://history.hanover.edu/texts/winthmod.html.
3. "Address of President-Elect John F. Kennedy Delivered to a Joint Convention of the General Court of the Commonwealth of Massachusetts, January 9, 1961," JFK Library, accessed October 20, 2025, https://www.jfklibrary.org/archives/other-resources/john-f-kennedy-speeches/massachusetts-general-court-19610109.
4. "Farewell Address to the Nation," Ronald Reagan Presidential Library and Museum, accessed October 20, 2025, https://www.reaganlibrary.gov/archives/speech/farewell-address-nation.
5. Anders Stephanson, *Manifest Destiny: American Expansionism and the Empire of Right* (Hill and Wang, 1998), 57.
6. Stephanson, *Manifest Destiny*, 57.
7. Ezra Stiles, *The United States Elevated to Glory and Honor* (New Haven, CT: Thomas & Samuel Green, 1783), 7, https://digitalcommons.unl.edu/cgi/viewcontent.cgi?article=1041&context=etas.
8. Stiles, *The United States Elevated*, 34.
9. David Humphreys, *A Poem on the Happiness of America: Addressed to the Citizens of the United States* (New York Printing Company, 1871), 11.
10. Ernest Lee Tuveson, *Redeemer Nation: The Idea of America's Millennial Role* (University of Chicago Press, 1968), viii.
11. Yii-Jan Lin, *Immigration and Apocalypse: How the Book of Revelation Shaped American Immigration* (Yale University Press, 2024), 5.
12. Lin, *Immigration and Apocalypse*, 183.

CHAPTER FIVE: SPEAKING WITH THE DEAD

1. Cathy Gutierrez, "Spiritualism," in *The Occult World*, ed. Christopher Partridge (Routledge, 2015), 197.
2. E. E. Lewis, *A Report of Mysterious Noises, Heard in the House of Mr. John D. Fox, in Hydesville, Arcadia, Wayne County, Authenticated by the Certificates, and Confirmed by the Statements of the Citizens of That Place and Vicinity.* (Canindaigua: E. E. Lewis, Printed on the Power Press of Shepard & Reed, 1848).

3. Ann Braude, "Unbroken Communication Between the Infinite and All Beings," in *Radical Spirits: Spiritualism and Women's Rights in Nineteenth-Century America* (Indiana University Press, 2013).
4. Arthur Conan Doyle, *The History of Spiritualism* (Cassell & Co., 1926), 86–87.
5. Harry Houdini, *A Magician Among the Spirits* (Harper & Brothers, 1924), 8.
6. Mary T. Longley, *Teachings and Illustrations as They Emanate from the Spirit World* (The Progressive Thinker Publishing House, 1908), 47–48.
7. Longley, *Teachings*, 31.
8. Longley, *Teachings*, 31.
9. Cathy Gutierrez, *Plato's Ghost: Spiritualism in the American Renaissance* (Oxford University Press, 2009), 30.
10. Marlene Tromp, "Queering the Séance: Bodies, Bondage, and Touching in Victorian Spiritualism," in *Handbook of Spiritualism and Channeling*, ed. Cathy Gutierrez (Brill, 2015), 90.

CHAPTER SIX: THE NEW WITCHES OF ENDOR

1. Martha Rampton, *Trafficking with Demons: Magic, Ritual, and Gender from Late Antiquity to 1000* (Cornell University Press, 2022).
2. James Porter, *The Spirit Rappings, Mesmerism, Clairvoyance, Visions, Revelations, Startling Phenomena, and Infidelity of the Rapping Fraternity Calmly Considered, and Exposed* (James P. McGee, 1853), 39.
3. Porter, *The Spirit Rappings*, 41.
4. Z. Campbell, *The Spiritual Telegraphic Opposition Line, Or, Science and Divine Revelation Against Spiritual Manifestations* (Springfield: H.S. Taylor, 1853), 224.
5. Jedediah M. Grant, "The Power of God and the Power of Satan," in *Journal of Discourses*, vol. 2 (Liverpool: F. D. Richards, 1855): 11, 14.
6. Grant, "The Power of God and the Power of Satan," 15.
7. J. D. Cox, *Modern Spiritualism Compared with Christianity: In a Debate Between Joel Tiffany, Esq., of Painesville, O., and Rev. Isaac Errett, of Warren, O., Upon the Following Questions—I. Are the Phenomena and Teachings of Modern Spiritualism Identical in Character with Those of Jesus of Nazareth? II. Is the Denomination Known as Disciples, Anti-Christ in Faith and Practice? : A Phonographic Report* (Warren, OH: George Adams, 1855), 168–69.
8. John Rose, "Moral Chemistry; Or Modern Spirits Analysed," in *The Local Preachers' Magazine and Christian Family Record*, vol. 25 (London: Chaloner and Cooke, 1875), 74.
9. Rose, "Moral Chemistry," 109.
10. Rose, "Moral Chemistry," 109.

11. Carlyle B. Haynes, *Spiritualism Versus Christianity: An Account of the Origin, the History, the Work, the Character, and the Destiny of the Remarkable Movement Which at the Present Time Is Attracting the Attention of the World* (Southern Publishing Association, 1918), 74.
12. Owen Davies, "The Witch of Endor in History and Folklore," *Folklore* 134, no. 1 (2023): 16, https://doi.org/10.1080/0015587X.2022.2152252.
13. Quoted in Davies, "The Witch of Endor in History and Folklore."

CHAPTER SEVEN: THE WAGES OF SIN IS DEATH

1. Carlyle B. Haynes, *Spiritualism Versus Christianity: An Account of the Origin, the History, the Work, the Character, and the Destiny of the Remarkable Movement Which at the Present Time is Attracting the Attention of the World* (Southern Publishing Association, 1918), 71.
2. John C. Bywater, *The Mystery Solved; Or, a Bible Expose of the Spirit Rappings. Showing That They Are Not Caused by Spirits of the Dead, But by Evil Demons, Or Devils* (Rochester, NY: Advent Harbinger Office, 1852), 103.
3. Bywater, *The Mystery Solved*, 108.
4. *The Medium and Daybreak*, January 13, 1882, 27.
5. *The Medium and Daybreak*, April 7, 1882, 215.
6. Quoted in Joseph Franklin Rutherford, *Can the Living Talk with the Dead? A Clear Explanation of Spiritism* (International Bible Students Association, 1920), 106.
7. Quoted in Rutherford, *Can the Living Talk with the Dead*, 120.
8. Quoted in Rutherford, *Can the Living Talk with the Dead.*
9. James Porter, *The Spirit Rappings, Mesmerism, Clairvoyance, Visions, Revelations, Startling Phenomena, and Infidelity of the Rapping Fraternity Calmly Considered, and Exposed* (James P. McGee, 1853), 50.

CHAPTER EIGHT: ABOMINABLE BELIEFS, ABOMINABLE POLITICS

1. Mary Wollstonecraft, *A Vindication of the Rights of Woman* (Peter Edes for Thomas and Andrews, 1792), https://oll.libertyfund.org/titles/wollstonecraft-a-vindication-of-the-rights-of-woman.
2. Wollstonecraft, *A Vindication of the Rights of Woman.*
3. Wollstonecraft, *A Vindication of the Rights of Woman.*
4. Nancy Levit and Robert R. M. Verchick, *Feminist Legal Theory*, 2nd ed. (New York University Press, 2016), 192.
5. Victoria Woodhull, "Victoria C. Woodhull, 'And The Truth Shall Make You Free' Speech Text," Voices of Democracy, accessed November 4,

2025, https://voicesofdemocracy.umd.edu/victoria-c-woodhull-and-the-truth-shall-make-you-free-speech-text/.

6. Thomas Nast, Artist, "Get Thee Behind Me, (Mrs.) Satan!" / *Th. Nast.* United States, 1872. Photograph. https://www.loc.gov/pictures/item/95512460/.
7. Charles Pettit McIlvaine, *The Truth and Life: Twenty-Two Sermons* (New York: Robert Carter & Brothers, 1854), 347.
8. Theodore Parker, "The Moral Character of Jesus," ed. Moncure Daniel Conway, *The Dial* 1, no. 9 (September 1860): 531.
9. Laurence W. Scott, *A Hand-book of Christian Evidence* (St. Louis, MO: John Burns, 1880), 123. Italics in original.
10. Scott, *A Hand-book of Christian Evidence*, 123.
11. J. W. Daniels, *Spiritualism Versus Christianity: Or, Spiritualism Thoroughly Exposed* (New York and Auburn: Miller, Orton & Mulligan, 1856), 255–56.
12. Daniels, *Spiritualism Versus Christianity*, 253. Italics in original.
13. Daniels, *Spiritualism Versus Christianity*, 259.
14. Miles Grant, *Spiritualism Unveiled and Shown to Be the Work of Demons: An Examination of Its Origin, Morals, Doctrines, and Politics* (Boston: The "Crisis" Office, 1866), 41.
15. Grant, *Spiritualism Unveiled.*
16. Grant, *Spiritualism Unveiled*, 42.
17. Grant, *Spiritualism Unveiled.*
18. Elizabeth Cady Stanton, "Preface," in *The Woman's Bible* (New York: European Publishing Company, 1895), 7.
19. E. P. Thorndyke, *Astrea: Or, Goddess of Justice* (San Francisco: Amanda B. Slocum, Book and Job Printer, 1881), 13.
20. Thorndyke, *Astrea*, 14.
21. Thorndyke, *Astrea*, 14.
22. Orestes Brownson, *The Spirit-Rapper: An Autobiography* (Boston: Little, Brown and Company, 1854), 72.
23. Brownson, *The Spirit-Rapper.*
24. Brownson, *The Spirit-Rapper*, 101.
25. Brownson, *The Spirit-Rapper*, 115–16.
26. Brownson, *The Spirit-Rapper*, 172.
27. Brownson, *The Spirit-Rapper*, 73.
28. Brownson, *The Spirit-Rapper*, 223.
29. Brownson, *The Spirit-Rapper*, 223–24.
30. Patrick W. Carey, "Orestes Brownson and the Civil War," *U.S. Catholic Historian* 31, no. 1 (2013): 5.
31. Gerrit Smith, *Three Discourses on the Religion of Reason* (New York: Ross & Tousey, 1859), 40.
32. Anonymous, "Steadfast, Unmovable," *The Presbyterian Expositor* 2, no. 6 (1859): 323. Italics original.

33. Quoted in Z. Campbell, *The Spiritual Telegraphic Opposition Line, Or, Science and Divine Revelation Against Spiritual Manifestations* (Springfield: H.S. Taylor, 1853), 112.
34. Campbell, *The Spiritual Telegraphic Opposition Line*, 113.
35. Campbell, *The Spiritual Telegraphic Opposition Line*, 117.
36. A Citizen of Ohio, *Interior Causes of the War: The Nation Demonized, and Its President a Spirit-Rapper* (M. Doolady, 1863), 42.

CHAPTER NINE: ABRAHAM LINCOLN'S PACT WITH THE DEVIL

1. Edward J. Blum and John H. Matsui, *War Is All Hell: The Nature of Evil and the Civil War* (University of Pennsylvania Press, 2021), 32.
2. Blum and Matsui, *War is All Hell*, 5.
3. Quoted in Stephen J. Vicchio, *Abraham Lincoln's Religion: An Essay on One Man's Faith* (Wipf and Stock Publishers, 2018), 15.
4. Vicchio, *Abraham Lincoln's Religion*, 32.
5. Christopher Grasso, *Skepticism and American Faith: From the Revolution to the Civil War* (Oxford University Press, 2018), 16–17.
6. Grasso, *Skepticism and American Faith*, 490.
7. Vicchio, *Abraham Lincoln's Religion*, 62.
8. Vicchio, *Abraham Lincoln's Religion*, 41.
9. Quoted in Jay Monaghan, "Was Abraham Lincoln Really a Spiritualist?," *Journal of the Illinois State Historical Society (1908–1984)* 34, no. 2 (1941): 209–32, 222. Italics in original.
10. Monaghan, "Was Abraham Lincoln Really a Spiritualist?," 230.
11. Citizen of Ohio, *Interior Causes of the War: The Nation Demonized, and Its President a Spirit-Rapper* (M. Doolady, 1863), 3. Capitalization in original.
12. Citizen of Ohio, *Interior Causes*, 5.
13. Citizen of Ohio, *Interior Causes*, 6.
14. Citizen of Ohio, *Interior Causes*, 8.
15. Citizen of Ohio, *Interior Causes*, 30.
16. Citizen of Ohio, *Interior Causes*, 69.
17. Citizen of Ohio, *Interior Causes*, 72.
18. Citizen of Ohio, *Interior Causes*, 97.
19. Citizen of Ohio, *Interior Causes*, 6–7, 98.
20. Fayette Hall, *The Copperhead: Or, The Secret Political History of Our Civil War Unveiled* (F. Hall, 1902), 13.
21. Fayette Hall, *The Secret and Political History of the War of the Rebellion* (F. Hall, 1890), iii.
22. Hall, *The Secret and Political History of the War of the Rebellion*, 8.
23. While the books represent two printings decades apart, there is a distinct similarity of title and whole paragraphs are nearly identical between the two books.

24. Hall, *The Copperhead*, 14.
25. Hall, *The Copperhead*, 56–57.

CHAPTER TEN: THE NEW BLACK MAGIC

1. Kate Field, ed. *Planchette's Diary* (New York: J. S. Redfield, 1868), 7.
2. Originally in Gregory Raupert, *A Convert from Spiritualism: J. Godfrey Raupert* (Dublin: Irish Messenger Office, 1932). Can be found preserved in Gregory Raupert, "A Convert from Spiritualism," *Psypioneer Journal* 7, no. 10 (2011): 303.
3. Raupert, *A Convert from Spiritualism*, 305.
4. John Godfrey Raupert, *The New Black Magic and the Truth About the Ouija-Board* (The Devin-Adair Company, 1920), 60–61.
5. Raupert, *The New Black Magic*, 209–10.
6. Raupert, *The New Black Magic*, 210.
7. Raupert, *The New Black Magic*, 211
8. Raupert, *The New Black Magic*, 224–25.

THE MODERN TAKEAWAY: GENDER AND CONSPIRACY

1. Man Camp: Jason Rogers, "He-Men and Holy Rollers," *Men's Health*, April 2, 2024, https://www.menshealth.com/trending-news/a60258262/crossroads-church-man-camp/; "Biblical Truths & Practical Training," The School of Biblical Womanhood, accessed October 23, 2025, https://schoolofbiblicalwomanhood.com/about.
2. David Edwards, "'God Has an Order': Head of Trump's Faith Office Says Women Must 'Submit' to Men," Raw Story, April 23, 2025, https://www.rawstory.com/paula-white-2671833752/.

INTERMISSION: THE SHAPE OF THINGS TO COME

1. For a vivid example, see "The Return of Christ," *End Times*, accessed December 14, 2025, https://rapture-watch.com/.

CHAPTER ELEVEN: MERRILL UNGER

1. It is not my intention to trivialize the death camps of Nazi Germany by offering so little commentary or context upon them. Rather, it would take another book entirely to cover the atrocities. Others have done so much better than I could. See for instance, Daniel Blatman, *The Death Marches: The Final Phase of Nazi Genocide* (Harvard University Press, 2011) and John

C. McManus, *Hell Before Their Very Eyes: American Soldiers Liberate Concentration Camps in Germany, April 1945* (JHU Press, 2015).

2. Merrill Unger, *Biblical Demonology: A Study of Spiritual Forces at Work Today* (Van Kampen Press, 1952), 19.
3. Unger, *Biblical Demonology*, 20.
4. Unger, *Biblical Demonology*, 206
5. Unger, *Biblical Demonology*, 149–50.
6. Unger, *Biblical Demonology*, 39.
7. Unger, *Biblical Demonology*, 40.
8. See for instance, Unger, *Biblical Demonology*, 87–90.
9. Unger, *Biblical Demonology*, 196.
10. Unger, *Biblical Demonology*.
11. I was reminded by a colleague the other day of Karl Barth—the famous, anti-liberal theologian who argued for a God that was radically transcendent from the world and revealed through the Bible—as he attended a conference in post-WWII Germany. At the conference, he relates that many people claimed to have "looked Satan in the eye" and the halls were filled with discussions of the demonic. Finally, Barth snapped at his friends "Why do you keep talking only about demons? Why don't you say outright that you were political fools?" (Eberhard Busch, *Karl Barth: His Life from Letters and Autobiographical Texts* (Wipf and Stock, 2005), 328).
12. Unger, *Biblical Demonology*, xiii.
13. Unger, *Biblical Demonology*, 198.
14. Unger, *Biblical Demonology*, 196.
15. Unger, *Biblical Demonology*, 198.

CHAPTER TWELVE: MICHAEL HARPER

1. Michael Harper, *Spiritual Warfare* (Hodder and Stoughton, 1970), 13.
2. Harper, *Spiritual Warfare*, 6.
3. Harper, *Spiritual Warfare*, 24–6.
4. Harper, *Spiritual Warfare*, 50.
5. Harper, *Spiritual Warfare*, 42.
6. Harper, *Spiritual Warfare*, 5.
7. Harper, *Spiritual Warfare*, 42.
8. Harper, *Spiritual Warfare*, 97.
9. Compare for instance Jessie Penn-Lewis, *War on the Saints: A Text Book for Believers on the Work of Deceiving Spirits Among the Children of God* (The "Overcomer" Office; Marshall Brothers, 1912), which discusses the notion of war and warfare, but uses none of the strategic or siege-based language that Harper does.
10. Harper, *Spiritual Warfare*, 108.
11. Harper, *Spiritual Warfare*, 118.

12. Harper, *Spiritual Warfare*, 50, 97.
13. Harper, *Spiritual Warfare*, 63.
14. Harper, *Spiritual Warfare*, 124.

CHAPTER THIRTEEN: FERTILIZING FEAR THROUGH FILM

1. Emma Jones, "The Chosen: The Christian-Funded Hit About Jesus Taking the US by Storm," BBC, January 24, 2024, https://www.bbc.com/culture/article/20240124-the-chosen-the-christian-funded-hit-about-jesus-taking-the-us-by-storm.
2. Joseph P. Laycock and Eric Harrelson, *The Exorcist Effect: Horror, Religion, and Demonic Belief* (Oxford University Press, 2023).
3. Michael Barkun, *A Culture of Conspiracy: Apocalyptic Visions in Contemporary America* (University of California Press, 2006), 55–57.
4. "ONE BILLION Chick Tracts," *Chick Publications,* accessed November 2, 2025, https://www.chick.com/information/article?id=one-billion-chick-tracts.
5. The book written on the subject is much more detailed: Mike Hertenstein and Jon Trott, *Selling Satan: The Evangelical Media and the Mike Warnke Scandal* (Cornerstone Press, 1993).
6. "Who We Are," Mike Warnke Celebrations of Hope, accessed December 14, 2025, http://www.mikewarnke.org/about/who/.
7. See for instance, Jesse Walker, *The United States of Paranoia: A Conspiracy Theory* (Harper, 2013), ch. 8.
8. Michael E. Heyes, *Demons in the USA: From the Anti-Spiritualists to QAnon* (Routledge, 2024), 59.
9. Billy Graham, "Spiritual Warfare," speech given in Phoenix, AZ, in 1974. See https://www.youtube.com/watch?v=0X6xFMRrLGY.
10. See for instance, Heyes, *Demons in the USA*, ch. 3.
11. See for instance, Laycock and Harrelson, *The Exorcist Effect*, ch. 4.
12. See for instance, Laycock and Harrelson, *The Exorcist Effect*, chs. 4 and 5.
13. Hal Lindsey, *The Late Great Planet Earth* (Zondervan, 1970), 110.
14. Lindsey, *The Late Great Planet Earth*, 105.
15. Lindsey, *The Late Great Planet Earth*, 111.
16. Lindsey, *The Late Great Planet Earth*, copyright page.

CHAPTER FOURTEEN: BILLY GRAHAM

1. Billy Graham, "Down on the Farm," in *Just as I Am: The Autobiography of Billy Graham* (Harper-Collins, 2011).
2. Thomas G. Long, "Preaching the Good News," in *The Legacy of Billy Graham: Critical Reflections on America's Greatest Evangelist*, ed. Michael G. Long (Westminster John Knox Press, 2008), 3.

3. "Billy Graham: We Must Talk About Hell," *Decision: The Evangelical Voice for Today*, January 1, 2023, https://billygraham.org/decision-magazine/articles/billy-graham-we-must-talk-about-hell.
4. Long, "Preaching the Good News," 9. The elements of Graham's sermons can be found on pages 6 to 9.
5. Karen Lebacqz, "'Keep Yourself Pure': Social Justice and Sexual Ethics," in *The Legacy of Billy Graham: Critical Reflections on America's Greatest Evangelist*, ed. Michael G. Long (Westminster John Knox Press, 2008).
6. Billy Graham, *Truth for Each Day* (Thomas Nelson, 2023), 182.
7. Ellen Ott Marshall, "A Matter of Pride: A Feminist Response," in *The Legacy of Billy Graham: Critical Reflections on America's Greatest Evangelist*, ed. Michael G. Long (Westminster John Knox Press, 2008), 82.
8. Quoted in Gary Dorrien, "Niebuhr and Graham: Modernity, Complexity, White Supremacism, Justice, Ambiguity," in *The Legacy of Billy Graham: Critical Reflections on America's Greatest Evangelist*, ed. Michael G. Long (Westminster John Knox Press, 2008), 152.
9. Billy Graham, "Satan's Religion," *The American Mercury*, August 1954, 41.
10. Graham, "Satan's Religion," 41–42.
11. Graham, "Satan's Religion," 45.
12. Graham, "Satan's Religion," 45.
13. Graham, "Satan's Religion," 45.
14. Graham, "Satan's Religion," 45–46.
15. Graham, "Satan's Religion," 46.
16. Graham, "Satan's Religion," 46.
17. Graham, "Satan's Religion," 46.
18. The sermon can be found in its entirety on several YouTube channels, a testament to both Graham and the sermon's enduring appeal. Footnote 9 of chapter 13 offers a sample link.
19. While Graham never actually tells us the gender of the social worker, it is one of the few professions that are women-dominated.

CHAPTER FIFTEEN: FRANK (AND IDA MAE) HAMMOND

1. Frank Hammond and Ida Mae Hammond, *Pigs in the Parlor: The Practical Guide to Deliverance* (Impact Christian Books, 1990), 11.
2. See for instance Hammond and Hammond, *Pigs in the Parlor*, ch. 14.
3. Hammond and Hammond, *Pigs in the Parlor*, 53.
4. Hammond and Hammond, *Pigs in the Parlor*, 39.
5. Hammond and Hammond, *Pigs in the Parlor*, 59.
6. Hammond and Hammond, *Pigs in the Parlor*, 36.
7. For examples, see Merrill Unger, *Biblical Demonology: A Study of Spiritual Forces at Work Today* (Van Kampen Press, 1952), 173, 183–89. The closest that Unger comes to this worldview appears on page 194 when he discusses

the "Prince of Persia" as a singular demonic entity over Persia but then moves back into generalities a few pages later.

8. For example see, Billy Graham, *The Collected Works of Billy Graham* (Inspirational Press, 1993), 55 (struggle against an "organized kingdom of satanic darkness"), 128 (discussion of Satan as influencer over nations). Both of these quotes emerge from his work *Angels*, included in the volume.
9. Hammond and Hammond, *Pigs in the Parlor*, 28.
10. Hammond and Hammond, *Pigs in the Parlor*, 28.
11. Hammond and Hammond, *Pigs in the Parlor*, 28.

CHAPTER SIXTEEN: THE SATANIC PANIC

1. Michelle Smith and Lawrence Pazder, MD, *Michelle Remembers* (Congdon & Lattès, 1980), 117.
2. Megan Goodwin, *Abusing Religion: Literary Persecution, Sex Scandals, and American Minority Religions* (Rutgers University Press, 2020), 44.
3. Goodwin, *Abusing Religion*, 55.
4. Debbie Nathan and Michael Snedeker, *Satan's Silence* (Author's Choice Press, 2001), 89.
5. Jeffrey S. Victor, *Satanic Panic: The Creation of a Contemporary Legend* (Open Court, 1999), 15.
6. Goodwin, *Abusing Religion*, 46.
7. Linda Charlton, "Women Seeking Equality March on 5th Ave. Today," *New York Times*, August 26, 1970, https://www.nytimes.com/1970/08/26/archives/women-seeking-equality-march-on-5th-ave-today.html.
8. It would be issues of race and not abortion that would largely change this. See for instance, Randall Balmer, *Bad Faith: Race and the Rise of the Religious Right* (Eerdmans, 2021).
9. Smith and Pazder, *Michelle Remembers*, 146.
10. Lauren Stratford, *Satan's Underground: The Extraordinary Story of One Woman's Escape* (Harvest House, 1988), 93.
11. All quotes from "Ronald Reagan's 'Evil Empire' Speech to the National Association of Evangelicals—1983," National Center for Public Policy Research, Historical Documents, November 4, 2001, https://nationalcenter.org/ncppr/2001/11/04/ronal-reagans-evil-empire-speech-to-the-national-association-of-evangelicals-1983/.
12. Tim Alberta, "How the GOP Gave Up on Porn," *Politico Magazine*, November/December 2018, https://politi.co/2JTHVAp.
13. Stratford, *Satan's Underground*, 16.
14. Stratford, *Satan's Underground*, 56.
15. Stratford, *Satan's Underground*, 68.
16. Stratford, *Satan's Underground*, 79.

17. Jay Sharbutt, "Cauldron Boils Over Geraldo's 'Devil Worship': 'Satan' Wins Ratings, Loses Advertisers," *Los Angeles Times*, October 27, 1988, https://www.latimes.com/archives/la-xpm-1988-10-27-ca-449-story.html.
18. Noah Caldwell, Ari Shaprio, Patrick Jarenwattananon, and Mia Venkat, "America's Satanic Panic Returns—This Time Through QAnon," NPR, May 18, 2021, https://www.npr.org/2021/05/18/997559036/americas-satanic-panic-returns-this-time-through-qanon.
19. Dan Shewan, "Conviction of Things Not Seen: The Uniquely American Myth of Satanic Cults," *Pacific Standard* (blog), September 8, 2015, https://psmag.com/social-justice/make-a-cross-with-your-fingers-its-the-satanic-panic/.
20. Richard Beck, *We Believe the Children: A Moral Panic in the 1980s* (PublicAffairs, 2015), 192.
21. Daniel Goleman, "Proof Lacking for Ritual Abuse by Satanists," *New York Times*, October 31, 1994, https://web.archive.org/web/20181125122537/https://www.nytimes.com/1994/10/31/us/proof-lacking-for-ritual-abuse-by-satanists.html?sq=satanic+ritual+abuse&scp=1&st=nyt.
22. Goleman, "Proof Lacking."

THE MODERN TAKEAWAY: SATANIC PANIC REDUX

1. Daniel Goleman, "Proof Lacking for Ritual Abuse by Satanists," *New York Times*, October 31, 1994, https://web.archive.org/web/20181125122537/https://www.nytimes.com/1994/10/31/us/proof-lacking-for-ritual-abuse-by-satanists.html?sq=satanic+ritual+abuse&scp=1&st=nyt.
2. Paul Kengor, *The Devil and Karl Marx: Communism's Long March of Death, Deception, and Infiltration* (TAN Books, 2020), dust jacket.
3. Kengor, *The Devil and Karl Marx*, xx–xxi.
4. Jake Kail, *Setting Captives Free: How to Break the Chains of Demonic Influence* (Destiny Image, 2020), 92.
5. Quotations taken from Q's tweets, which can be found collected at "Q-Posts," QResearch.ch, accessed December 15, 2025, https://qresear.ch/q-posts.
6. "Q-Posts," #3.
7. "Q-Posts," #1432, #1886, #2403, #2904, #3593, #3594, #3887, #4207, #4429, #4463.
8. "Q-Posts," #3683, #4397.

CHAPTER SEVENTEEN: OUT WITH THE OLD AND IN WITH THE NEW APOSTOLIC REFORMATION

1. "How to Spot a NAR Church," Holly Pivec (blog), March 22, 2013, https://www.hollypivec.com/blog/2013/03/how-to-spot-an-nar-church/2805.
2. For more information, I recommend John Weaver's excellent book, *The New Apostolic Reformation: History of a Modern Charismatic Movement* (2016). It

is one of the most thorough on the subject and forms a significant backdrop for this and future chapters.

3. George H. Warnock, *The Feast of Tabernacles* (2002), 10.
4. Warnock, *The Feast of Tabernacles*, 181.
5. Warnock, *The Feast of Tabernacles*, 181.
6. Michael Cuneo, *American Exorcism: Expelling Demons in the Land of Plenty* (Doubleday, 2010), 83.
7. Cuneo, *American Exorcism*, 84.
8. Cuneo, *American Exorcism*, 122.
9. Cuneo, *American Exorcism*, 122.
10. See for instance, Cuneo, *American Exorcism*, 122–23; Weaver, *The New Apostolic Reformation*, 42–47.
11. Cuneo, *American Exorcism*, 123.
12. Weaver, *The New Apostolic Reformation*, 45.
13. C. Peter Wagner, *The Third Wave of the Holy Spirit: Encountering the Power of Signs and Wonders Today* (Vine Books, 1988), 22.
14. "History & Legacy," Vineyard USA, accessed August 13, 2025, https://vineyardusa.org/about/history/.
15. Wagner, *The Third Wave of the Holy Spirit*, 24.
16. Wagner, *The Third Wave of the Holy Spirit*, 24.
17. C. Peter Wagner, *Churchquake! How the New Apostolic Reformation Is Shaking up the Church as We Know It* (Regal, 1999), 14.
18. Wagner, *The Third Wave of the Holy Spirit*, 58.
19. See for instance, René Holvast, *Spiritual Mapping in the United States and Argentina, 1989–2005: A Geography of Fear* (Brill, 2009).

CHAPTER EIGHTEEN: SPIRITUAL MAPPING

1. Sean McCloud, *American Possessions: Fighting Demons in the Contemporary United States* (Oxford University Press, 2015), 10.
2. Wagner, *Churchquake!: How the New Apostolic Reformation Is Shaking up Church as We Know It*, 47.
3. C. Peter Wagner, *Warfare Prayer: How to Seek God's Power and Protection in the Battle to Build His Kingdom* (Regal Books, 1992).
4. Fresh Air, "A Leading Figure in the New Apostolic Reformation," NPR, October 3, 2011, https://www.npr.org/2011/10/03/140946482/apostolic-leader-weighs-religions-role-in-politics.
5. See for instance, Wagner, *Warfare Prayer*, 14–15.
6. Wagner, *Warfare Prayer*, 15–16.
7. Wagner, *Warfare Prayer*, 15.
8. Wagner, *Warfare Prayer*, 202.
9. Wagner, *Warfare Prayer*, 22.

10. Cindy Jacobs, *Deliver Us from Evil: Putting a Stop to the Occultic Influence Invading Your Home and Community* (Gospel Light, 2001), 18.
11. All quotes from Jacobs, *Deliver Us from Evil*, 22. "Just how much influence did the occult and those who are demonically inspired who work in the media have on instances such as the Columbine massacre and other school shootings?"
12. Jacobs, *Deliver Us from Evil*, 88.
13. Jacobs, *Deliver Us from Evil*, 109.
14. John Weaver, *The New Apostolic Reformation: History of a Modern Charismatic Movement* (McFarland & Company, 2016), 75.
15. Weaver, *The New Apostolic Reformation*, 75.
16. Wagner, *Warfare Prayer*, 62–63.
17. Wagner, *Warfare Prayer*, 16–17.
18. For context, see for example George Otis, *Informed Intercession: Transforming Your Community through Spiritual Mapping and Strategic Prayer* (Renew, 1999), 49. For explanation, see André Gagné, *American Evangelicals for Trump: Dominion, Spiritual Warfare, and the End Times*, trans. Linda Shanahan (Routledge, 2023), 57–58.
19. Wagner, *Warfare Prayer*, 16–17.
20. C. Peter Wagner, "Territorial Spirits," in, *Wrestling with Dark Angels: Toward a Deeper Understanding of the Supernatural Forces in Spiritual Warfare*, ed. C. Peter Wagner and F. Douglas Pennoyer (Regal Books, 1990), 86.
21. "Activating Generals," Generals International, accessed August 11, 2025, https://www.generals.org/.
22. Originally found on "Shields Up—Call 911!," Generals International, October 24, 2023, https://www.generals.org/shields-up-call-911-october/. Jacobs appears to have edited her webpage since then (prophetic figures are ever careful of failed prophecies), but the unedited version can be found on the Wayback Machine (https://web.archive.org/web/20250118040630/https://www.generals.org/shields-up-call-911-october/) and Breaking Christian News (https://www.breakingchristiannews.com/articles/display_art.html?ID=38474). Apparently, it was unsettling enough to Jacobs to re-record the video that accompanies the statement: at this time, the video offers a verbatim statement for the text recorded on the October 24, 2023, entry, but was clearly recorded according to the title on February 5, 2025.
23. "Shields Up—Call 911!," Generals International.
24. "Shields Up—Call 911!," Generals International.
25. "Shields Up—Call 911!," Generals International.
26. Compare for instance Emma Stark of the Global Prophetic Alliance's use of the term to refer to a demon who steals "health, wealth, and relationships" from people. *Break the Robbing Spirit Attacking Your Health, Finances & Relationships | The War Rooms EP31*, directed by Global Prophetic Alliance, May 8, 2025, https://www.youtube.com/watch?v=yFp46CNng2Y.

27. E.g., Wagner, *Warfare Prayer*, 28, 30, 36, 43, 78, 79.
28. C. Peter Wagner, *Breaking Strongholds in Your City: How to Use Spiritual Mapping to Make Your Prayers More Strategic, Effective, and Targeted* (Regal Books, 2015), 19–21.
29. Wagner, *Breaking Strongholds in Your City*, 19–21.
30. René Holvast, *Spiritual Mapping in the United States and Argentina, 1989–2005: A Geography of Fear* (Brill, 2009), 12.
31. George Otis Jr., *The Twilight Labyrinth: Why Does Spiritual Darkness Linger Where It Does?* (Chosen Books, 1997), 55.
32. Otis, *The Twilight Labyrinth*, 91.
33. Otis, *The Twilight Labyrinth*, 97.
34. Otis, *The Twilight Labyrinth*, 109.
35. Otis, *The Twilight Labyrinth*, 118.
36. Otis, *The Twilight Labyrinth*, 124–25.
37. Otis, *The Twilight Labyrinth*, 135.
38. See for instance Otis, *The Twilight Labyrinth*, 191–98.
39. See for instance, Otis, *The Twilight Labyrinth*, 172–81.
40. See for instance Otis, *The Twilight Labyrinth*, 181–90.

CHAPTER NINETEEN: DOMINION, HE WROTE

1. George Otis, *The Last of the Giants: Lifting the Veil on Islam and the End Times* (Chosen Books, 2002), 161.
2. Lance Wallnau, "The Seven Mountain Mandate," in *Invading Babylon: The 7 Mountain Mandate*, ed. Lance Wallnau and Bill Johnson (Destiny Image Publishers, 2013), 54.
3. Wallnau, "The Seven Mountain Mandate," 57–58.
4. Wallnau, "The Seven Mountain Mandate," 63.
5. Wallnau, "The Seven Mountain Mandate," 65.
6. Wallnau, "The Seven Mountain Mandate," 58.
7. Wallnau, "The Seven Mountain Mandate," 65–66.
8. "If a majority feels that heterosexual marriage is the best choice for a happy and prosperous society, those in the minority who disagree should conform—not because they live in a theocracy, but because they live in a democracy" (Peter C. Wagner, *Dominion! How Kingdom Action Can Change the World* [Chosen, 2008], 17).
9. Wagner, *Dominion!*, 138–39.
10. Wallnau, "The Seven Mountain Mandate," 65.
11. Wallnau, "The Seven Mountain Mandate," 71.
12. Wallnau, "The Seven Mountain Mandate," 58.
13. Wallnau, "The Seven Mountain Mandate," 72.
14. Wallnau, "The Seven Mountain Mandate," 73.
15. Wallnau, "The Seven Mountain Mandate," 73.

16. Wallnau and Johnson, *Invading Babylon*, 75.
17. The full thirty minute monologue can be found at https://www.facebook.com/LanceWallnau/videos/774821525234419/, but I highly recommend the good work of the people over at Right Wing Watch, who do an excellent job of just distilling the most alarming bits of many right-wing media figures: Kyle Mantyla, "Lance Wallnau Says God Is Using Trump to Give Right-Wing Christians Control Over The Seven Mountains," Right Wing Watch, August 14, 2025, https://www.peoplefor.org/rightwingwatch/lance-wallnau-says-god-using-trump-give-right-wing-christians-control-over-seven.
18. Wagner, *Dominion!*, 143–44.
19. Wagner, *Dominion!*, 64.
20. Wagner, *Dominion!*, 65.
21. Wagner, *Dominion!*, 64.
22. Wagner, *Dominion!*, 65.
23. Wagner, *Dominion!*, 68.
24. Wagner, *Dominion!*, 71.
25. Wagner, *Dominion!*, 73.
26. Wagner, *Dominion!*, 40.
27. Wagner, *Dominion!*, 40.
28. Wagner, *Dominion!*, 37.
29. Wagner, *Dominion!*, 59.
30. Wagner references this idea several times in his work, the first instance is in Wagner, *Dominion!*, 46.
31. Wagner, *Dominion!*, 46–47.
32. A colleague and I like to refer to this idea as *Christian sharia*, sharia being the theonomic systems of governance in Islam based on the Quran.
33. Michael J. McVicar, *Christian Reconstructionism: R. J. Rushdoony and American Religious Conservatism* (The University of North Carolina Press, 2015), 131. Italics mine.
34. Kerwin Lee Klein, *From History to Theory* (University of California Press, 2011), 154.
35. Wallnau, "The Seven Mountain Mandate," 65.
36. Wagner, *Dominion!*, 17.
37. John Weaver, *The New Apostolic Reformation: History of a Modern Charismatic Movement* (McFarland & Company, 2016), 98, 161.
38. Wagner, *Dominion!*, 76.
39. Wagner, *Dominion!*, 80.
40. Wagner, *Dominion!*, 95.
41. Wagner, *Dominion!*, 103.
42. Wagner, *Dominion!*, 112.
43. Wagner, *Dominion!*, 112–13.
44. Wagner, *Dominion!*, 116–17.

45. Wagner, *Dominion!*, 144.
46. Wagner, *Dominion!*, 138.
47. Wagner, *Dominion!*, 140–41.
48. Wagner, *Dominion!*, 145.
49. Wagner, *Dominion!*, 140–41.
50. Wagner, *Dominion!*, 150.
51. Wagner, *Dominion!*, 18.
52. Wagner, *Dominion!*, 182.
53. Wagner, *Dominion!*, 183.
54. Wagner, *Dominion!*, 183.
55. Wagner, *Dominion!*, 158.
56. Wagner, *Dominion!*, 158.
57. Wagner, *Dominion!*, 158.
58. Wagner, *Dominion!*, 158.
59. "Project 2025 Tracker," Project 2025 Tracker, accessed August 19, 2025, https://project2025.observer/en.

CHAPTER TWENTY: WHATEVER IT TAKES

1. Sarah McCammon, "Inside Trump's Closed-Door Meeting, Held to Reassure 'The Evangelicals,'" Politics, *NPR*, June 21, 2016, https://www.npr.org/2016/06/21/483018976/inside-trumps-closed-door-meeting-held-to-reassures-the-evangelicals.
2. The post has been preserved on MyCharisma.com, a website that caters to charismatic Christian interests: "C. Peter Wagner: I Like Donald Trump," *Charisma Magazine Online*, June 10, 2016, https://mycharisma.com/culture/c-peter-wagner-i-like-donald-trump/.
3. Matthew D. Taylor, *The Violent Take It by Force: The Christian Movement That Is Threatening Our Democracy* (Broadleaf Books, 2024), 76.
4. Lance Wallnau, *God's Chaos Candidate: Donald J. Trump and the American Unraveling* (Killer Sheep Media, 2016), 7. Italics original.
5. Chris Mitchell, "Trump: A 'Wrecking Ball' for Political Correctness," CBN, November 17, 2016, https://cbn.com/news/news/trump-wrecking-ball-political-correctness.
6. Lance Wallnau, "I sent this prophetic prayer to Donald J. Trump via his partner and attorney Michael Cohen," Facebook, October 27, 2015, https://www.facebook.com/LanceWallnau/videos/prophetic-prayer-sent-to-donald-trump/10153729859919936/.
7. "Tonight on The Hal Lindsey Report," The Hal Lindsey Report, accessed August 22, 2025, https://www.hallindsey.com/hlr-3-20-2015/.
8. Wallnau, *God's Chaos Candidate*, 9.
9. Wallnau, *God's Chaos Candidate*, 10–11.
10. Wallnau, *God's Chaos Candidate*, 11. Underline original.

11. Wallnau, *God's Chaos Candidate*, 12.
12. Wallnau, *God's Chaos Candidate*, 15.
13. Wallnau, *God's Chaos Candidate*, 16.
14. Wallnau, *God's Chaos Candidate*, 18.
15. "President Trump: 'I am the Chosen one,'" BBC, August 21, 2019, https://www.bbc.com/news/av/world-us-canada-49429661.
16. André Gagné, *American Evangelicals for Trump: Dominion, Spiritual Warfare, and the End Times*, trans. Linda Shanahan (Routledge, 2023), 13.
17. "Trump Champions the 'Silent Majority,' But What Does That Mean In 2016?," NPR, January 22, 2016, https://www.npr.org/2016/01/22/463884201/trump-champions-the-silent-majority-but-what-does-that-mean-in-2016.
18. Taylor, *The Violent Take It by Force*, 99.
19. Sunnivie Brydum, "A President 'Anointed by God': POTUS Shield and the Religious Right's Affair with Trump," Religion Dispatches, August 4, 2017, https://religiondispatches.org/a-president-anointed-by-god-potus-shield-and-religious-rights-affair-with-trump/.
20. "The Eight Prayer Watches—Three Hour Cycles of Prayer," POTUS Shield, accessed December 17, 2025, https://www.potusshield.com/prayer-watches.
21. Gagné, *American Evangelicals for Trump*, 41.
22. Gagné, *American Evangelicals for Trump*, 42.
23. Taylor, *The Violent Take It by Force*, 103.
24. Taylor, *The Violent Take It by Force*, 105.
25. Taylor, *The Violent Take It by Force*, 103.
26. Taylor, *The Violent Take It by Force*, 105–6. Italics mine.
27. Taylor, *The Violent Take It by Force*, 107.
28. Andy Kroll and Nick Surgey, "Inside Ziklag, the Secret Organization of Wealthy Christians Trying to Sway the Election and Change the Country," *ProPublica*, July 13, 2024, https://www.propublica.org/article/inside-ziklag-secret-christian-charity-2024-election.
29. Kroll and Surgey, "Inside Ziklag."
30. "Restriction of Political Campaign Intervention by Section 501(c)(3) Tax-Exempt Organizations," IRS, August 20, 2025, https://www.irs.gov/charities-non-profits/charitable-organizations/restriction-of-political-campaign-intervention-by-section-501c3-tax-exempt-organizations.
31. Kroll and Surgey, "Inside Ziklag."
32. Kroll and Surgey, "Inside Ziklag."
33. Damon T. Berry, *The New Apostolic Reformation, Trump, and Evangelical Politics: The Prophecy Voter* (Bloomsbury Academic, 2023), 89.
34. Berry, *The New Apostolic Reformation*, 93.
35. Berry, *The New Apostolic Reformation*, 93.
36. Right Wing Watch offers a condensed version of Wallnau's video here: "RWW News: Lance Wallnau Says Kamala Harris Is Being Used by the

Devil 'To Take Trump Out,'" Right Wing Watch, YouTube, accessed December 17, 2025, https://www.youtube.com/watch?v=gKY1L-d2654.

37. There is perhaps a touch of irony here, in that televangelist Rick Joyner wrote in *The MorningStar Journal* (March 2017) after the 2017 Women's March, "Some estimated that a million women gathered in the different cities where the Women's March was held. Perhaps, but even if there were that many, it was just a fraction of one percent of the women in America. I don't think the March was a reflection of the women in America. There was a baseness, depravity, and lack of basic dignity on the Women's March in DC. This could hardly have been a more clear manifestation of the Jezebel spirit."
38. Frederick Clarkson, "Packed with Threats of Political Violence, Media Largely Ignore the NAR's 'Million Women' Rally in DC," Religion Dispatches, October 17, 2024, https://religiondispatches.org/packed-with-threats-of-political-violence-media-largely-ignore-the-nars-million-women-rally-in-dc/.
39. Clarkson, "Packed with Threats of Political Violence."
40. "Trump vs. The Jezebel Spirit: How Trump Can Still Win," The Lance Wallnau Show, YouTube, accessed December 17, 2025, https://www.youtube.com/watch?v=qiMBXw0J2VI.
41. "The Modern-Day Elijah: Rising Against the Spirit of Jezebel," The Lance Wallnau Show, YouTube, accessed December 17, 2025, https://www.youtube.com/watch?v=QsW68RLSDhE.

CHAPTER TWENTY-ONE: THE MONSTER MANUAL

1. "Leviathan Unmasked: Ancient Demonic Spirit Behind Media's Lies | Lance Wallnau," Sid Roth's It's Supernatural, YouTube, accessed December 17, 2025, https://www.youtube.com/watch?v=F59ykujqHqo.
2. "Leviathan Unmasked," 10:29–10:48.
3. "Leviathan Unmasked,"11:32–12:57.
4. "Leviathan Unmasked,"15:17–15:23.
5. Lance Wallnau, podcast, episode 980, "Breaking the Power of Leviathan: Spiritual Warfare," accessed December 17, 2025, https://lancewallnau.com/episode-980-breaking-the-power-of-leviathan-spiritual-warfare/.
6. S. Jonathon O'Donnell, *Passing Orders: Demonology and Sovereignty in American Spiritual Warfare* (Fordham University Press, 2020), 115.
7. O'Donnell, *Passing Orders*, 115–16.
8. O'Donnell, *Passings Orders*, 115.
9. Ron Phillips, *Everyone's Guide to Demons & Spiritual Warfare: Simple, Powerful Tools for Outmaneuvering Satan in Your Daily Life* (Charisma House, 2010), 149.
10. Phillips, *Everyone's Guide to Demons & Spiritual Warfare*, 150.
11. See for instance Frederick Clarkson, "New Apostolic Reformation Faces Profound Rift Due to Trump Prophecies and 'Spiritual

Manipulation of the Prophetic Gift'" Religion Dispatches, August 9, 2022, https://religiondispatches.org/new-apostolic-reformation-faces-profound-rift-due-to-trump-prophecies-and-spiritual-manipulation-of-the-prophetic-gift/.

12. Jennifer Leclaire, *The Spiritual Warfare Battle Plan: Unmasking 15 Harassing Demons That Want to Destroy Your Life* (Charisma House, 2017), 28.
13. LeClaire, *Spiritual Warfare*, 27.
14. LeClaire, *Spiritual Warfare*, 25.
15. Jonathan Cahn, *The Return of the Gods* (FrontLine, 2022), 95.
16. Cahn, *The Return of the Gods*, 104.
17. Cahn, *The Return of the Gods*, 105. Italics original.
18. Peter C. Wagner, *Dominion! How Kingdom Action Can Change the World* (Chosen, 2008), 183.
19. J. Matthew Wilson, ed., *From Pews to Polling Places: Faith and Politics in the American Religious Mosaic* (Georgetown University Press, 2007), 141.
20. See for instance, Tara Isabella Burton, "The Prosperity Gospel, Explained: Why Joel Osteen Believes that Prayer Can Make You Rich," *Vox*, September 1, 2017, https://www.vox.com/identities/2017/9/1/15951874/prosperity-gospel-explained-why-joel-osteen-believes-prayer-can-make-you-rich-trump; Laura Fitzpatrick, "Pastor Joel Osteen," *TIME*, November 5, 2009, https://time.com/archive/6915412/pastor-joel-osteen/.
21. Wagner, *Dominion!*, 185. Italics mine.
22. Wagner, *Dominion!*, 191.
23. Rick Joyner, *Overcoming the Spirit of Poverty* (MorningStar Publications, 1996), 22.
24. Joyner, *Overcoming the Spirit of Poverty*, 46.
25. Bill Johnson, *Breaking the Spirit of Poverty: The Revival Collection Transcript* (Destiny Image, n.d.), Kindle Edition, 37.
26. Johnson, *Breaking the Spirit of Poverty*, 38.
27. Johnson, *Breaking the Spirit of Poverty*, 38.
28. Wagner, *Dominion!*, 194–95.
29. C. Peter Wagner, ed., *Freedom from the Religious Spirit* (Regal Books, 2005), 12.
30. Wagner, *Freedom from the Religious Spirit*, 13.
31. Jim Anderson, "The Corporate Spirit of Religion in Action—A Case Study," in *Freedom from the Religious Spirit*, ed. C. Peter Wagner (Regal Books, 2005), 27–29.
32. Anderson, "The Corporate Spirit of Religion in Action," 28–29.
33. Anderson, "The Corporate Spirit of Religion in Action," 30.
34. Anderson, "The Corporate Spirit of Religion in Action," 31.
35. John Weaver, *The New Apostolic Reformation: History of a Modern Charismatic Movement* (McFarland, 2016), 153.
36. LeClaire, *The Spiritual Warfare Battle Plan*, 18.

37. Michael McVicar, *Christian Reconstruction: R. J. Rushdoony and American Religious Conservatism* (University of North Carolina Press, 2015), 15. Also, the entirety of chapter 4 covers this analytical point.
38. Cahn, *The Return of the Gods*, 133.
39. Cahn, *The Return of the Gods*, 155.
40. Cahn, *The Return of the Gods*, 177–79.
41. Cahn, *The Return of the Gods*, 167–68.
42. Thaddeus Russell, *A Renegade History of the United States* (Free Press, 2010), 327.
43. Rick Joyner, "Combating the Spirit of Religion," in Wagner, *Freedom from the Religious Spirit*, 48.
44. Tony Semerad, "Why the LDS Church Soon May Not Need Tithing Anymore to Cover Its Global Programs," *Salt Lake Tribune*, April 1, 2025, https://www.sltrib.com/religion/2025/04/01/lds-church-wealth-day-soon-may/.
45. David Frankfurter, *Evil Incarnate: Rumors of Demonic Conspiracy and Satanic Abuse in History* (Princeton University Press, 2018).

CHAPTER TWENTY-TWO: CONSPIRACY!

1. See for instance, Anahad O'Connor, "Coca-Cola Funds Scientists Who Shift Blame for Obesity Away From Bad Diets," *New York Times*, August 9, 2015, https://archive.nytimes.com/well.blogs.nytimes.com/2015/08/09/coca-cola-funds-scientists-who-shift-blame-for-obesity-away-from-bad-diets/; Paulo Serodio, Gary Ruskin, Martin McKee, and David Stuckler, "Evaluating Coca-Cola's Attempts to Influence Public Health 'in Their Own Words': Analysis of Coca-Cola Emails with Public Health Academics Leading the Global Energy Balance Network," *Public Health Nutrition* 23, no. 14 (2020): 2647–53, https://doi.org/10.1017/S1368980020002098.
2. Retraction Watch, accessed December 18, 2025, https://retractionwatch.com/.
3. Frederik Joelving, "Signs of Undeclared ChatGPT Use in Papers Mounting," Retraction Watch, October 6, 2023, https://retractionwatch.com/2023/10/06/signs-of-undeclared-chatgpt-use-in-papers-mounting/. "Papers and Peer Reviews with Evidence of ChatGPT Writing," *Retraction Watch*, March 18, 2024, https://retractionwatch.com/papers-and-peer-reviews-with-evidence-of-chatgpt-writing/.
4. See https://theconversation.com/us.
5. Michael Barkun, *A Culture of Conspiracy: Apocalyptic Visions in Contemporary America* (University of California Press, 2003), 26–29.
6. Barkun, *A Culture of Conspiracy*, 3.
7. Barkun, *A Culture of Conspiracy*, 3.
8. See Michael E. Heyes, *Demons in the USA: From the Anti-Spiritualists to QAnon* (Routledge, 2024), ch. 6.

CHAPTER TWENTY-THREE: WHAT HAPPENS NEXT

1. Meg Anderon, Rachel Treisman, and Russel Lewis, "The Suspect in the Shooting of 2 Minnesota Lawmakers Had a 'Hit List' of 45 Officials," NPR, June 16, 2025, https://www.npr.org/2025/06/16/nx-s1-5433748/minnesota-shooting-suspect-vance-boelter-arrested-melissa-hortman-john-hoffman.
2. Lou Raguse, "'Dad Went to War': Alleged Killer's Message Shocks Family and Officials," KARE11, June 17, 2025, https://www.kare11.com/article/news/local/acting-us-attorney-shares-details-of-vance-boelter-case-in-one-on-one-interview-minnesota/89-82633b77-386b-4c21-ad45-1d4ddbbb1af6.
3. Shaun Rabb and Adam Fullerton, "Vance Boelter Graduated from Dallas Religious School," Fox4, June 16, 2025, https://www.fox4news.com/news/vance-boelter-dallas-christ-for-the-nations-institute.
4. Eric Killelea, "Dallas Bible School Condemns Actions of Minnesota Shooter Alum," *Chron*, June 17, 2025, https://www.chron.com/culture/religion/article/vance-boelter-texas-bible-college-alum-20381262.php.
5. Chris Hippensteel, Nicholas Bogel-Burroughs, Ernesto Londoño, Mike Baker, and Mark Walker "What We Know About the Minnesota Shooting Suspect," *New York Times*, June 14, 2025, https://www.nytimes.com/2025/06/14/us/politics/minnesota-shootings-gunman-suspect.html.
6. Paul O'Donnell, Religion News Service, "Suspected Assassin Preached on Spiritual Warfare," *Christianity Today*, June 16, 2025, https://www.christianitytoday.com/2025/06/suspected-assassin-minnesota-vance-boelter-evangelical-spiritual/.
7. "Minnesota Shooting Suspect had Target List of Abortion Providers," National Abortions Federation, news release, June 14, 2025, https://prochoice.org/minnesota-shooting-suspect-had-target-list-of-abortion-providers/.
8. Dominick Bonny, "Cashmere's 'Collective' Kicks Off 'Kingdom Defense' Survival Workshop This Saturday," Dominick Bonny Reports, April 23, 2024, https://dominickb.substack.com/p/cashmeres-collective-kicks-off-kingdom.
9. "The Rising Tide," The Collective, accessed December 17, 2025, https://www.thecollectivewa.com/rising-tide; emphasis mine.
10. Mark Potok, "Doug Wilson's Religious Empire Expanding in the Northwest," *SPLC*, April 20, 2024, https://www.splcenter.org/resources/reports/doug-wilsons-religious-empire-expanding-northwest/.
11. Mariya Manzhos, "Is America a Christian Nation?," *Desert News*, August 16, 2025, https://www.deseret.com/faith/2025/08/16/pastor-doug-wilson-idaho-christian-nationalism/.
12. Jack Jenkins, Religion News Service, "At Doug Wilson's DC Church Plant, 'Worship Is Warfare,'" *Christianity Today*, July 15, 2025, https://www.christianitytoday.com/2025/07/christ-church-dc-doug-wilson-pete-hegseth/.
13. "What to Know About the Archconservative Church Defense Secretary Pete Hegseth Attends," PBS, August 12, 2025, https://www.pbs.org/newshour/

nation/what-to-know-about-the-archconservative-church-defense-secretary-pete-hegseth-attends.

14. Amanda Grace, *The Revelationary War: The Epic Battle Against False Prophecy and Deception* (Charisma House, 2025), 149–50.
15. Grace, *The Revelationary War*, 91–95.
16. Grace, *The Revelationary War*, 163.
17. "WWIII or US Split? Amanda Grace Unpacks Israel-Iran Clash and Civil-War Prophecy," Revival Nation, YouTube, https://www.youtube.com/live/dP7TzycAJ0M?si=4uN64QDMiqohMGWJ (at approx. 31:01).
18. "WWIII or US Split?," at approx. 30:35.
19. For example, James Scaminaci III, "Battle with Bullets: Advancing a Vision of Civil War," Political Research Associates, August 31, 2020, https://politicalresearch.org/2020/08/31/battle-bullet-advancing-vision-civil-war; James Lasher, "Is America on the Brink of Civil War? Shocking Insights from Military Insider," *Charisma*, June 13, 2025, https://mycharisma.com/culture/is-america-on-the-brink-of-civil-war-shocking-insights-from-military-insider/.
20. Diane Winston, *Righting the American Dream: How the Media Mainstreamed Reagan's Evangelical Vision* (University of Chicago Press, 2023), 7.
21. See @itsdeaann and @parkergetajob.
22. For example, "Right-Wing Influencers Were Duped to Work for Covert Russian Operation, US Says," *AP News*, September 5, 2024, https://apnews.com/article/russian-interference-presidential-election-influencers-trump-999435273dd39edf7468c6aa34fad5dd; William Marcellino, Christian Johnson, Marek N. Posard, and Todd C. Helmus, *Foreign Interference in the 2020 Election: Tools for Detecting Online Election Interference* (RAND, 2020), https://www.rand.org/pubs/research_reports/RRA704-2.html.
23. And if you need a primer on evaluating unfamiliar sources, a lot of university libraries have already prepared these. See for instance, https://library.uwgb.edu/evalinfo.
24. Robert P. Jones, "Not a Single Senator Probed the Most Dangerous Part of Pete Hegseth's Background: His Ties to White Christian Nationalism," *Religion Dispatches*, January 16, 2025, https://religiondispatches.org/not-a-single-senator-probed-the-most-dangerous-part-of-hegseths-background-white-christian-nationalism/.
25. Mike Baker and Ruth Graham, "Pete Hegseth and His 'Battle Cry' for a New Christian Crusade," *New York Times*, December 5, 2024, https://www.nytimes.com/2024/12/05/us/hegseth-church-crusades.html.
26. Pete Hegseth, *American Crusade: Our Fight to Stay Free* (Center Street, 2020), 2.
27. Hegseth, *American Crusade*, 30.
28. After first mentioning a "holy war," Hegseth writes by way of explanation "One thousand years ago, after years of ceding land to conquering Muslim

hordes, the pope ordered military action to save Europe. 'Deus vult' ('God wills it') was the rallying cry of Christian knights as they marched to Jerusalem. Two hundred and fifty years ago, as King George III exercised more power over the colonists in North America, they rebelled. 'Give me liberty or give me death!' they exclaimed. America was born and then battle tested. The most important rallying cry of our era—'Make America Great Again'—catalyzed a political miracle of similar proportion and consequence so shocking that it still confounds those who proclaimed it. Like crusaders and patriots past, Donald Trump's red hat rebellion demonstrates that unapologetically going on offense is the only tenable strategy for the defense of our republic. Surrounded by the Left, with the odds stacked against us, only a crusade will do" (*American Crusade*, 2).

29. Jones, "Not a Single Senator Probed the Most Dangerous Part of Pete Hegseth's Background."
30. Christal Whelan, *The Beginning of Heaven and Earth: The Sacred Book of Japan's Hidden Christians* (University of Hawai'i Press, 1996), 39.